INFANTRY
SOLDIER

GEORGE W. NEILL

INFANTRY SOLDIER

Holding the Line at the Battle of the Bulge

University of Oklahoma Press • Norman

This book is published with the generous assistance
of Edith Gaylord Harper.

2 3 4 5 6 7 8 9 10

The paper in this book meets the guidelines for permanence
and durability of the Committee on Production Guidelines for
Book Longevity of the Council on Library Resources, Inc. ∞

Library of Congress Cataloging-in-Publication Data

Neill, George W.
    Infantry soldier : holding the line at the Battle of the Bulge
/ George W. Neill.
        p. cm.
    Includes bibliographical references and index.
    ISBN 0-8061-3222-1 (alk. paper)
    1. Neill, George W.   2. Ardennes, Battle of the, 1944 –
1945—Personal narratives, American.   3. World War,
1939–1945—Personal narratives, American.   4. World War,
1939–1945—Campaigns—Western Front.   5. United
States. Army. Division, 99th—History.   6. Soldiers—United
States—Biography.   I. Title.

D756.5.A7 N45 2000
940.54'21431—dc21
                                                            99-048506

To those who served on the front line

CONTENTS

ILLUSTRATIONS

PHOTOGRAPHS (*Following page 248*)

MAPS (*on pages as shown below*)

PREFACE

A MEETING OF OLD FRIENDS, BOTH DEAD AND ALIVE, IS about to occur on a field in Belgium—their first get-together since the battlefields of 1944–45. The date and time: October 2, 1990, 2:30 P.M.

Tour buses drive into an attractively landscaped parking lot surrounded by trees and shrubs. Ninety-six elderly former U.S. soldiers—many with wives, children, and grandchildren—emerge from the buses and proceed slowly along a path. The old men, in their late sixties and seventies and early eighties, find themselves fighting to control powerful, long-buried emotions.

I am one of them. We are survivors of the 99th Infantry Division's battles of 1944 and 1945, including the Battle of the Bulge in which the division played a major role. As we approach our destination, the reason for our journey quickly comes into focus: the Henri-Chapelle American Cemetery and Memorial, located near Aubel, Belgium, a few miles west of Aachen, Germany. It was the second largest of the thirty-seven World War II U.S. military cemeteries in western Europe and the United Kingdom when the war ended in 1945.

Our misty eyes tell the story. We suffer from fast-emerging memories of pain from the distant past—pain caused by terrible experiences and far-from-forgotten recollections of close buddies cut down in the bloom of youth. Since tears are not natural for us, they make the moment all the more poignant.

Simultaneously, with our first glimpses of a sight we have only imagined for forty-six years, a wild combination of emotions races to the surface—great sorrow, enormous respect, and, yes, guilt. The American flag flies at half-staff. We gasp at the awesome yet strangely beautiful sight: 7,989 white crosses and Stars of David, row after row, stretching out on a carpet of gloriously green freshly-mowed lawn. The dark green forests, so typical of the Belgian Ardennes, provide an appropriate background.

One of these dead won the Congressional Medal of Honor. In thirty-three sets of graves, two brothers lie side by side. In one instance, three brothers rest next to each other. We all have friends in that field of graves.[1]

Chills run up and down my back. I'm not prepared for such a strong reaction. I expected to be moved, not overwhelmed. "My God!" I whisper to my eighty-year-old former colonel, McClernand Butler, who walks beside me. He remains silent. Everyone speaks in the hushed voices we would use in a great cathedral. To us, this is sacred ground. Henri-Chapelle is "our cemetery" because so many of our comrades in the 99th Division, U.S. First Army, lie buried here. Only incredibly good luck kept us from sharing this cold earth.

Each grave represents a death suffered from September 1944 to May 1945 during the Battle of the Bulge or the Rhineland or Central Europe campaigns. I try to visualize how the cemetery looked at the end of the war when the number of graves totaled 17,323, more than double the current number. By the end of 1951, 9,334 soldiers had been "repatriated" to the United States by next of kin for reburial in hometown or military cemeteries.[2]

We stand for a few minutes on an overlook at the front of the cemetery. I think of the devastated parents, wives, brothers and sisters, of children never born, of the never-attained contributions to families, community, and nation. I keep asking myself,

"Why did we live, and why did they die?" I do not believe it was the will of God.

After viewing this scene of appalling loss, we line up in the cemetery's office to get exact locations of those we want to "visit." For example, I find that my friend Gene Oxford, L Company, 395th Regiment, 99th Division, is buried in Section B, Row 10, Grave 28. A German land mine killed him while he was on a combat patrol near Höfen, Germany, on December 13, 1944, three days before the Germans launched the Battle of the Bulge.

Soon our group spreads out in ones, twos, and threes, seeking old friends. Under a gray, solemn afternoon sky, we pay respects to our dead comrades. As I kneel at Gene's grave, my mind flashes back to the strong, determined face of the nineteen-year-old I knew throughout 1943 and 1944. Another flashback takes me to the rear of our truck as we drove through Belgium from Normandy to the front line. Gene and I talked about a long American hospital train headed the other way, toward France. We pondered that sight and wondered if we would soon be on a similar train.

A Belgian visitor, on tour with a group of his countrymen, walks up to me and asks why so many in my group are so emotionally upset. "Many of the men buried here were our friends," I answer. "We were like brothers. We lived together under incredible hardships. We dug foxholes together. We fought together. We grieved for fallen comrades together. Some of those buried here saved our lives. And this is the first chance we have had to rejoin them since they were carried off the battlefield forty-six years ago. We have lived full lives, and they—" I could not finish the sentence. Then I add, "We have come back to honor them." The Belgian understands. Mist fills his eyes, too, as he turns to interpret my answer for his group.

During a ceremony for the occasion, Roger V. Foehringer, a former American prisoner of war in Germany and a member of the 99th Division in 1944, asks the audience to listen carefully for the voices of their dead. "You will hear them say, 'What took you so long? Where have you been? Gee, we are glad to see you.'" Looking out to the grave markers, he waves to two fallen friends. "Goodbye, Tommy [Hutton]. Goodbye, Bernie [Pappel]. So long, fellows!"

The haunting sound of taps drifts across the silent graves. Colonel Butler and I walk back to our tour bus in silence. The passengers remain quiet all the way back to our hotel in Liege. Our minds are far away. Mine strays back to December 16, 1944, when all of us in the 99th Division shared the traumatic beginning of the Battle of the Bulge. Most of us had friends who died in the first few minutes of that bloody six-week battle.

The timing of the ceremony, held almost within sight of the German border, was particularly poignant. At midnight, church bells all over Germany rang in celebration of an historic moment in German history—the official reunification of a nation held partially in bondage by the Soviet Union for forty-five years. The peace we fought for was finally achieved. The soldiers who lie in Henri-Chapelle had not died in vain.

Almost everyone knew that life in the infantry would be rough and dangerous, but few knew how rough and how dangerous. General Omar N. Bradley estimated that based on casualties in Normandy, the infantry as a whole would incur 83 percent of U.S. casualties.[3] It was much worse for the infantry's rifle platoons. They made up only 6 percent of all U.S. Army personnel in the European Theater of Operations (ETO) in November 1944.[4] This "handful," as Bradley pointed out, took most of the casualties.[5]

I describe in this book what it was really like for the forgotten, expendable infantry soldiers who did most of the fighting and dying. I was one of them. We manned the front line. Few realize the enormously disproportional burden of the war we carried. Only by understanding our predicament can one really understand the human effort involved in World War II, the so-called "good war."

I draw the reader into the everyday lives of young soldiers in the foxholes and reveal how we lived, how we felt, and what happened to us. I report only indirectly about the war itself. That's already been well covered by generals and historians in a plethora of thick books. In the process of telling my story, I provide the close-up view—a side that usually isn't reported. I believe strongly that the experiences I relate need to be told before we who lived them—and can tell them best—fade away.

I tell my story through my experiences in an infantry rifle platoon and through the experiences of friends who served with me in the bottom ranks of the 99th Infantry Division in Texas, Oklahoma, Belgium, and Germany. Our lives and those of comrades in many other American infantry divisions in Europe were similar and extraordinary. One writer described the life of a combat infantryman as the most extreme experience a person can live through.

While trying to sleep in a frozen foxhole along the Western Front in the winter of 1944–45, I vowed to tell our story to as many people as possible. It builds to a climax in the Battle of the Bulge. I make no claim to heroics because there were none by me. But I introduce the reader to some real heroes.

My research helped me solve mysteries that I had encountered during my service with the 99th. I report them in this book.

My many letters home, all saved by my farsighted parents, provided an accurate timeline and many helpful details. I have also incorporated the narratives and memories of many comrades. For example, two friends, referring to notes they wrote immediately after the war, describe how they and sixteen other men of their platoon successfully delayed a German parachute battalion for the first day of the Battle of the Bulge. Combined with other stubborn small-scale American defenses all along the Ardennes Front, they doomed Hitler's offensive only four days after it started.

I relate tales of soldiers risking their lives to save buddies, of the horror of watching friends—and enemies—die, of smart and stupid leadership, of greed and corruption in the rear echelon, of young American soldiers learning the killing trade, and of an enemy both surprisingly humane and incredibly cruel.

Because I am a journalist and because I had all my wartime letters, my wife and friends urged me to start writing. In essence, they said, get it on paper before it's too late. I hesitated, thinking of the time and energy it would take. (It took seven years.) But, as if preordained, I was drawn to it. I began researching and writing when I had time, at age seventy—after college, raising children, career. Only at that stage of life did I find time to learn more about this dramatic part of my youth.

As I worked on the book, I wanted to find out what part the war had in shaping me and fellow infantrymen and put to rest the demons from our collective past. Among my army friends, some have deliberately wiped out almost all memory of their military service. Others are so haunted they cannot talk about their experiences, even among old army buddies. Some wives know, nevertheless, that something traumatic happened. They know because their husbands still have nightmares.

I wanted to remember. During the most traumatic events, particularly the first four days of the Battle of the Bulge, I told myself, "This should never be forgotten." Each year after the war, as the anniversary dates of these events occurred, I would review what happened to me and my friends and try to solve mysteries that still bothered me. These efforts to remember helped me greatly when I began work on this book.

Haunted by my experiences, I returned to my part of the front line four times—in 1955, 1977, 1990, and 1993. Much to my surprise, I discovered that many of my comrades had also made multiple return trips.

Many of us were incredibly innocent when we entered the service. I used the term "boys" to describe my group up to the time we started serious training for combat. Then, subconsciously, I started to call us "men." Underneath, however, we remained boys in many ways. What else explains why so many soldiers, on both sides, cried out for their mothers as they lay dying on the battlefield? In my own case, I realized how sheltered my life had been growing up in comfortable Pasadena, California.

Some of the treatment we experienced from our own people was inhumane. I cite numerous examples. Sending rifle platoons, those most exposed to the weather, onto a freezing front without appropriate winter clothing and footwear is an egregious example. Sometimes the nearest neighbors to our rifle platoons were the Germans who manned foxholes and Siegfried Line fortifications. They, too, were cold, hungry, exhausted, and dirty. In many ways, we had more in common with them than we had with Americans behind our lines.

I include official "Morning Reports" from my 3rd Battalion to my regiment (the 395th Infantry). These reports, though brief and bureaucratic, provide timelines and summaries of events involving my battalion. They omit the human chronicle. I also include top-secret decisions of the German high command concerning the Western Front. Summaries of these decisions document how my 99th Division gradually moved into the center of Hitler's last-gasp offensive through the Ardennes Forest.

The on-the-spot quotes I attribute to myself and others obviously cannot be exact. But I keep the flavor and meaning as close as possible to reality.

During World War I, a commentator declared that if common soldiers suddenly became articulate and could write and describe their experiences, the war would not last a month. Exaggerated, yes. But I believe the thought has validity. In that spirit, I wrote this book.

George W. Neill

Carmichael, California
January 1, 2000

ACKNOWLEDGMENTS

W ITHOUT THE EDITORIAL SKILLS AND PATIENT, LOV-
ing encouragement of Shirley B. Neill, my wife, this
book would never have happened. My college room-
mate, William Commerford, and his wife, Betty, convinced me
that I had a story to tell worthy of a book and provided encouragement throughout the seven years of research and writing.

There are so many others I want to thank and recognize
for their help that I must list them mostly by name only. They
are: Helen Adams, Warner Anthony, Harry Arnold, Rosemary
Boes, Lyle Bouck, Mitchell Brooks (cartography), Ivan Bull,
McClernand Butler, Richard Byers, the California State Univer-
sity (Sacramento) Library, Rod and Marlene Cecchettini, Joe and
Judy Culley, Vincent Demma (U.S. Army Center of Military His-
tory), Vince Dudzinski, Don Fuller, Manfred Geisler (translation
from German to English), John Gilroy, Jackson Goss, Stephen
Guise, James Hare, Sydney Harriet (literary agent), Rudolph
Jansen (Monschau, Germany), Lewis Kemper (photo reproduc-
tion), Heinze Kerkmann (Höfen, Germany), Leonard Kreidt,
Bud Lembke, Delrose McGeehan, John and Beverly Mellin, Bill
Meyer (editor, *Checkerboard*, 99th Infantry Division Associa-
tion), Robert Mitsch, the National Archives, Suzanne Neill,
William and Sadhna Neill, Max Norris, Louis Pedrotti, George
Prager (translation from German to English and much more),

Thor Ronningen, the Sacramento Public Library Telephone Reference Service, Sy Saffer, Duane Shipman, Bert Skaggs, Don and Jean Stafford, Paul Sweet, Robert Trimingham, John and Ruth Turner, Karin and Anton Uhl (Höfen, Germany), Bruce Waterman, Michael Winey (U.S. Army Military History Institute, Carlisle Barracks), Doug Witt. To them, I offer my most grateful thanks.

INFANTRY
SOLDIER

1 • The Beginning

THE NEWS ARRIVED BY MAIL IN A BRIEF MIMEO-graphed, unsigned letter from the dean of students, University of California, Berkeley. It directed ninety of us in the U. S. Army's Enlisted Reserve Corps (ERC) to report for active duty.[1]

At first glance, the letter hardly looked important—another bureaucratic exercise. Dated March 16, 1943, it told us to re-port on March 24, only eight days later. The meaning was clear: the army wanted to move from inactive to active duty most of the young, healthy manpower it held in reserve in institutions of higher education. The order ended months of uncertainty. I was nearing the end of my junior year as a major in Ameri-can diplomatic history. In addition, as required by ERC, I par-ticipated in ROTC (infantry) and an intensive, daily, army-style physical fitness program that included running, swimming, and a demanding obstacle course. Al Regan, the university's track coach, served as our trainer.

For months, rumor after rumor had spread through the large campus about the imminent call-up of the ERC. Now the call-up was a fact. I was happy the suspense was over. Many others felt the same way. With so much uncertainty about when we would be called up, trying to concentrate on our studies had been impossible.

Our new adventure began as all ninety of us—mostly strangers—gathered in front of the university's Harmon Gymnasium. At this point we were a milling, quiet crowd of "boys," the term often used in those days to describe male college students. We ranged in age from eighteen to twenty-one years old. This gathering represented a rare breed in 1943. Only 25 percent of the total population of the nation twenty-five years of age and older had completed four years of high school, and only 5 percent had completed four years of college.[2]

I was excited and nervous at the same time. I knew this was an historic moment for me. After a call of the roll, we moved by rapid transit train from Berkeley to San Francisco, then by railroad to the Presidio at Monterey, California. It was dusk as we marched up a hill into the hands of the Presidio's induction officers and noncoms (noncommissioned officers).

Since all of us had enlisted in the ERC during the summer of 1942, we were already in the army months before we arrived at the Presidio. (Turned down in Los Angeles by the draft in the spring of 1942 because of hemorrhoids, of all things, I volunteered to undergo a painful operation at the university's hospital so the army would accept me. Thus, I entered the army as a volunteer, not as a draftee.)

At Monterey, our days of freedom ended. We arrived with one weakness. Three or four in our group tended to be cocky. After all, they rationalized, we came from Cal, one of the nation's most respected universities. I think some expected the Presidio to roll out a red carpet. The army quickly discouraged such silly notions.

We ate our first army meal soon after our arrival. The cooks dished out generous, good-tasting portions—a promising beginning because food was very important to us. After dinner, our last vestige of civilian life began to disappear when noncoms ordered us to take off our civilian clothes; place them in a bag; write our home address on an attached label; and don the attire of an army private, including olive drab underwear. Each of us also received an army toilet kit that included a toothbrush, shaving brush, razor, and comb.

Next, our noncoms led us to a nearby two-story barracks and assigned us to steel-framed beds. A thin pad served as the mattress, and its cover served as the only sheet we had. We picked up two blankets and a pillow, and a corporal taught us how to make our beds—army-style. The army had a certain way of doing it and allowed no leeway for individuality. (More than fifty years later I still make beds that way.) Each barracks room had twenty beds, ten on each side. No privacy here. We had time to get a postcard at the Post Exchange (PX) and write a note home. Then showers and lights out. We slept in our new olive drab underwear—a T-shirt and briefs.

We awoke abruptly to the sound of a bugle playing reveille at what seemed an ungodly hour. It was still dark. In minutes, we dressed and raced outside for roll call. Then we returned to our barracks to make our beds and race to the latrine. The urinal was a long troughlike container. The toilets were lined up, out in the open, in the same room with the urinal and sinks. All bathroom activities were done in one room by eight to ten men at one time. I was surprised to find that we defecated out in the open room, with other men passing back and forth. Five or six of us sat on toilets simultaneously.

We had a busy schedule for the rest of the day, starting with a long questionnaire that sought detailed personal information.

One question gave us an opportunity to list the branch of service we would prefer. "Infantry," I answered. That was the branch most of those with me wanted to avoid. I knew it was the toughest, most dangerous part of the army, and that is why I wanted it. The vigorous life would toughen me up physically, I thought, just as it had Theodore Roosevelt when he worked as a young man on a primitive ranch in North Dakota.

We stripped and lined up for a physical examination and shots. I learned that a "short arm" inspection consisted of a close-up look at one's genital area to determine the presence or absence of venereal disease. The fact that we all passed the physical was hardly surprising. To get into the ERC, we had already passed careful exams at Cal's hospital.

As buck privates, we had earned $1.67 for our first day in the army, which translated into $50.00 per month.

On our second day at the Presidio, the army attempted to determine our mental capabilities by giving us an IQ-type assessment called the AGCT (Army General Classification Test). It consisted of 150 multiple-choice questions with a forty-minute time limit. The tests were machine-graded and included three types of questions: block counting, matching synonyms, and simple arithmetic. The following is an example from the arithmetic portion: "Mike had 12 cigars. He bought 3 more and then smoked 6. How many did he have left?"[3]

Our AGCT score had much to do with our army future. Taking the test was, in fact, our most important chore at the Presidio. Personnel officers would use the results to decide assignments. So it was crucial that we be in top form—plenty of sleep the night before and no headaches. Fortunately, I felt fine. When the exam was over, we lined up to get our hair shorn army-style—a severely short crewcut. Our civilian look disappeared.

I spent the remaining time in the PX and the service club, watching landing craft carrying troops from ships onto the sandy beaches at nearby Fort Ord. The infantry was training its men for beach invasions like the one the United States and Britain had launched five months earlier in North Africa.

Throughout the day, I kept singing under my breath a new song called "As Time Goes By," from the recently released *Casablanca* starring Humphrey Bogart and Ingrid Bergman. Amazingly, it was released at the same time the North African campaign began. Many of us were obsessed with the song and could not get it out of our minds: "You must remember this, a kiss is just a kiss, a sigh is just a sigh. . . ."

Among several other induction chores in the next four days, we picked up our two identical, newly-minted "dog tags"— metal identification plates attached to a short metal necklace. Information on the tags included our blood type (for blood transfusions), army serial number, religion ("P" for Protestant, "C" for Catholic, "H" for Hebrew or Jewish), first and last names, and a middle initial if we had a middle name or "NMI" (no middle initial) if we didn't have one. The "H" helped Germans spot U.S. Jewish soldiers they captured. My serial number was 19119300 (a number I knew better than my social security number more than fifty years later). The first number—"1"— disclosed that I enlisted (volunteered) for the army. The first number of draftees was "3." We wore both tags. In case of death, the army removed one for record keeping. The religious designation indicated the appropriate chaplain to provide last rites. The other tag remained with the body for identification at an army cemetery.

We waited anxiously for personnel officers to decide our fates, based on our physical condition, test scores, and which branch of service we preferred. Sometimes, influence helped. In a few cases, the personnel specialists considered requests for favorable assignments for certain soldiers whose parents knew "the right people," such as a general or an important politician or business mogul.

After five days, we received our shipping orders. The largest part of the Berkeley group, including me, was assigned to the infantry. We were to depart the following day on a troop train going to Camp Wolters, Mineral Wells, Texas, the largest all-infantry replacement training center in the United States. We were scheduled for a three-month infantry basic training program. That didn't bother me, since I had asked for it. However, the news of infantry assignment upset many of my new friends. Others actually received assignments to branches they requested, such as artillery, engineers, and Signal Corps. For the most part, they had gone farther in math and physics than the rest of us. We departed by troop train late in the afternoon, bound for Texas. Many were excited because this was their first long-distance train trip. We stopped the next morning in Los Angeles, where we picked up additional cars of recruits. Approximately forty of the draftees were blacks.

When our train reached Texas, it stopped. A new conductor, a Texan, came aboard and declared: "Negroes in Texas do not ride in the same railroad passenger car with whites." Most of the Californians on the train were stunned. When the blacks were segregated, the train proceeded. Fifty years later at a reunion of my UC-Berkeley army group, Jack Dowell added this comment: "There was a great deal of unhappiness among the Californians. We did not find this segregation order at all pleasant. Amazingly, the African Americans accepted it. They were unhappy, but they knew what was coming. If we had been on a civilian train, it would have been easier to accept."

When our train stopped in El Paso's railroad station to pick up food for lunch, we received two more shocks. There were two rest rooms for men, one labeled "White" and one labeled "Colored." Another surprise: drinking fountains labeled "For Colored Only" and "For Whites Only."

My good friend, Craig Armstrong (a member of our Berkeley group), told me the priorities for serving food. "After the whites had been provided for, they started bringing food aboard for the Negroes. Unfortunately," he added, "they quickly ran out of food." The train pulled out with most of the now-segregated California blacks getting nothing to eat! Our introduction to Texas drove home to us the practice of segregation in the South. Seeing something in person made a far bigger impact than reading about it.

Finally, on April 1, our train moved slowly on a spur line that led into Camp Wolters. The noncoms in charge of our cars yelled, "Gather your belongings and form on the platform next to this car. Camp Wolters cadre will take over." After sitting up for two nights without much sleep, we looked like what we were—a bedraggled bunch of raw recruits.

Noncommissioned officers separated us into three groups—blacks, white draftees, and the ERC group, also all-white. Then they separated the ERC group into platoons. I was now part of the 1st Platoon, C Company, 52nd Battalion. A corporal named Gerwiner looked at us with disgust and marched us off to our new home amid the mass of new two-story barracks that made up Camp Wolters. They looked almost exactly like those at Monterey.

Ten bare, steel-framed single beds, each with a footlocker in front of it, lined both sides of the long rectangular wood-floored room. Our second corporal, Corporal Whitmore, called out bed assignments. We picked up a thin pad, a mattress cover, a blanket, and a pillow. Whitmore showed us how Camp Wolters wanted beds made. It was the same as at the Presidio of Monterey. He added one new wrinkle: "Make the blanket so tight that when I drop a quarter on it, the quarter will bounce."

We ate dinner in the mess hall, checked out the PX, and returned to our barracks before lights out. Someone on our floor had a radio. He turned the dial from bottom to top, and virtually every station was playing country music.

Next morning, lights went on at 6:10 A.M. One of our two

corporals walked through our big room yelling the same crude message we heard at Monterey: "Drop your cocks and grab your socks!" He added another colorful order: "Let's move it, you bastards!" We lined up for roll call and daily calisthenics (including twenty-five fast push-ups) and met our platoon leader for the next three months, Lieutenant Shoup. He led us through a series of about seven other brisk exercises. Shoup was about twenty-four or twenty-five years of age and looked the part of the "gentleman" that officers are supposed to be. He made a good impression. Although decidedly aloof, Shoup still appeared pleasant and friendly, quite a contrast to our noncommissioned officers. He informed us that we would be taking basic infantry training with specialization in front-line radio and telephone communications.

After breakfast, we showered and shaved. Three or four of my group were not ready on time for our big chore of the day—to pick up basic infantry equipment. Our two corporal drill instructors went into apoplexy. They snarled, yelled, and threatened us with everything short of a firing squad. Such viciousness over such a small thing really bothered me. Both corporals and Sergeant Sekulovitch, our platoon sergeant, appeared dedicated to making us fear them. Their tactics certainly had the desired effect on me.

The climate the officers and noncommissioned officers established at Camp Wolters was the direct opposite of views expressed by General Eisenhower. He declared that "an Army fearful of its officers is never as good as one that trusts and confides in its leaders. . . . If men can naturally and without restraint talk to their officers, the products of their resourcefulness become available to all. Moreover, out of the habit grows mutual confidence, a feeling of partnership that is the essence of esprit de corps."[4] It sounded as though our army had a split personality on important points of conduct.

"When we tell you to do something, you do it immediately

and without hesitation," one corporal yelled. "You obey your superiors instantly, automatically. You don't question us. If you want to think differently, we'll knock that out of you in ways you won't like." Drill and what GIs called "chicken shit" concerning dress, haircuts, and inspections were all tools to turn independent-minded civilians into obedient troops.

Our noncoms became even tougher when they discovered that most of us came from colleges. They made it unmistakably clear they didn't like "college boys." They seemed to delight in wielding almost unlimited power over us. I decided we were at the mercy of sadists who hated us without really knowing anything about us, except that we went to college.

After the corporals cooled down, they marched us over to a supply room to pick up infantry tools and clothes. Each of us received a blanket, fatigues, a steel helmet and helmet liner, a shelter half and tent pegs to make half of a two-man pup tent, leggings, an entrenching tool (a small shovel to dig foxholes), a rifle belt, a bayonet, and a semiautomatic M1 Garand rifle (first manufactured in 1936).[5]

At the 99th Infantry Division Association convention in 1993, much of our army equipment of 1943 was on display. I tried on the 2.75-pound steel helmet for the first time in forty-nine years and was surprised at how heavy it felt. I remembered the entrenching tool as small, but not as small as it really was. In actuality, it was only twenty-eight inches long. With this midget shovel, we were supposed to dig five-foot-deep foxholes, often in rocky, root-infested ground. I was also surprised at how much heavier the 11.25-pound rifle felt. A highly respected semiautomatic rifle, the M1 accepted a clip of eight 30-caliber bullets. Each squeeze of the trigger fired a bullet. It ejected the fired bullet casing by gas action and automatically inserted a new bullet into the firing chamber. (Rifles with these characteristics are now called "assault weapons.") The M1 clearly outgunned the German Mauser, the standard rifle in the German infantry.

Noted for accuracy, the Mauser fired a clip of five 32-caliber bullets, three less than the M1. Each time a bullet was fired, the German rifleman had to push the bolt back to eject a shell and then forward to insert a new bullet in the firing chamber.[6]

When we returned to our barracks with our new equipment, we discovered that more ERC boys, many from City College of New York, had moved into the second floor. They tended to be aggressive, abrasive, loud, profane, extremely self-confident, fun loving, and very smart. The New Yorkers from upstate seemed more like the rest of us. Our noncoms especially disliked the New York City contingent.

Although many of the New Yorkers didn't mix much initially with the first-floor boys, one happy-go-lucky eighteen-year-old New Yorker from White Plains became our close buddy. He had a tongue-twisting name—William James ("Sack") Tsakanikas. Sack was outgoing, friendly, athletic, sometimes brash, and a fast learner with a great sense of humor. He liked to make fun of the antics of our corporals, but he managed to avoid their wrath most of the time by being disrespectful only when they weren't around. From this early stage of our army careers, Tsakanikas and I and many of my comrades converged on a single path that eventually led us to the Western Front in Belgium and Germany. For gutsy Tsakanikas, that path led to heroism and years of suffering.

Some of the bolder soldiers on both floors of the barracks fought back against the abusive treatment we received. The meanness of the sergeant and the corporals continued, as they snapped at the slightest imperfection and dealt out swift punishment to anyone with the wrong look on his face. I'm sure the noncoms would have acted differently if we had been going overseas together. With live ammunition on the battlefield, they would have been likely targets.

One noncom snapped at Bob Mitsch, my new friend from St. Thomas College, St. Paul, Minnesota. Mitsch didn't say a word, but his body language revealed hostile resistance. This was too much for the corporal. He gave Mitsch permanent latrine duty for the next thirteen weeks in addition to his already-heavy regular training schedule. Apparently he targeted Mitsch as an example for others. Forty-eight years later, Mitsch commented on his troubles with the sergeant and the two corporals: "I simply resented leaving my freedom at home when entering the service. I also harbored the mistaken idea that the army was trying to make fools of us young recruits."

Our training schedule moved up to full speed. My parents wanted a description of a typical day. I sent the following:

> Camp Wolters
> Mineral Wells, Texas
> April 18, 1943

Dear Mother and Dad,

At 5:15 A.M., the cook came through our dark barracks with his little flashlight picking recruits for the day's KP ["kitchen police"] duty. [KP included washing dishes, pots, and pans as well as cleaning the kitchen.] He wakes everyone in the process. At 6:10 A.M., we get dressed and make our beds "on the double." Before we can finish, a whistle blows for roll call and calisthenics. Then we run back into the barracks to finish our beds, polish our shoes, straighten the shelves, and button all buttons of shirts and jackets on the clothes hangers. We do all of this in just a few minutes. Again a whistle blows, and we rush to breakfast. After eating, we sweep and mop the floor of the barracks, fix a light battle pack, and "fall in" for extended-order drill at 7:50 A.M. Few of us have time to get to the latrine.

We then march three miles in platoon formation. When we reach our destination, we organize into squads and follow a second lieutenant, running across the countryside.

We also practice firing our rifles. At 11:30 A.M., we march back to our barracks for mail call and lunch. Immediately after a hasty meal, we make a full field pack. By 12:45 P.M., with all this equipment on our backs, we march two miles to a gas chamber to test our gas masks. Various poison gases, in diluted form, are released so we can learn them by smell. We march through the smoke with full field pack still on our backs.

At 4 P.M., we march back to the barracks and the parade ground for "close order" drill, executing orders of left face, right face, about face, forward march, to the rear march, etc. At 5:30 P.M., we eat. As soon as we finish, we have a "GI Party" at the barracks. This consists of taking all the beds outside and scrubbing the floors, washing windows, etc. When the place is spotless, we move to our last required task of the day: cleaning our rifles.

I just get the parts back together when the lights go out at 10 P.M. We then spend the next hour cleaning up in the latrine. By 11 P.M. I go to bed—dead tired. This is a typical day. . . .

Love, George

I think I lived in a dream world as we moved through the nitty gritty of the infantry training program. My main concern was to do well on all the skills being taught. The terrible reality that we were cannon fodder seemed to escape me.

At the end of April, an epidemic of German measles hit the camp, and I was one of its victims. I lay in bed in the Camp Wolters hospital for two stays, one for four days and one for thirteen. During those days in bed, I lost much of the good physical conditioning I had achieved.

The patients had to do KP just like the soldiers who were not ill. Another thing that seemed ridiculous to me was the daily inspections of the wards. At 9 P.M., we all got up, made our beds according to strict regulations, straightened things on our bedside tables, and placed our polished shoes on a certain spot with the laces tied tightly. Then we slipped back into our beds as carefully as possible, trying not to disturb the tightly drawn blankets. We lay quietly until someone yelled "Attention." The inspection officer stomped into the ward, checking for dust and wrinkled beds. "Attention," by the way, meant lying on our backs, both arms outside the blankets and extended stiffly parallel to our bodies, fingers extended. Our eyes stared, without wavering, at the ceiling immediately over our heads. (We were permitted to breathe.) When the officer left our ward, following an "at ease" order, we could relax and go to sleep.

I was pronounced well and ready to return to my platoon after a four-day stay in the hospital. When I reported for duty, I quickly learned that our corporals considered time in a hospital bed as "gold-bricking" (in other words, malingering). Still a bit shaky, I joined the platoon just in time for a double-time march.

I went straight from my hospital bed to the speedy schedule of the platoon. In a few hours, I was involved in an exercise that required me to go over the side of a mock troopship thirty feet above a waiting landing craft. I faltered. I was halfway over the side of the "ship." But with the added weight of the load on my back and the rifle, I could tell I was not strong enough to hold on. Lieutenant Shoup urged me to go ahead. "You can do it," he yelled. I pulled myself back onto the deck. "Try it again," Shoup urged. I refused. I was not going to kill myself for him. He apparently had forgotten that I had been lying in a hospital bed for four days. He gave me a dirty look, which made me feel like a shirker. He ordered me to get off the "ship" and continue the rest of the obstacle course.

At the end of the day I felt sick and was sure I had a fever. I finally talked the corporals into letting me report to the medics at the dispensary. After a quick check, they told me to report to the hospital—again. My temperature was 102 degrees.

After another thirteen days in the hospital, I returned for a second time to my platoon, weak from being in bed so long. My weight had dropped 14 pounds—from 154 to 140. Since I am six-foot-one, I looked skinny. Shoup finally recognized the mistake of putting me on full schedule so quickly. This time he eased me back into our rugged program.

I missed two weeks of communications technical training and the last week of basic training. I even missed three days at "Hell's Bottom," the toughest part of basic training at Camp Wolters. It included advancing on the "enemy" with live bullets snapping over soldiers' heads. I made it up by going out with another training cycle. When my group went through the "live" fire, one fellow raised his hand too high while crawling under the barbed wire. It met a bullet.

Lieutenant Shoup decided to let me graduate with my platoon at the end of our three-month training period. I completed one of his favorite workouts, a five-miles-in-one-hour, up-and-down-hill speed march (120 steps per minute) carrying sixty pounds of weight, including a field pack and a rifle. I was again one of the fastest in the platoon on the obstacle course. He said I recovered quickly and could accomplish much of the makeup required. That meant I didn't have to repeat the hellish program with strangers.

As we completed the last month of basic infantry we discovered a new enemy—hot, humid weather. It arrived with June in Mineral Wells. Fast marches with both the temperature and the humidity in the nineties were tough to survive without passing out en route. To keep us on our feet during these ordeals, the cooks sometimes placed salt tablets in our breakfast coffee and in lemonade served at lunch and dinner. On particularly hot days, our leaders ordered us to put a salt tablet in our water canteens after breakfast. I managed to complete most of the marches without collapsing.

One march took us over a four-mile trail of rocky ups and downs. It was one of the roughest afternoons I had experienced at Camp Wolters. The temperature was ninety-four degrees, and the humidity was nearly as high. Our bodies and clothes were soaking wet with sweat before we started. To make it even hotter, an officer ordered us to wear our gas masks. At times we had to run to keep up. Very few could make the march without stopping to rest, including two second lieutenants with their much lighter loads. They had put wads of toilet paper in their packs to make them look full and heavy. Instead of carrying M1 rifles, they carried the lighter carbines.

Near the halfway mark, our columns thinned out as members of our platoon started collapsing along the dusty trail. Then came the steepest and longest hill of all. It seemed almost straight up. We continued at the same fast pace. Near the top I began to lose my position in line. I fell into the dust at the side of the trail just beyond the crest but regained consciousness quickly when two friends gave me salty water from their canteens. After resting for ten minutes, I was back on my feet and made the bivouac area in time to go back to camp with the company. Soldiers littered the trail, trying to catch their breath or recover from heat exhaustion. Medics carried some to the hospital on stretchers.

We wound up our three-month training program with a maximum test of endurance, a twenty-mile march. I marched across from my friend Bob Mitsch, and every time I looked over at him I would see a big droplet of sweat clinging to the end of his nose. His face and clothes looked as if he just stepped out of a shower. He said I looked the same. When we returned to the barracks we could wring sweat out of our clothes.

The training marches behind us, we learned that we had something new to worry about. Lieutenant Shoup announced that Camp Wolters would select some of us for the new Army Specialized Training Program (ASTP). Those picked would go to college to study certain subject areas of interest to the army, including engineering, medicine, dentistry, and foreign languages. Those going into ASTP, he suggested, would have better opportunities for advancement in the army. That sounded great to me.

On our last day of training at Camp Wolters, Lieutenant Shoup posted a list of 1st Platoon men with orders to ASTP. About 50 percent made the list, including me. Most of us were assigned to the ASTP engineering program. To qualify for ASTP consideration, we had to have at least a high school diploma and a score of 115 or more on the Army General Classification Test—five points higher than the minimum for officer candidate schools. The men not ordered to ASTP received an immediate furlough. Then, many of them joined infantry divisions scheduled for the invasion of Italy.

On July 9, we said a heartfelt farewell to our friends not going into ASTP, boarded trucks, and left Camp Wolters. Our destination: Camp Maxey, located north of Paris, Texas, near the Red River border with Oklahoma.

2 • A Brief Diversion

*In June 1943, I graduated from Exeter. In July, I was in
the ASTP as an engineering student at V.M.I. . . . I flunked
out in November '43 (deliberately). I had figured out that
the program was useless for me. I was not an engineer. Also,
I knew that when the troubles began along the Rhine, we'd
be the cannon fodder. . . . Our original (ASTP) group was
nicely slaughtered.*

—GORE VIDAL, NOVELIST

JULY 9, 1943–MARCH 19, 1944

OUR ASSIGNMENT TO THE ARMY SPECIALIZED TRAIN-
ing Program started on a strange note. We marched
into Camp Maxey in the dark. Noncoms led us to our
new home within the grounds of the large army base. It looked
like a concentration camp surrounded by two high fences,
barbed wire, and guard towers. As we approached, its inhabitants started screaming. "Let us out," they howled. "The guards
are killing us!" Then, much to our amazement, a gate opened,
and we marched into a prison compound. As we passed through
two fences and barbed wire, the "inmates" started cheering:
"Welcome to the Jap Trap!"

We quickly learned that the "inmates" were ASTPers playing a joke on us. But the Jap Trap was not a joke. It was a real
prison facility the army had constructed for Japanese prisoners
of war. But since few Japanese soldiers surrendered, the army
found other uses for the facilities. In the Jap Trap, everything

was miniaturized to fit Japanese men, including the length of beds and the height of doorways. This customization presented a real problem for most of us. We kept forgetting to duck when we walked through doorways, and many of us had bloody bruises on our foreheads.

After twenty days of tests, interviews, marches, calisthenics, and loafing, we learned our fate. "Most of the Camp Wolters contingent are assigned to an ASTP engineering program at John Tarleton College at Stephenville," an officer told us. Stephenville is located forty miles southwest of Fort Worth.

Six days later, we arrived on the peaceful campus (now known as Tarleton State University). At this point, I was not sure ASTP made any sense for the army, but it meant more education and relatively good living conditions for us. I was delighted that most of my Camp Wolters group stayed together.

Since the population of Stephenville in 1943 was only 4,768 (17,000 in 1995) and enrollment in the college was about 400 (6,400 in 1995), the sudden arrival of 500 soldiers caused a big social and economic impact on both the town and the college. The theater and local food establishments were jammed on weekends, and females in the town could have as many dates as they wanted.

The only other students at Tarleton were civilian females, 4F males, and some seventeen-year-old civilian male ROTC cadets. Many of the other male students had already left for military service. As the first (and only) soldiers stationed in Stephenville, we were accepted wholeheartedly by many townspeople. They could not understand, however, how we were going to help win the war.

Our ASTP program was designed for overstudious bookworms. ASTPers had higher average test scores than air cadets and candidates for West Point and Annapolis, according to Brig. Gen. Walter L. Weible, the army's director of military training.[1]

The program was a terror, especially for liberal arts majors like me. My schedule called for thirty-four hours of class work, military drill, and physical workout during each six-day week: seven hours of physics, six hours of math (algebra to begin with), three hours of chemistry, three hours of American history, three hours of English, two hours of geography, and ten hours of military drill and physical conditioning. This did not include the hours required to complete daily homework. All courses were conducted at double- and triple-time. A friend in ASTP declared, "If you dropped a pencil in class, by the time you picked it up you were three weeks behind."

We completed the first half of our algebra program in nine days, which I figured set some kind of speed record. After another nine days for the other half, we moved on to trigonometry, then to analytical geometry and calculus. I quickly discovered that college-level physics and chemistry were tough for the 40 percent of us who had avoided them in high school. Our physics teacher formerly taught music, so he was having as much trouble as we were. The army, perhaps feeling defensive about having so many healthy young men in college with a war going on, made certain we did not have an easy life. Some of our teachers said they thought the program covered too much ground too quickly.

A new directive from the commanding officer (CO) in early February required us to take daily tests in physics, calculus, and history. The army wanted to identify those who received failing grades as quickly as possible. A failing grade in any course—a "D" (below 70 percent)—meant a quick transfer to a regular army unit. The commanding officer also required teachers to post grades in the hall for all to see. Several who failed were sent to the Signal Corps Officer Candidate School.

Nine months after starting ASTP, the army decided to close most of the program. Chalk this up to a costly error in manpower needs. Gen. George C. Marshall, army chief of staff, said the army had to fill manpower shortages in ten stateside divisions or be forced to dissolve them.[2] Since no one wanted to do that with the invasion of Normandy looming, the answer was obvious. Transfer the ASTPers. They were just what the infantry needed: vigorous young men in A-1 physical shape who, for the most part, had already taken infantry basic training. In an official letter to ASTP engineering students, the army said bluntly: "The time has come for the majority of you to be assigned to other active duty. The ASTP will be reduced to 35,000 trainees [from 140,000]."[3]

The army did not admit to its big, expensive mistake that involved more than 100,000 men. If it had calculated carefully, it would never have started Secretary Stimson's dream (ASTP) in the first place.

The army could not argue that it needed college-trained men as much as it needed fighting men on the front line, with one exception. The army wanted more medical doctors. It offered all interested ASTPers in the closing engineering program an opportunity to take a medical aptitude test. Those who passed would be transferred to colleges with ASTP pre-medical programs. Several at Tarleton passed. One was Stanford University's Norman E. Shumway, who credits ASTP and the medical aptitude test for his going into medicine. Shumway, from Michigan, pioneered in heart bypass surgery at Stanford University Hospital and became known as the "father" of heart transplantation. Thus, ASTP and the medical aptitude test made a major contribution to American medicine. ASTPers in other colleges who became famous included Henry Kissinger, secretary of state in the Nixon and Ford administrations; Edward I. Koch, former mayor of New York City; Gore Vidal, novelist; Kurt Vonnegut, novelist; George Kennedy, actor; and Harry Reasoner, news journalist with CBS News and "Sixty Minutes." In addition, "ASTP proved extremely important to several technical branches of the Army," said Lt. Gen. Brehon B. Somervell, army chief of supply and procurement. A report prepared by his command cited the example of sixteen hundred former ASTPers who helped make the first atomic bomb.[4]

Some in the Tarleton ASTP group were bitter about the army's decision—with good reason. They had already earned the rank of sergeant before the ASTP began. They gave up their rank because success in ASTP was supposed to increase their chances of becoming second lieutenants. They left ASTP as privates. The army needed enlisted personnel, not officers. I do not want to leave the impression that we ASTPers believed we were elite and should not be asked to risk our lives in battle. Looking back from the vantage of more than fifty years, I think we should not have been surprised at the outcome. Our country did to the ASTP what it had done previously in emergencies. It placed the perceived welfare of the many before the sanctity of the contract with the few.

The army decided our next assignment. We received orders to return to Camp Maxey to join the 99th Infantry Division. As we pulled up stakes to leave Tarleton, the major part of ASTP—the largest single college training program the U.S. government ever implemented—came to a close. We were now on our way to some distant battlefield.

3 • From Boys to Men— In the Infantry

*The ties that bind soldier and unit are strong. There is
a sense of home, of belonging.*
—PFC. HARRY S. ARNOLD, E COMPANY,
393RD REGIMENT, 99TH DIVISION

MARCH 20–SEPTEMBER 13, 1944

WE WAVED GOODBYE TO FRIENDLY CROWDS OF
college officials, teachers, and school children who
cheered us as our buses left Stephenville. Several hours
later, we rolled into the drastically different world of the seventy-
thousand-acre Camp Maxey. No tree-lined streets here.

We were part of the 3,200-man ASTP infusion into the 99th
Division. At full strength, it had 14,253 men. We were replacing
3,000 riflemen and others the 99th Division had contributed to
the 85th and 88th Divisions to make up for combat losses in
Italy.

As "bus leader," I marched my group into a company area
where the 99th Division noncoms waited. A belligerent looking
sergeant stepped forward and greeted us with curt orders. We
could feel his hostility immediately. He let us know he didn't
think much of college students as soldiers. He marched us to the
headquarters for L Company, 3rd Battalion, 395th Regiment,

one of the 99th's three regiments. A company clerk called us, one by one, into the office to answer required questions on army forms. It was similar to a mass hotel registration.

As we waited, we speculated on the nature of L Company. In making assignments, the 99th would surely take into account the infantry communications training many of us had received at Camp Wolters. That would not be so bad, we thought. But our optimism faded quickly. Someone yelled, "It's a rifle company, and we are going into rifle platoons!" Our new assignment had a special finality to it. Rifle platoons meet the enemy face to face, either to advance on the ground or to hold ground already taken. The rest of the army existed to support them.

Thanks to our infantry basic training, we had a good idea about life in a rifle platoon. We knew it was one of the most dangerous outfits we could get into. Its main purpose was to kill— close up—as many of the enemy as possible. We would learn a skill of no value in civilian life, unless we became bank robbers or gangster hit-men. I never saw so many dejected faces.

Within a week, most of us had recovered from the depression that overcame us when we joined the 99th. We started to fight back in a positive way as we went through a refresher training program as an all-ASTP unit. Pride of group began to influence our behavior. Taunting from our noncommissioned officers spurred most of us to excel at every task—drills, fast marches, the obstacle course, even neatness of dress and bed making.

The physical education program we had received in ASTP helped our standing with some sergeants. When we arrived at Camp Maxey, we were in better shape than most of the army not serving in the infantry. Fortunately, not all of our leaders disliked us. The animosity came from some of the sergeants and lieutenants but not from most of the higher ranking officers, including Maj. Gen. Walter E. Lauer, division commander, age fifty-one. Unfortunately, we rarely saw our colonels and generals. We saw the sergeants every day.

The top brass liked the idea of having many young, healthy, well educated, highly motivated men in the bottom ranks of their rifle platoons. They knew they had a plentiful supply of potential leaders. ASTPer Paul Putty, I Company, 395th Regiment, said he overheard Col. Alexander J. Mackenzie, commanding officer of the 395th, tell two other colonels that he had never seen such intelligent enlisted men. Mackenzie said his ASTP men learned twice as fast as the typical training group and created no discipline problems. Lt. James Hare, a liaison officer for the 3rd Battalion on the front line in Germany, credited part of our battalion's strong combat performance to the large infusion of ASTP students it received before going overseas. "These kids made damn fine soldiers. They had guts, vigor, smarts, and performed very, very well," Hare said.[1]

We ASTPers were beginning to look and feel like hardened infantry. Each day we got up at 5 A.M. and left for the rifle range to fire the M1 rifle. For three days we worked in the pits running targets for another battalion of ASTPers. Then we spent three days firing. We marched out in freezing weather wearing overcoats, gloves, and wool caps, and we marched back in the heat of a Texas late afternoon. In the early morning the wind was so cold the glue we used on the targets froze.

Lt. Col. McClernand Butler, our battalion commander, said we broke all known records in any U.S. Army camp. All but two of us made "sharpshooter" or "expert" (the best). These two exceptions made "marksman." At Camp Wolters I had barely made sharpshooter, but this time I was nearly expert by making high sharpshooter. At Wolters the qualifying rate for the entire camp was about 65 percent, but in this outfit it was 100 percent.

Life got tougher every day. I wrote my parents in early April about what it was like: "Already, I have fired my rifle more here than during the three months at Camp Wolters. During the past two weeks, we have had knife fighting, hand grenade throwing, bayonet practice, compass reading, first aid, and practice in crawling and creeping. Beginning Monday we go on two weeks of maneuvers, so don't expect any mail from me."

Bayonet practice worked us into a particularly bloodthirsty mood. Our bayonet trainers told us over and over that every German we killed would bring the war closer to an end. They repeatedly said, "The only good German is a dead German." My instructor advised: "Stick them in the abdomen, chest, or neck, and don't go too deep. A deep thrust may be difficult to withdraw. In case the bayonet gets stuck, put your foot against your opponent's body, and then pull with both hands. Do it quickly. If that does not work, fire your rifle. The shot will blast him off the bayonet."

During this phase of our training, we learned all about venereal disease (VD). Sitting in soaked clothes resulting from a downpour on our way to a camp theater, we viewed a new army film featuring an older army doctor who personified credibility. He showed us ghastly photos of syphilis and gonorrhea cases, and calmly suggested we would be wise to avoid sexually transmitted diseases. The only sure way, he added, was abstinence. If not abstinence, he added, use army-prescribed protection before and after sexual intercourse. "This is a must," he asserted. "Protection," the film doctor continued, "means to use a condom and report to a prophylactics station." An enlisted man demonstrated use of a condom by rolling one down a broom handle. We squirmed in our soaked clothing. The cool, calm doctor, by speaking in a quiet, professional-sounding voice, did a good job of scaring us.

Colonel Butler and a middle-aged 99th Division chaplain sat on the stage during the film. When it ended, the Baptist chaplain gave us an impassioned speech about the importance and rightness of abstinence. "Save the intimate act of love for your marriage," he declared. Following the chaplain's appeal, Colonel Butler stepped to the podium. With the chaplain now back in his chair listening, Butler made it clear that he didn't care what we did, as long as it didn't hurt our effectiveness as soldiers. Then he added succinctly: "I don't want any 'promiscuous fucking' in this battalion!" ("Promiscuous" meant not using prescribed protection.) I just about fell off my chair. I wondered what the chaplain thought about the colonel's earthy comments.

With Butler's memorable quote reverberating in our heads, we filed out, water still squishing inside our shoes, right past an army VD poster on the theater wall. It declared: YOU CAN'T SLAP A JAP WITH THE CLAP! It featured a drawing of a grotesque Japanese Army officer happily looking at a graph showing a sharp rise in venereal disease in the U.S. Army. In addition to advising us that "prophylactics prevent venereal disease," it listed nearby "Pro Stations": AT ALL DISPENSARIES [at Camp Maxey]. IN PARIS [Texas]—WHITE, II N. 2OTH ST.; COLORED, III TUDOR ST. IN HUGO [Oklahoma]—206 S. BROADWAY. No separation by color was mentioned for Hugo.

Our ASTP training battalion completed the refresher basic infantry course in only two and a half weeks, instead of the five to seven weeks originally planned. Some of our company officers told us they were impressed, but most of our noncoms remained silent.

During the training period, the former ASTP students occupied the first floor of a barracks, and the regulars occupied the second floor. We rarely saw each other because we followed one schedule and they followed another. But now we became one outfit. With about 60 percent ASTP and 40 percent regulars, we made up a full-strength 2nd Platoon, one of L Company's three rifle platoons. A similar merger of ASTP and regulars occurred in all the other eighty rifle platoons of the 99th. Thanks to the ASTP transfusion, the 99th Division and nine other undermanned infantry divisions became viable again.

Never were two more dissimilar groups of men pooled together in an army unit that required absolute teamwork for survival. The old-timers were mostly two or three years older than the ASTPers, and they looked several years older than their actual ages. These riflemen came to the 99th Division when it was formed in Mississippi in late 1942.

The marriage of the two groups was a culture shock for both sides, and neither liked the other by the end of the first hour together. We had little in common except that we both served in the same platoon, carried rifles and bayonets, and were very good shots. Many of the regulars, often hard drinkers, thought the ASTP men were not real men and would not make good soldiers because many drank only milk, milk shakes, or soda pop. Real men, they said, drank hard liquor or beer. Another difference: most of the regulars smoked cigarettes; a high percentage of the ASTPers did not. Many of the old-timers chewed tobacco, a habit no ASTPer had. These small differences added up to a big difference to many of the regulars. To increase the friction, a few ASTPers made fun of the noncoms behind their backs and acted superior. Many of the regulars had not graduated from high school, and a few could neither read nor write. Most were good soldiers—tough and mean when it was necessary (and often when it was not).

My squad leader, about twenty years old, was a short, smart, remarkably strong and tough sergeant named Joseph Mysliewiec. We called him Sergeant Mike. I rated him excellent as an infantry soldier. Before entering the army, he had graduated from high school. Initially, he was neutral toward ASTPers, revealing a cool "show me" attitude. He exhibited no direct hostility. During our infantry refresher course, he turned from cool to friendly. He discovered that most of us were excellent riflemen, and that we brought an upbeat spirit to the platoon. He treated both old-timers and newcomers firmly but fairly. Remarkably calm in tough spots, he actually smiled once in a while, an uncommon trait among many infantry sergeants. We felt lucky to have him.

My platoon sergeant, Eugene E. Thompson, about twenty-four years old, was moody and brusque. Also a good, dedicated soldier, he demanded strict obedience.

We ASTPers and the regulars began working together as a

team doing typical infantry training activities. We followed the "buddy system" in the field. This meant that assigned pairs dug foxholes together, pitched pup tents together, slept in the same tiny pup tent, and supported each other in simulated combat.

In one of our typical war games, we left the camp on a Monday morning for a wilderness area about ten miles away. We spent the first day digging foxholes and marching six miles with a full field pack. We ate late (about 11:30 P.M.). The next day, we shoved off at 5:30 A.M. More digging was on our agenda, plus war maneuvers that included attacking machine gun positions and capturing farmhouses. At night we took turns as sentinels. My shift was from 2:30 to 4:24 A.M.

One night six of us went on patrol into "enemy" territory. We were surrounded at once, but it was so dark we escaped. After cutting up the "enemy's" wire communications, we returned at 1 A.M. only to be sent out again to get some prisoners. Instead, an "enemy" patrol captured us and marched us back to their headquarters. We didn't get back to our side until 6 A.M., just in time to participate in the main attack—and miss breakfast. At 8 A.M., live shells from the 81-mm mortars and 105-mm howitzers whistled over our heads. Added to this was live rifle fire. By noon we captured our objective and got our first food in twenty-four hours and first water in eighteen hours. The experience left us exhausted, but Sergeant Thompson told us to fill in scores of foxholes. Other highlights of the week included experiencing a gas bomb attack in the midst of a chow line and constant attack by Texas chiggers.

We continued the rugged field problems into a full second week, during which we fought a "battle," found hidden machine guns, and dug foxholes—all with minimum food, water, and sleep and maximum rain, mud, and discomfort. During these two weeks, we marched 130 fiercely hot miles, partly in Oklahoma and partly in Texas. A highlight in Oklahoma was a rest period in a farmer's watermelon patch. By the time we pulled out, we had eaten most of his crop. During this period in the field, Sergeant Mysliewiec appointed me Browning Automatic Rifle (BAR) assistant gunner for my squad.

The BAR, first manufactured in 1918, was the powerhouse of American rifle squads in World War II. Gas operated, it was a mix of machine gun and rifle. Each squad of twelve men had one BAR. Infantry specialists considered it an especially good defensive weapon. I agree.

In combat, the BAR man usually drew enemy fire because he was in charge of the rifle squad's most dangerous weapon. As a result, the other men in the platoon tried to keep a safe distance from him. Two men, an assistant gunner and an ammunition bearer, supported the BAR gunner.

Usually used with a bipod at the front-end of its barrel to improve accuracy, the BAR could fire a maximum of three hundred rounds (bullets) per minute, according to the BAR field manual. Its sustained rate of fire was forty to sixty rounds per minute. Maximum range was two miles, but its maximum effective range was fifteen hundred feet.

In contrast, the M1 rifle was a manual, single shot, semiautomatic weapon with a maximum firing rate of about thirty-four rounds per minute. To hit a specific enemy soldier, its maximum effective range was 225 feet. When used to spray an area, it was effective at 1,095 feet.

The BAR was rough on the gunner because it weighed twenty-one pounds seven ounces loaded, compared to eleven pounds four ounces for an M1 rifle. The BAR gunner also carried 240 rounds in twelve magazines in his ammunition belt. They weighed a minimum of seventeen pounds, bringing the total weight for the weapon and its bullets/magazines to more than thirty-eight pounds. Each loaded magazine of twenty rounds weighed one pound seven ounces. If the gunner carried a bandoleer for extra ammunition, as he sometimes did, that added nine pounds. That load, plus the full field pack, brought the total weight carried by a BAR gunner to approximately seventy pounds. No wonder I felt like an overloaded moving van.

Every day the former college students and the "old men" worked better as a team, and we began to respect each other as good soldiers. But the ASTP men and the regulars rarely went together to the service club or on passes to Paris, Hugo, or Dallas.

In a few cases, however, highly positive personal relationships developed. One example was my platoon's medic, former ASTPer Warner Anthony, and Willie Cates, age twenty-seven, ammo bearer on our BAR team and former coal miner from Kentucky. My squad called Cates "Pop" because he was much too old, we thought, for a rifle platoon. Anthony discovered that Cates could not read the letters his wife sent him, nor could he write to her. Anthony offered to teach Cates, and Cates accepted. During the next few months, Cates learned the basics of reading and writing.[2]

My new job as assistant BAR gunner gave me a new "buddy." He was Pfc. John Smith (name changed), about twenty-three years old. He looked thirty and was illiterate. Smith served as my squad's BAR gunner. In civilian life he was a coal miner and moonshiner.

I joined Smith after a stop to set up defensive positions on a ridge line. We were told to dig a hole among four-foot-high bushes that camouflaged our location. I sat on the ground and waited until Smith had dug one shovel-blade deep. When he sat down, I started digging the depth of another blade. As I dug, he began to talk, mostly about his former civilian life. I noticed immediately that one four-letter word dominated his speech. He could use three or more forms of the word in one short sentence. He was a bitter, angry man with a sadistic, dehumanized outlook on virtually everything, including sex. He talked continuously, and I listened for two hours. He recounted how he had fooled revenue agents trying to destroy illegal distilleries hidden in the woods at home. Later, he told me he had shot a man who was having sex with his girlfriend. At that point, I had heard too much.

As soon as we completed the foxhole, Smith pulled from his pocket a smooth, flat piece of stone and, from under his fatigues, a knife with a six-inch blade. When he started sharpening the knife on the stone, I was afraid to ask him why he needed such a sharp knife. I soon learned that the sharpening stone and the knife were Smith's trademarks. Later, I saw him use the knife to cut the shell from a live turtle and watch its naked body squirm in agony. He performed this surgery so skillfully that it had to be something he had done many times before. I began to think he could do likewise to people. Fortunately for me, Smith did not become my pup tent/sleeping buddy as well as my foxhole buddy. Before we ASTPers arrived, Smith had been teamed up for sleeping with Willie Cates. They continued that arrangement.

In early May, we participated in our first field exercise involving both infantry and tanks. The army wanted us to know first-hand the problems of tank crews in combat. We learned by climbing inside and riding at the machine gunner's spot in a light tank and a medium Sherman, the mainstay tank for American ground forces. The idea was to show us how little tank gunners could see when bumping over rough ground.

This experience taught me the great difficulty of firing accurately from a moving tank and how vulnerable the tank is from the sides and rear. The exercises were intended to give us greater confidence if confronted by enemy tanks. I shuddered to think of the results when a shell penetrated the tank's armor and exploded inside. To illustrate this phenomenon, the army sprayed the inside of a Sherman with white paint and then fired a shell through its side. The explosion sent thousands of pieces of shrapnel ricocheting back and forth inside until all their energy was spent. Each shrapnel strike was recorded on the white paint. Crew members would be shredded by pieces of steel. Many enemy and American tank crews met that ghastly fate.

After our experience with the tanks, we were scheduled for

a big march—the toughest physical endurance test required to win the Expert Infantry Badge. It ranked with excellent marksmanship as one of the most important infantry tests. We marched twenty-five miles in eight hours carrying full field packs and rifles. Unfortunately, the weather was unseasonably hot and humid. Before we left the battalion area, we dropped salt tablets into our canteens of water.

As we marched out of the barracks area at 8 A.M., the temperature was in the high seventies. Our return deadline was 4 P.M. We formed two columns and, heading north toward the Red River, followed a dirt road into a vast unoccupied wilderness of scrubby forests, small fields, and dilapidated, unoccupied farmhouses. We kept a steady pace of 3.5 miles per hour, somewhat faster than the traditional infantry pace of 2.5 miles per hour. At the end of each hour we took a ten-minute break. The first couple of hours went easily. Smith carried the BAR during the first hour. Then he traded with Cates, our BAR ammunition carrier.

By 10 A.M., as the temperature rose, the weight of our rifles and packs seemed to increase. I traded my M1 rifle for the onerous BAR Cates was carrying. We traded back a half-hour later. The trail was now sprinkled with sweat. About 11 A.M., I took the BAR from Cates again. As we waded through a small creek, we took off our heavy steel helmets, filled them with dirty water, and placed them back on our heads. The water poured over our faces and down over our fatigues. It cooled us for a moment and felt wonderful. This was the first time I had carried a BAR for any distance. No wonder no one wanted to be BAR gunner.

At the halfway mark, we stopped to eat our bag lunches, consisting of the usual two sandwiches and the salty water in our canteens. Then we were on our way again. Nineteen-year-old Ensign Williamsen, our squad's second scout, volunteered to carry the BAR for two hours. As the strain increased, the column spontaneously began singing "Volga Boatman," "I've

Been Working on the Railroad," "Birmingham Jail," and other songs. "Volga Boatman" seemed most appropriate for an endurance march, so we sang it most often.

At about 2 P.M., Williamsen returned the BAR, and Smith quickly took it. He wanted to avoid carrying it for the last—and toughest—hour. With both the temperature and humidity now in the mid-nineties, our clothing became soaked with sweat. We passed a handful of men who had fallen out and lay exhausted under trees along the roadside. At the 3 P.M. break, Smith gave me the BAR to carry during the last hour.

We became silent as each man concentrated on completing the march without collapsing or becoming a straggler. The road rose steadily as it approached Camp Maxey, and the gaps between the marching men gradually widened. Our orderly appearance faded as a few men pulled out of the lines to set a slower pace. One by one, men fell at the side of the road. Ambulances, nicknamed "meat wagons," waited to pick up those who needed medical help. I struggled with the BAR, but I managed to keep up. So did everyone around me. As we marched into Camp Maxey, we closed ranks.

The men in camp watched as we neared our barracks with heads up, trying mightily to disguise our overwhelming exhaustion. After roll call, we headed straight for our beds to take off our dripping clothes and rest. I had a tremendous feeling of accomplishment, especially since I carried the BAR for the final hour. We all felt elated as we raced into the shower room. I was in my best-ever physical condition and, despite the fatigue, I felt marvelous.

The 99th's old-timers quietly noted that the college boys performed very well—better than they did. But, we had an advantage. We were younger. This ordeal marked a major step in bringing our two groups together as a successful team.

Training, training, and more training. By mid-May, we feared that we would burn out from the heavy dose of marching and battle exercises before we arrived on a real battlefield. However, the division wanted to make sure we would not arrive on the front line inadequately trained. Pressure to get us into top shape continued. We marched another seventy-five miles during the next seven days of war games.

One afternoon, a terrific thunder and lightning storm hit us as we moved across an open slope bracketed by thick forests. We stopped in our tracks, terrified by the lightning. Sergeant Mysliewiec stretched out on the ground and covered himself and his rifle with his raincoat. We copied him. Another series of lightning bolts must have hit very close, because the sound of the thunder followed the lightning in one or two seconds. At this point, I decided that having a wet, dirty rifle was much better than being struck by lightning attracted to the metal. So I gently tossed it out into the open field, as far away from me as possible. Others did the same thing. It was dark when the storm passed. We picked up our muddy rifles and moved by platoons into the nearby woods. After trying to clean our rifles in the dark and eating K rations (small packets of prepared food), we set up a perimeter guard. Then we placed our blankets on the wet ground and tried to make up for the previous night, when none of us had slept more than three hours.

Sometime in the middle of the night I woke up. The moon shone brightly, and shafts of light filtered through the tree branches. I spotted something moving over a fallen log in our midst. I suspected a large snake. Finally, convinced I was not seeing things, I shook Mysliewiec's shoe and pointed to where I had seen "it." We started searching and, in the process, woke the entire platoon. For the rest of the night, all forty of us sat up imagining a big snake in our midst. As dawn arrived, many dirty looks were directed my way. Thanks to me, the platoon got off to an early start in our continuing search for the elusive "enemy infantry."

In late morning, our scouts sensed the "enemy" was on the

other side of a nearby woods. We moved off a dirt road and spread out in a skirmish line. As soon as we were among the trees, Smith and another man took off their shoes and bounced barefoot through the rough forest bottom. As assistant gunner, I ran behind him, with my shoes on. When we exited the other side of the forest without spotting the "enemy," we moved back to the road.

In the afternoon we set up a defensive position on a ridge. I quickly dug a shallow hole just deep enough for me to lie below ground level. As I was getting ready to fire (blanks), a thin black snake dropped from a branch above me, fell across my rifle, and skittered off my left arm. I was so startled I jumped up and gave away my concealed position. Sergeants Mysliewiec and Thompson both told me to stop being so jumpy about snakes. "Get used to them." Earlier that day, however, word had passed through our company that a soldier in another 395th battalion was in serious condition from a poisonous snakebite incurred several nights earlier. Apparently the snake slid over his face while he slept, and he attempted to brush it off. That incident made us much more nervous about snakes.

On June 6, we were getting ready to depart on a two-day, 330-mile motor (truck) march to hill country near Abilene, Texas, where we were scheduled for a mock battle with the 12th Armored Division. It would launch an attack against defensive positions we were going to prepare and defend. After breakfast, we heard on the mess hall radio that the invasion of France had begun on the beaches of Normandy.

Our journey ended in a desolate mountainous area. The trucks dropped us off at the foot of rough, hilly terrain. After a march of a few miles into higher ground, we halted and pitched our pup tents. The only sign of civilization was a dilapidated ranch windmill that actually produced good water. After a quick C-ration dinner of canned beef stew, we lined up for showers under the cool water pouring out of a pipe about eight feet above the windmill's platform. Hot, tired, and sweaty after the two-day truck ride, we stood waiting our turns, one platoon at a time, in a long, naked line. We all used the same bar of soap. We had no towels, but we dried quickly with the help of wind blowing over our bodies. Rustic as it was, the shower gave us a great feeling of rejuvenation.

Early the next morning, we marched about five miles east to an escarpment with a long-range view of Abilene and beyond. At the edge of this lookout, Capt. Paul Price, commanding officer of L Company, ordered Smith, Cates, and me to dig deep foxholes with good lines of fire. When we started digging, our entrenchment tools bounced more than dug. The ground was mostly rock. Finally, after much yelling on our part, Sergeant Mysliewiec found us a real pick and shovel.

Around noon, we decided to eat the brown-bag lunches of two peanut butter and jelly sandwiches, which we had placed on a rock. Small ants swarmed over and inside the sacks. "Just a few piss ants," Smith declared. I returned my bag to the rock, but Smith and Cates picked up their sandwiches and began to eat. "Why don't you eat?" Smith asked. "I won't eat anything covered with ants," I replied. Both Cates and Smith doubled over in fits of laughter. "Are you afraid of a few piss ants?" Smith asked. Cates jumped in: "Ants won't hurt you," he taunted, as he bit into ants and sandwich. If Smith had been the only one there, I would not have listened. But, with Cates also giving me a hard time, I pulled out the ant-covered sandwiches, flicked off a few ants, and quickly ate them both.

That night Bill Parmelee and I had barely fallen asleep when a pouring rain awakened us. The ground had become so drenched that our tent pegs would not hold, and our pup tent collapsed on top of us. As we put things back together in the dark, water flowed inside our tent, soaking our blankets and rifles. Worn out from the uncomfortable night of semi-sleep, we staggered back to finish our half-done foxholes. This time, I kept my lunch in my pocket. By the end of the day, our foxholes were shoulder-deep, a major accomplishment in light of our lack of sleep and the difficult terrain.

To boost our morale and build camaraderie, Captain Price ordered the company cooks to serve a "Texas barbecue" accompanied by a "beer bust" around a camp fire. He sent a company Jeep into Camp Barkley to pick up a trailer full of bottled beer (Texas Pearl). With the beer and the singing, we forgot our troubles. This was the first alcoholic beverage some of us had ever tasted. Some, including Ensign Williamsen, a Mormon, would not touch it.

To make an attack even costlier for our "enemy," we prepared a second line of defense two or three miles behind our forward foxholes. When we finished digging, we strategically placed antipersonnel mines and booby traps to "kill" as many of the "enemy" as possible before they reached our first line of defense. We also spread miles of barbed wire to slow down their attack. Our combat engineers constructed tank traps and placed fifteen thousand antitank mines armed with puff (smoke) charges on roads and trails.

Captain Price said combat conditions would prevail (breakfast before dawn, no lunch, dinner near midnight, and no tents or fires) for the next week. Thus, while the war swayed in the balance in Normandy, the 395th prepared for a sham battle. To add realism, both sides fired blank shells, but they sounded like the real thing. Referees decided who was captured, wounded, or killed.

Our efforts to stop the 12th Armored Division paid off. We beat back its attack decisively. I think we won because of the large number of defenses we used and our favorable high-ground location. "We" consisted of only one infantry regiment (the 395th) with additional attached engineers and artillery. Our opponent, the 12th, consisted of three flexible combat commands, each of which had considerably more firepower and ability to maneuver than an infantry regiment.

Our success helped to boost our pride in the 395th. With

our "battle" won, we relaxed and stretched out on our blankets under the stars for a good night's sleep. Just after daylight, we awoke and ate a K-Ration breakfast (biscuits and food tins in a cardboard pack). A rustle in the bushes only twenty feet away alerted us to the largest rattlesnake I had ever seen. It coiled up, ready to strike. Smith grabbed my rifle and thrust the barrel at the snake's head. It struck, but not close enough for Smith. Twice more he taunted it. Then, when it struck again, closer to the end of the barrel, Smith pulled the trigger. The concussion from the exploding blank shell smashed the snake's head, killing it instantly. Not satisfied with just killing the great rattler, Smith pulled out his knife, grabbed the dead snake just below its shattered head, and started skinning it. He hung the skin over his backpack and ran to catch up. Smith's gait indicated that he was very proud of his trophy. He kept the skin looped over his backpack for the next three days. My "buddy" was obviously a five-star sadist.

We returned to Camp Maxey after fifteen days in the wilderness. Our success over the 12th Armored Division was so great that it had to undergo additional training before going overseas. We had created a "main line of resistance" (MLR) with an "enemy" on the other side. As part of building that front line, we learned the art of using booby traps and antipersonnel mines. We also learned the importance of having a second line of resistance in case the first line collapsed. (This lesson helped us greatly a few months later when we used it against the Germans.) These experiences brought us closer to readiness for a real front.

On our return to camp, we found that we had a new platoon leader, a six-foot-four, lanky, shy second lieutenant named Jackson W. Goss, age twenty. Goss enlisted in the army at age eighteen, right after completing high school in Lamar, Missouri, his birthplace. (President Harry Truman and Goss were born in the same house.) A graduate of Ft. Benning's Infantry Officer Candidate School, he knew infantry basics upside down. Nineteen at the time, Goss was one of the youngest graduates of that tough school. Although he had the final word, he gave Sergeant Thompson, our platoon sergeant, much leeway in running the platoon.

A forty-man platoon included three squads of twelve men each. Mysliewiec, my squad leader, reported to Thompson, platoon sergeant, who reported to Goss, who reported to Captain Price. He reported to Colonel Butler, commander of the 3rd Battalion. An infantry rifle company had four platoons: three rifle platoons and one weapons platoon (machine guns and mortars). A rifle company consisted of 193 men.

In late June, after fifteen months in the army, I finally received a promotion. This happened at the same time that John Smith disappeared from our ranks. When I asked his whereabouts, Sergeant Mysliewiec told me he was in the Camp Maxey stockade. "He got drunk and disorderly in a bar in Paris. When the Military Police went to pick him up, he pulled out his knife and dared them to take him. Before they subdued him, he had badly cut up several MPs. So, Smith is gone, as far as we are concerned. We don't want him back. We think he could be dangerous to the officers and noncommissioned officers in a battle situation. If he got angry at an order he didn't like, he might turn his gun on us."

Mysliewiec announced that I was the new BAR gunner, replacing Smith. Thus, I became a Private First Class. Willie Cates, the former ammunition bearer, became my assistant gunner, and John R. Karchner, ASTPer with me at Tarleton College and a former civilian student at Gettysburg College in Pennsylvania, replaced Cates as ammunition bearer. I noted to myself that the old-timers were gradually being replaced by ASTPers as BAR gunners. That made the old-timers happy.

I was proud of my new assignment. It showed that my sergeants thought I could perform well in this rugged job. My ego was deflated years later when I discovered that several good men in my squad deliberately tested poorly with the BAR on the firing range so they would not be given the job. No one wanted to carry this heavy weapon. Another reason it was unpopular: the Germans always wanted to knock it out. Its distinctive sound (da-da-dum), moreover, told the enemy its location.

In July, I received a two-week furlough and, around the same time, on a staggered schedule, everyone else received furloughs as well. This fact told a big story, because the army usually gave furloughs before a unit shipped overseas. Departures from home at the end of these furloughs were usually wrenching affairs. Mothers, wives, and girlfriends shed many tears. Even unemotional dads were often stressed, trying not to cry.

Back at Camp Maxey, our officers and noncoms alerted us to things we should do before leaving the country. One was to check the beneficiary of the $10,000 government life insurance policy given all soldiers. Another was to increase the amount deducted from our paychecks for savings. When my father promised me a dollar for every dollar I saved, I considered his offer a good incentive for saving.

On September 10, trains began moving the 14,253 men of the 99th Division to an unknown port of embarkation. General Lauer ordered all of us to remove unit patches from our shirts and jackets so no one could identify us.

As the trains departed, Lauer reported on the mood of his men. "The urge to see strange places and real combat was getting stronger," he said. His analysis was certainly different from mine. I knew of no riflemen who had an urge for "real combat." Perhaps Lauer was reflecting his own feelings and those of his fellow generals, who usually kept a safe distance from the front line. Our gung-ho general added: "Surely the war would not be over before they [his men] could get into it. Eagerly and impatiently they awaited the day to get going but, with the stoical philosophy of the soldier who had much training in 'hurry-up-

and-wait,' they felt they probably would be disappointed." I don't know who Lauer talked to in reaching these conclusions.[3]

ON THE OTHER SIDE. On July 31, 1944, Adolph Hitler, looking much older than his fifty-four years, revealed to a small group of intimates the first hint of his plan for a great German offensive on the Western Front in the fall. He said "it would decide the fate of the war." This was the same day Gen. George Patton's U. S. Third Army achieved its decisive Normandy break-through at Avranches. Also on July 31, in preparation for the arrival of American infantry at his doorstep, Hitler ordered im- mediate strengthening of the Siegfried Line along Germany's western border. Concrete bunkers required the digging of support trenches and foxholes, installation of new machine guns, and removal of brush to provide clear lines of fire from pillboxes.[4]

On September 6, Col. Gen. Alfred Gustav Jodl presented a plan to Hitler for the all-out German winter offensive on the Western Front. He listed two requirements: (1) overwhelming superiority in men and supplies for the sector chosen for the at- tack, and (2) an attack date that would ensure bad weather to deter Allied air superiority. "A major offensive of this type will not be possible before November 1," Jodl advised.[5]

ON OUR SIDE. General Omar Bradley reported that infantry and tanks of the U. S. First Army crossed into Germany ten miles south of Aachen on September 13. "We go into Germany as conquerors, and there will be no fraternization"—meaning with enemy civilians— General Eisenhower said at a press conference in Paris.[6]

4 • To the Front

THE TRAIN CARRYING L COMPANY PULLED OUT OF Camp Maxey on September 15, after more than a month of rumors of imminent departure. Much to my surprise, each platoon immediately established a twenty-four-hour guard duty schedule. Two men, with loaded rifles and fixed bayonets, stood guard at both ends of each car. They had orders to prevent anyone from leaving or boarding the train. Did they think we would try to escape?

The movement of an infantry division, 14,253 men and their equipment, required forty trains. We followed different routes to reach our destination, which turned out to be Camp Miles Standish, the port of embarkation for Boston.

Railroad workers tipped off local citizens about arrival times of troop trains. Consequently, at all hours of the day or night, when our train slowed down to pass through a town, men and women stood by the tracks waiting to greet us. They tried to give us food and candy if the train stopped or slowed to a walking pace, but we couldn't accept anything to eat. The army worried about possible efforts to poison us.

My train arrived at Camp Miles Standish on September 18, three days after leaving Texas. To keep us busy, the division started extensive training programs, including demonstrations on how to abandon a sinking troop ship and how to escape from enemy capture. We had to pass a physical inspection, and we also received additional immunization shots. From now on, we were told, all our letters would be censored. (Unbeknownst to us, censorship of letters actually began in April at Camp Maxey. I discovered that fact years later when I read the letters my parents saved. One letter in April had two words deleted, and a letter written on May 1 had five lines cut.)

Division units issued twelve-hour passes to towns within a fifty-mile radius. On this, our last fling in the United States, I went to Boston with three friends. We treated ourselves to lobster dinners, including our first Old-Fashioneds, and elaborate desserts. Fully stuffed, we made the standard historical walk around Boston before the entertainment of the evening, a one-person show (with orchestra) by Lena Horne.

Our situation was not always somber, even at our port of embarkation. There was still some of the boy left in us, and it came out during an evening orientation about conduct on troopships. The entire division was assembled on bleachers at an outdoor athletic field. In typical military fashion, we were in place an hour before the scheduled time on a beautiful fall evening. A gentle breeze blew from left to right across the assembled mass of men.

A friend, Sgt. Dick Byers of the 99th artillery, described the scene: "Most everyone was in good humor, with a lot of grousing for being delayed from taking off for evening passes to Boston. Because of the liberal pass policy," he noted, "many GIs had condoms. They were ordered to carry them whether they wanted them or not. Suddenly, a large white balloon floated up on the left above the heads of the audience. As it drifted, a waiting hand batted it back into the air. A murmur of laughter went through the crowd upon recognizing the balloon. Within seconds, another balloon appeared. Then another and another, until the air was filled with them." [1]

GIs roared with laughter as they jumped up to keep the balloons moving along. Officers ran up and down the stairs giving orders to stop, but the men ignored them. The field to the right was white as snow with condoms dancing across the grass and swirling around the legs of civilians waiting at a bus stop. Passing cars popped them. Then, just as suddenly as the deluge began, it stopped, and we settled back into boredom as the lectures began.

On our tenth day at Camp Miles Standish, Lieutenant Goss told us to have all packs and equipment ready for departure the following day to an awaiting troopship in Boston harbor. Because of the tragic sinking of the troopship *Dorchester*, security at Camp Miles Standish was tight. Apparently, authorities thought a spy tipped off the Germans about the *Dorchester*'s sailing schedule. They used that tragedy to scare us into silence.

The fate of the 5,252-ton *Dorchester* was a fearful reminder of the dangers from German U-boats in the North Atlantic. On its way from St. Johns, Newfoundland, to Greenland at reduced speed due to ice, it was torpedoed shortly after midnight on February 3, 1943, despite the protection of two U.S. Coast Guard escorts. It had 904 men on board, including 751 soldiers. The *Dorchester*'s master gave orders to "abandon ship" three minutes after it was struck. The ship sank rapidly, bow first. It fired no rockets or flares. The escort ships learned of the torpedoing only after the troopship disappeared into the dark waters. A total of 299 men were rescued, and 74 of them later died, bringing the total lost to 679 men.

We heard reports that nearby public phones were being monitored by army security to intimidate us from telling where we were and when we might ship out. The telephone company could not divulge the location of our calls. Posters depicting a sinking ship carried variations of this message: LOOSE LIPS SINK SHIPS.

If we had known the full story of the *Dorchester*, with all its horrors, I don't think we would have tried to get around the censors' efforts to protect us. But, we knew none of the details. I learned them fifty years later.

Our stay at Camp Miles Standish came to an end on September 29. With the feel and smell of fall in the air, troop trains moved into the camp's spur lines by late morning. The load each of us carried was so large we could barely get through the doors into the train. It included a full field pack, a rifle, and a heavy duffel bag. It was a miracle we could walk.

We were excited. A big new adventure was unfolding. By 3 P.M., we reached a dock area of Charlestown, across the Charles River from Boston. As we left the train, we searched for a likely ship. We could see part of one on the water side of a warehouse we were approaching. She was not very imposing, and no one would call her an ocean liner. Approximately eleven thousand tons, she came into full view as we marched out the other side of the warehouse. *Marine Devil* was painted on the bow. Newly built for the United Fruit Company to carry bananas, she prepared for her maiden voyage—without bananas. Members of our regiment were already boarding. Cheerful Red Cross ladies passed out coffee and donuts as we waited our turn to go aboard. "Let's go, men," yelled Sergeant Thompson. We marched up the gangplank in single file as a loudspeaker blared the stirring music of "Over There." This was a scene right out of the movies, and I was surprised to be in it. I wondered—casually—if I would ever step onto American soil again.

Following the men in front, we descended into one of the ship's cargo compartments. It had been turned into a giant barracks, with rows of stacked canvas shelves serving as beds. Each stack had seven or eight shelves, one on top of the other. The space between the shelves was approximately eighteen inches, barely enough for a man to turn over without hitting the man above him. The aisles between the stacks were about three feet wide. Sergeant Mysliewiec assigned us our shelves for the eleven-day crossing. "I'll tell you when you can move about the ship," he added. Although we complained loudly, I think morale, overall, remained high. We did what we had to do despite continual griping.

We figured out quickly that if the Germans torpedoed the ship, most of the men in the holds would drown, unable to get through the traffic jam at exits. Officers moved into cabins on the upper decks. They had easy access to lifeboats. Fortunately for us, the danger from U-boats was much lower than in 1942 and 1943. After January 1944, the Allies considered the Battle of the Atlantic essentially won. The U.S. Navy credited the victory to the use of escort aircraft carriers and effective radar.

At approximately 9 P.M., I could feel the ship moving slowly. Not wanting to miss our departure, I went up to the deck. It was dark now. I could see wartime-dim lights along the shoreline as we glided through the calm waters of the harbor—a beautiful, silent scene. We moved toward the open Atlantic, and lights faded from sight. With only a glimpse of the coast still visible, I said goodbye to the United States and promised myself I would return. I knew some of us might not make it back. However, the odds looked good since I figured the fighting was almost over.

The *Marine Devil* rolled with the gentle sea. It carried the 2nd and 3rd Battalions of the 395th Infantry Regiment, approximately seventeen hundred men. Our first battalion sailed on the *Explorer.* Many of us stayed on deck for a couple of hours after the lights disappeared. I was looking for other ships, but I could not see any.

When I returned to the hold, most of the men were already

on their shelves. Some were participating in noisy, high-stakes poker or craps on the floor. No one could write letters or read letters except those who had top shelves, which had both lights and room to lie sideways. I was on the fifth or sixth shelf from the bottom, which meant that I had to climb four or five other shelves to reach mine. I was so close to the man in the next shelf that I had to watch where I put my arms to avoid hitting him. The latrine, or "head," was a long way off, up to the deck area— a tough run for those who suffered from seasickness! We slept fully dressed, including shoes. Tired from the day's excitement, I quickly fell asleep.

I awoke early in the morning with the creaking and rolling of the ship and the noise of ventilator fans. I could hear numerous men suffering from sea sickness. Fortunately, none was in my immediate area. The weather was windy, overcast, and cold. The sea was gray. Surprisingly to me, we appeared to be alone, except for a coastal antisubmarine navy blimp hovering overhead like a worried mother. German U-boats would not reveal themselves with the blimp looking down on them. I noticed that the *Marine Devil* had deck guns to fight off U-boats and planes. I stayed on deck with some of my buddies for most of the day. We enjoyed the endless waves, looked for other ships and U-boats, and watched our ship's navy crew practice firing deck guns. We also participated in lifeboat drills. Evening in the hold went much the same as the first night, but the gamblers became more raucous as the stakes got higher. On the deck level above our hold, a recent movie was shown. For me, films provided a great escape.

I awoke early again on the third day and headed for the fresh air of the outdoor deck. The weather was the same—windy, overcast, cold. But something was different. We were no longer alone. We had joined a great convoy during the night. It was one of the largest military convoys to cross the Atlantic during World War II. Immediately in front of us rolled a baby aircraft carrier, loaded with new two-engine bombers tied to its landing deck. Other troopships in our convoy included the former passenger liner *Argentina,* the *George W. Goethals,* the *Exchequer,* and the *Excelsior.* We could see ships in every direction, extending to the horizon. On distant flanks, destroyers raced back and forth on alert for German U-boats that attacked in groups. Navy personnel warned us not to fall overboard because no ships would stop to pick us up.

Discomfort was rising. Cold saltwater showers with only a gritty pumice soap left us feeling uncomfortable and dirty. A most unpleasant situation developed in the "head." Several victims of seasickness vomited mistakenly in the ten-foot-long troughlike metal urinal instead of in the toilets. That clogged the exit drain for urine—which became a hazard to everyone trying to urinate. With each rise and fall of the ship, the urine rushed back and forth. When the flow hit either end of the urinal, it shot six feet into the air, spraying anyone nearby. Urinating became a timing game. Urinate fast at one end and run before the flow returned for another splash. Soon the urine and vomit mix was draining down into our sleeping quarters. The smell caused more men to become seasick. It took hours before crew members fixed the drains.

At about this time in our voyage, the convoy, following a slow zigzag course, ran into some excitement. Pfc. Bob Mitsch, a friend from basic training and ASTP days, was lying on a top bunk in the hold of the *Explorer* when the public address system warned of possible torpedo wakes off the port bow. The *Explorer* was sailing on the fringe of the convoy, several miles from the *Marine Devil.* "I immediately jumped down and raced to the deck," Mitsch said. "I found the railing lined with GIs looking for torpedoes. Immediately adjacent to our ship, Canadian destroyer escorts dropped depth charges, which created geysers of water when they exploded." [2]

"We didn't see any torpedo wakes," Mitsch added, "but we

saw one of our ships slow down almost to a standstill. It slipped to the rear as our convoy continued its steady zigzag. It was left alone in a hostile sea, easy prey for U-boats. As far as we could see, no naval ship dropped back to protect it." (The convoy suffered no losses.)[3]

One of the more unpleasant assignments of the "cruise" was garbage duty. I reported after dark with other "volunteers" at the rear of the ship, where we found scores of overflowing garbage cans. "Start dumping the contents into the ocean," a duty sergeant yelled. The ship saved all its refuse during the day and dumped it overboard at night. "By daylight there will be no trail for subs to follow," the sergeant explained. It was impossible not to get the gook on our hands and clothing. By job's end, we were all stinking messes. We showered as soon as we finished, but the cold salt water and latherless soap weren't equal to the task. Even worse, we couldn't do anything about our clothes. We continued wearing them night and day, much to our discomfort and that of those sleeping near us.

When it came to KP duty, no one in L Company got the assignment more often than Pvt. John Brown (name changed), an ex-ASTPer from New York City. Whenever there was an onerous job, our officers and noncoms immediately thought of him. In their minds, he was the ultimate "gold brick" and "smart ass"—and they were right. They did not forget him on the *Marine Devil*. Whenever they got a call from the officers' mess for someone to do KP duty, they often included Brown. In addition to washing pots and pans, Brown had to help serve meals. In doing this, he found out how much better the officers ate than we did. The ultimate was real ice cream—an incredible luxury on the *Marine Devil*. As he served big dishes of chocolate ice cream, he got angrier and angrier. "Not fair!" he muttered to himself. When his job was finally over, he grabbed two one-gallon containers of the precious ice cream and managed to carry them, unseen, down to the crowded hold. Using mess gear spoons, his squad devoured the "forbidden fruit" before the officers knew what happened. Brown had a big smile on his face. "Justice" had prevailed, he thought, and he enjoyed a rare moment of popularity.

The first signs of land appeared on October 8. We spotted birds and a few fishing trawlers disappearing in the large waves. We now knew we were approaching our destination, but we didn't know what it was—England, Ulster, Scotland, Wales, or France. A heavy overcast blocked any view of the sun.

After eleven days in a mostly rough sea, we looked forward to getting off the smelly, forever-rolling ship. Some men suffered seasickness every day and desperately wanted relief. I was lucky.

Our great convoy had disappeared during the night, and we now sailed alone. Sea gulls, land birds, and fishing trawlers became more plentiful, so we knew the *Marine Devil* was nearing its destination. Soon, we saw a dark ridge to the distant northeast of the *Marine Devil*'s prow. The grapevine reported it was England. I felt elated. For years I had wanted to visit England, and there it lay in front of me—with all travel expenses paid by the U.S. government.

Within an hour, a port city appeared along the coast to our northeast. The grapevine, accurately again, said it was Plymouth. Other ships carrying the 99th arrived at other ports, including Liverpool and Gourock, Scotland.

As we eased into Plymouth harbor, I noticed an impressive battleship lying at anchor off to our right. As a "student" of battleships, I recognized the silhouette of a thirty-five thousand ton *King George*-class battleship, one of four of Britain's most powerful warships in October 1944. On the eastern lip of the harbor, a weathered pillbox sat offshore on stilts. Several barrage balloons hovered overhead. More than twelve concrete forts looked out to sea to stop a German invasion that never happened.

The *Marine Devil* turned left into a channel lined with docks. As we got closer, we noticed some open areas that had been bombed during the blitz of 1940–41. (The Royal Air Force estimated that four hundred acres of buildings had been destroyed, making Plymouth one of the most damaged cities in the United Kingdom.) This was our first sign of real war.

We docked about 1 P.M. Within an hour, a large crane started unloading cargo while we waited. At 3:30 P.M., the crane ceased functioning because the men operating it were taking their afternoon tea break. High in the crane's control compartment they had a teapot on a tiny stove. We couldn't believe they would stop their work for tea.

We remained aboard the *Marine Devil* until late that night. "Get all your belongings ready to go," ordered Sergeant Thompson. We boarded a strange-looking, toylike train, which moved out of the dock area just after midnight. After about two hours of traveling, including a wait on a sidetrack, we stepped out into an empty street in a place called Dorchester (population 10,030 in 1944, 14,000 in 1997). The blackout was complete in the town except for very dim covered lights at the station.

We marched a couple of miles to Camp Marabout, a castle-like building on the west edge of town. Rows of one-story, ill-kept military barracks spread out behind the main building. No lights here. Each platoon moved into an empty barracks, and L Company announced a guard duty schedule for the rest of the night. Fortunately, I didn't get picked.

As soon as the lights went out, we heard rats scampering across our floor. In the morning, we found that everything in the place was dirty. Rat droppings dotted the floor and some sleeping bags. Sergeant Thompson ordered a big cleanup "party." We went to work on hands and knees as the sergeants watched and criticized our lack of skill. Although we got to take badly needed freshwater showers, we still had no hot water. L Company posted a twenty-four-hour guard duty schedule just before dark to keep outsiders out and our men in.

The people of Dorchester discovered overnight that their

town was full of Yanks—again. We replaced the U.S. 1st Infantry Division, which had left Dorchester on the night of June 5 for Omaha Beach and, the next morning, D-Day. After four months of combat in France, most of the men in the 1st Division's rifle platoons, the men who had slept in our barracks before us, were now casualties.

We began a stringent program of getting back into shape. The division's answer was morning calisthenics, football, and long full-field-pack marches into the Dorset countryside, thirty-five miles west of Southampton. Our first march out of Camp Marabout took us down a two-lane country road leading to the coastal town of Weymouth (about ten miles round trip). Traffic was light; only an occasional car (usually military) or a public bus drove by us. While we were still near Dorchester, we passed a country manor house that looked as if it belonged in an Agatha Christie mystery. Later, we spotted Maiden Castle, a pre-Roman fortress that provided an excellent landmark for German bombers seeking the port of Weymouth. After an hour, we took our regular ten-minute break. Five hundred Americans on one side of the road and five hundred on the other turned away from the road and began urinating. At that moment, a crowded public bus drove by. I imagined they were saying, "Those Americans are so uncouth!" The light rain turned into a downpour for the last three miles back to Camp Marabout. It took hours to dry our clothes and clean our weapons. In the evening, we wrote our first letters from England. Mine follows:

> Somewhere in England
> With the 99th Division
> October 11, 1944

Dear Mother and Dad,

   Cheereo and all that. Your traveling offspring is now "Somewhere in England."

I'm enjoying every bit of new countryside, every new village, every new experience. The fields are crisp green, and the homes look warm and cozy, although the opposite is more the truth.

Our appearance on the streets is not accompanied by the applause you see in newsreels from France and Italy. But most of the people are friendly and industrious.

No other countryside I've seen resembles it. It features lines of chimneys, rolling hills, winding country roads, endless hedges, quaint little villages, and toylike trains. Above all, I'm impressed by the determined, patient people.

Two boys from town managed to sneak through the fence to visit us. One was 12, and his buddy was 11. We flooded them with questions, and they told us their favorite movie star was Hopalong Cassidy. We loaded them down with candy, soap, and even C and K rations. They'll probably return tomorrow—with friends. [The children of Dorchester surprised us with their pink cheeks and healthy looks. The boys appeared well mannered and wore short pants.]

We have been heating cocoa and beans, mixing lemonade, and frying ham all day.

Keep me informed on the U.C. football scores, politics, and anything else you might think interesting. Don't forget to send me some film.

Love, George

ON THE OTHER SIDE. On October 11, Hitler gave his newly created Sixth Panzer Army the most important assignment in his forthcoming winter offensive in the Ardennes. Its attack front covered the area from Höfen-Monschau, Germany, in the north, to the Losheim Gap, Belgium, about twenty miles by road to the south.[4]

Finally, after three days as prisoners within the camp fence (except for marches into the countryside), we received passes into downtown Dorchester. Three friends and I walked into town, where we found a place that specialized in fish and chips. There was nothing similar at home. We ate standing up in the dark, chilly street. We passed a pub that sounded like a lively, popular place. In we went. Half of the people inside the pub were from the 99th Division, and everyone was having a boisterously good time drinking, singing, throwing darts, and talking. Later, we plodded our way back to our barracks and talked about our first experience with the English. They weren't nearly as stuffy as we had thought.

Our daily routine continued, except for football. We had so many men temporarily disabled from injuries caused by falling on rocks that the game was changed from tackle to touch. While we were busy with our daily physical conditioning program, the supply personnel of the division worked frantically to get us ready for the front line.

Each platoon usually had at least one man who seemed to attract trouble. Pvt. John Brown, the man who stole ice cream on the *Marine Devil,* did something that displeased our officers so much they ordered him to dig a 6′×6′×6′ hole with his entrenching tool. He dug all night, but he had not completed his assignment when reveille sounded. With no sleep during the night, he joined us for calisthenics and for our usual march in the rain. At the end of the day, he went back to his hole. By morning he had finished. Then a sergeant told him, "Fill it in! Then join the platoon for the day's schedule." He barely made it through the morning march without collapsing. We hated to see anyone suffer such treatment, but Brown seemed to ask for it.

One night, I stood night guard for two hours, covering a stretch of the camp's fence perimeter. My job was to keep outsiders from getting into the camp and prevent our men from getting out. But I had a problem.

Nefarious activities were going on between a young woman (age eighteen or nineteen), who lived in a shack just outside the camp's fence, and as many as fourteen men from an L Company platoon (but not my platoon). Some of the platoon's men, including their sergeant, told me they had "this good thing going" and the guards on this post should look the other way when the men squeezed through a break in the fence. What to do? If I wanted to be extremely unpopular with many men in L Company, I would stop them. Since my own sergeants indicated a permissive approach might be wise, I let them go and watched in amazement. About every half-hour, one man would return to camp and another—carrying Cadbury chocolate bars, canned rations, nylons, or all three—would go out through the fence. Some of the men thought she really needed the food. During my two-hour guard stand, four men squeezed through the fence.

I never learned how this little enterprise got under way, but I knew many of the men in that platoon appeared highly pleased after their encounters. One of their favorite conversations was comparing notes on their experiences. The platoon kept the arrangement a monopoly.

Three of us went into Dorchester on October 20 for fish and chips and a stop at the same pub we had visited on the previous pass. Some local men whispered to us of a disaster in the English Channel offshore from the Dorset-Devon coast six months earlier. The mystery began, they said, when coastal people spotted bodies of American soldiers in combat gear washing up on Lyme Bay beaches. At Portland Island, others reported seeing wounded and dead Americans being brought ashore from ships. Rumors spread that the Americans had attempted an unsuccessful landing in France.

When I visited Dorchester in 1993, I learned that a disaster had really happened on the night of April 27–28, 1944, as a result of a bold German sea attack off the Dorset-Devon coast. Two LCTs (Landing Craft Tanks) were sunk and one was seriously damaged by nine fast German ninety-three-foot-long torpedo boats. The attack claimed the lives of 749 Americans participating in Exercise Tiger, a two hundred-ship rehearsal near Slapton Sands for the 4th Infantry Division's D-Day landings on Utah Beach. The death total surpassed the 549 killed in the three spearhead U.S. divisions on D-Day at both Utah and Omaha Beaches. Another 300 men were wounded, bringing total casualties in Exercise Tiger to more than 1,000. The 1st Engineer Special Brigade alone suffered 413 men killed and 16 wounded.[5]

The disaster resulted from German daring and Allied failure to provide adequate protection for the troop-laden ships. The convoy sailed near the coast without air cover and under protective escort of only one slow British ship, *HMS Azalea*. Unfortunately, *Azalea* could not communicate with the American ships because it was using a different radio frequency.

Sworn to lifetime secrecy, the survivors of Exercise Tiger did not begin to talk freely about the disaster until its fiftieth anniversary. Thanks in part to tight censorship surrounding the episode when it occurred, Exercise Tiger was one of the least known disasters of World War II. Supreme Headquarters Allied Expeditionary Force (SHAEF) placed such high priority on keeping the incident a secret that it would not authorize sending death and wounded notices to next of kin until after D-Day. The wounded were quarantined in hospitals.[6]

ON THE OTHER SIDE. On October 21, Adolph Hitler directed his favorite commando, Major Waffen-SS Otto Skorzeny, to play a risky role in his forthcoming Ardennes campaign.

Skorzeny's assignment included sending English-speaking German commandos in American uniforms behind U.S. lines to capture one or more bridges across the Meuse River, to spread misinformation, and to cut American communications lines. "Complete your preparations by December 2," he told Skorzeny. "The Ardennes offensive will begin sometime in December," Hitler added.[7]

On October 21–22, I received the best short leave one could get in this part of the world: a two-day pass to London. Pfc. George Kelly, BAR gunner, and Pfc. Bill Rogers, Berkeley buddy, accompanied me. Our train arrived at Waterloo Station, London, early Saturday afternoon. We raced for Rainbow Corner, the American Red Cross (ARC) headquarters and the Mecca for GIs visiting Britain. Through a milling mob of American servicemen, we worked our way to the information desk. In fifteen minutes, we had sleeping quarters reserved for the night (fifty cents per bed); tickets for a two-hour ARC-sponsored taxi tour of the major tourist sites; and good seats for a light opera at the Winter Garden Theatre. Our taxi driver spent two hours showing the three of us highlights of the city. He stopped so we could get out, take photos, and hear short accounts of such historical places as St. Paul's Cathedral and the Tower of London. The tour also included some of the most heavily bombed areas. Our driver pointed out a building just recently hit by a jet-propelled V-1 German buzz bomb, which was now a pile of rubble. Damage to London caused by German air attacks, although considerable in some areas, was much less than I expected—and vastly less than Allied bomb damage to German cities.[8]

Kelly, Rogers, and I had dinner in a modern restaurant near Piccadilly. I had rabbit as my main course, tea, cakes, and apple dumpling for dessert. After eating, I was still hungry. The bill came to one dollar each. Government regulations limited all restaurants in Britain to only one main course, and the cost could not exceed five shillings (one dollar). Some luxury restaurants got around this limit by adding a "cover charge."

Our night on the town continued with a walk to the theater. Sitting to my left was an attractive young WAAF (Women's Auxiliary Air Force, the women's branch of the British Royal Air Force, or RAF). I struck up a conversation with her and discovered we liked many of the same things. We had coffee together at intermission and, after the last act, made arrangements to meet the next day (Sunday) at 10 A.M. Since Kelly and Rogers had already gone, I was on my own in a London blackout to find my way back to our Dover Street hotel.

As I wended my way through crowds of people, going west to Piccadilly Road, I found myself being accosted by young women I could not see. At first, I failed to understand what they were saying, but my instincts told me to keep walking. After several approaches, I finally figured out what was going on— prostitution on a vast scale! By the time I reached Swan & Edgar's elegant store at Piccadilly Circus, I decided to count the number of propositions in the next block, just east of the famous Ritz Hotel. The figure was six. Piccadilly Circus and its immediate vicinity, the center of London, was one mass orgy. I had trouble believing what I was encountering—so many young women willing to expose themselves to numerous unknown dangers. Apparently they lured enough Yanks (and other military and civilians) each night to make it profitable from a money standpoint. The moral and health costs apparently didn't matter.

In describing the prostitutes of Piccadilly (often called Piccadilly Commandos), Edward R. Murrow, then CBS correspondent in London, called them "the bravest of the brave in London." He reported that they stayed on the streets in the heaviest raids.

Even General Eisenhower experienced the follies of Piccadilly when he arrived in London in 1942. His assistant, Navy Capt.

Harry T. Butcher, and George E. Allen, on special assignment for President Roosevelt, accompanied him. "After a fine dinner," Butcher said, "George insisted that we walk up Piccadilly to our hotel, if for no other reason than for the CG [commanding general] to know the morality conditions. George said that we would see at least three combat divisions of ladies of the street on our way back to the Dorchester Hotel. When the first one approached, she looked straight at George and purred: 'Hello, fat boy. Does your mother know you're out?'"[9]

When I finally reached the Dover Street Club, Kelly and Rogers had already gone to bed, but they were still awake. I said, "Guess what I just experienced," and they knew exactly what I was talking about. They, too, had met the same onslaught. When we finished talking about the prostitution madness and started to doze off, we experienced another London reality. Air raid sirens were sounding across the vast city. What were they warning us about? Enemy bombers or a flying V-1 bomb? (No warning was possible for the V-2 rocket.)

This called for a decision. Do we go to a bomb shelter? The odds, we thought, were tremendously in our favor. So we lay in bed waiting to see what would happen. The warning sirens stopped wailing, followed shortly by a deep grumbling and throbbing overhead that reminded me of a heavy truck with a cylinder or two missing. Then the noise stopped. The jet engine had shut off, and the V-1 was gliding to the ground. A heavy explosion followed at what sounded like a mile or two away from us. We had survived our first V-1 attack. During the next hour, we heard two more. They fell farther away than the first one. Ten minutes later, the all-clear wailing sounded. Although I didn't want to admit it, I felt uneasy lying in bed waiting for a bomb to hit the ground. We finally fell asleep, but air raid sirens awakened us again in early morning. Another V-1 flew over, shut off, and crashed, followed by another explosion. An all-clear siren followed.

In the morning, the three of us joined Gene Oxford and Bill Parmelee, L Company friends, in the dining room for breakfast. We decided we would come back to London again, if we got another chance.

Back at camp, in a letter to my folks, I raved about how well the people of Dorchester treated us. Many local people went out of their way to show their friendship and great appreciation for the sacrifices that American GIs were making to win the war. During my visit to Dorchester in 1993, however, I discovered that my conclusions about happy English-GI relations in Dorset were probably off target. In the Dorchester Public Library, I found the book *Dorset at War, 1939–1945* by John Murphy, a Dorchester resident. Although Murphy did not base his conclusions on scientific opinion polling, he talked to many 1943–45 residents of Dorchester and its environs.[10]

"I moved among the past-middle-aged of Dorset doing my research among those who remembered," Murphy wrote in his foreword. "The reaction of the majority shocked me. The German is forgiven, the wartime Italian [seen in England as a prisoner of war] has become a joke, but dislike for the American GI has survived through the years." Murphy's findings upset him because he felt that many of his countrymen, who owed so much to the GIs, reached an unfair verdict. He thought they had judged the GIs on the bad behavior of a small minority. Murphy was only twelve years old when he cycled excitedly to meet the first U.S. Army truck convoy threading its way through Dorset. "I met the young men who, as olive-drab clad ghosts, have plagued me ever since." Why such animosity toward us? The oft-repeated flip answer, which we GIs took more as a joke than a serious response, was this: "The Americans are overpaid, oversexed, and over here!" Much to my surprise, this remark had real basis in fact for many people in England.[11]

Our pleasant stay in Dorchester came to an abrupt end. In preparation for leaving, we cleaned and double-checked our weapons. Some men sharpened personal knives they carried in hidden places. I loaded my twelve BAR ammunition clips with 240 rounds of 30-caliber bullets. My assistant gunner loaded another 240. In addition, we each carried 160 rounds in bandoleers across our shoulders. Our ammunition bearer carried another 520 rounds. We interlaced the predominant antipersonnel bullets with a set pattern of armor-piercing and tracer bullets. (The tracers helped the gunner improve his accuracy, and the armor-piercing bullets sometimes proved effective against lightly armored vehicles.)

We marched out of Camp Marabout at 4 A.M. on November 1 and headed for Dorchester's railroad station. Each of us carried a full field pack, a duffel bag, and a rifle. The few people awake that early came out onto the sidewalks and waved goodbye. We arrived at the station about 4:30 A.M., but no train appeared until 11 A.M. Our destination was the busy port of nearby Southampton. Within an hour, we were at a dock for our second ocean voyage in a month. The weather was cold, wet, and overcast, par for the course. Unlike our boarding in Boston, no fanfare greeted us. Just "Speed it up, men!" from Sergeant Thompson.

By early evening, *HMS Empire Lance* (about eight thousand tons), an American-built and British-run troop carrier, moved us in darkness past the Isle of Wight, birthplace of my maternal great-grandfather, and out into the English Channel.

While we were crossing the Channel, our 99th Division was transferred to V Corps, U.S. First Army. Our sector on the front became much more specific—somewhere between the Ardennes Forest area along the German-Belgian border and Aachen, Germany. But, of course, we riflemen did not know this.

I awoke at dawn the next day, had breakfast—including dishwater-like English tea with milk and sugar—and then walked out on deck to look for signs of France or Belgium. The *Empire Lance* sailed alone—no blimp, no convoy, no other ships in sight—and there was no sign of land. Apparently those who decided our fate considered the Channel safe from German U-boats. I felt like an enthusiastic tourist (although armed to the teeth), anxious to experience a new country. I forgot—ever so temporarily—that I was going to the front line to be a target for German riflemen. As we looked across the calm, gray water, we discounted any danger from German submarines or mines. After all, wasn't the war almost over?

We didn't know it, but the U-boat menace had increased substantially by the end of October in the waters around England and France because of a new German secret weapon—the snorkel U-boat. The snorkel innovation permitted subs to stay under water longer, making them more difficult to detect. With its upcoming winter offensive in mind, the German high command sent the new U-boats out to sink as many U.S. reinforcements as possible before they set foot in France.

We took turns looking through field glasses. Gradually, we could see a coastal city and German Atlantic Wall emplacements. We were told that we were about twenty miles north of the Normandy invasion beaches. What at first looked like a normal city finally came into focus. Shocked into silence, we watched as the damage became clearer. Word spread through the troop-lined deck that we were looking at Le Havre (population 162,000 in 1936, 105,000 in 1946, 196,000 in 1997). Good God, what a mess. Vastly worse than any damage we observed in England, the devastation of most of Le Havre surprised us because we had heard nothing about it.

Approximately a mile from the harbor's entrance, a small boat came out to guide us slowly into the outer harbor. We spotted many intact German fortified gun emplacements at the end of the breakwater and much larger gun emplacements in great concrete forts in the inner harbor. Tops of sunken ships stood like silent sentries. Shattered warehouses, toppled loading cranes, and wrecked piers lined the waterfront as far as we could see. No crane stood upright. We figured, correctly, that German demolition teams caused much of the harbor damage to render the port useless to the Allies. The harbor was "almost 100 percent destroyed," including 288 cranes, most railway facilities, more than ten miles of dockside space, and practically all the lock and communication systems, according to Capt. Charles A. Olsen, United States Navy, commanding officer of the port following departure of the Germans.[12]

Our arrival signaled a major strategic achievement for the Allies: the opening of a second major port on the west coast of Europe to supply our advancing armies. The 99th Division pioneered as the first major Allied unit to enter the harbor since the Germans had surrendered. Few Allied personnel, other than port specialists, arrived before the end of September. Only 1,868 landed in October, but the total troop arrivals for November were 89,271, including 14,253 men of the 99th. Between our arrival on November 2, 1944, and November 1, 1945, 1,247,000 U.S. military personnel debarked and 1,123,081 embarked from the port.[13]

We actually were in great danger as soon as our ship approached the harbor entrance. The danger lay under the water. As a departing present, the Germans had sprinkled the harbor bottom and all approaches to it with new, almost revolutionary "oyster" mines. When a ship passed over one of these mines, the increased pressure caused it to activate. The Germans programmed some of them for delayed detonation. British surface mine sweepers cleared what they thought was a safe path into the harbor, but the oyster mines, lying on the bottom, remained undetected.

On September 25, 1944, only twelve days after the Germans in Le Havre had surrendered, oyster mines claimed the *U.S.S. Miantonomah*. It sank near the breakwater entrance with the loss of many navy men. On November 11, only nine days after we arrived, the *Lee S. Overman*, a Liberty Ship carrying trucks and six thousand tons of ammunition, was suddenly shaken as an oyster mine exploded underneath a hold filled with ballast sand. Amazingly, the vessel's vital but highly volatile cargo did not explode. On November 21, an oyster mine claimed another victim, the *Empire Cutlass*. No loss of life was reported.[14]

With no safe place to dock, we remained at anchor in the outer harbor until after nightfall. At about 9:30 P.M., a ten-foot-wide rope cargo net (matrix) was thrown over the railing of the ship for us to climb down about thirty feet into infantry landing craft. When my turn came, I nearly panicked. I had trouble with heights. Water movement complicated matters. One minute the landing craft was against the side of our ship, and the next minute four feet of water separated the two vessels.

As a BAR gunner, I carried my usual seventy pounds of gun, ammunition, full field pack, and other accouterments. This made my descent particularly difficult. The rope hugged the ship tightly, leaving no space for my fingers to get a grip or for my feet to get a foothold. Out went my right leg, trying to find a foothold. I grabbed the top of the railing with my right hand and the rope ladder below with my left hand. I did not dare look down. With both hands gripping successfully, the rest was easy. If any of us had fallen into the water, no one could have rescued us. We would plunge to the ocean bottom like a heavy sinker on a fishing pole.

In fifteen minutes, our landing craft scraped ashore on a stony beach. One of our officers checked some nearby wreckage with a flashlight and was surprised to spot the body of a civilian, apparently an undiscovered victim of the violence that destroyed Le Havre. The officer said several hundred bodies, trapped in the debris, remained unburied. When Cpl. Vince Dudzinski of the 99th Division artillery landed, he spotted rats "almost as large as opossums" feeding on a dead body under a partially destroyed dock.

We assembled by squads and marched single file on a narrow path bulldozed in the middle of a debris-laden street. Some buildings stood with outside walls gone, leaving plumbing and furniture hanging precariously over open space. There were few signs of inhabitants and virtually no lights. After a march through about five blocks of rubble, we reached a convoy of trucks and moved off again into the unknown.

In 1993, I visited the city hall and public library in Le Havre to learn what devastated the central and residential areas of the city. I found out that air attacks on the city occurred for more than four years, starting in May 1940 when Germany invaded France.

Beginning in April 1944, shortly before D-Day, planes from England attacked the city and port almost every day. When the U.S. First Army broke through German defenses in Normandy in late July 1944, Hitler ordered his troops in Le Havre to defend the city. On August 31, Col. Eberhard Wildermuth, the German commander in Le Havre, ordered demolition of all harbor installations. In an effort to force the Germans to surrender, the British stepped up their attack on the city. During September 4–6, they bombed it from the sky and shelled it from the sea. Seven attacks by the RAF dumped 9,750 tons of bombs in one week. Two RAF attacks by heavy Lancaster bombers on September 5 and 6 were particularly damaging. A ground attack against the Germans began on September 10. Two days later, the German garrison, with eleven thousand troops, surrendered to the British and the Canadians.[15]

Le Havre's four-year ordeal ended at an appalling cost: a total of 5,126 French civilians killed (2,053 during September 5–6); 35,000 rendered homeless; the business district wiped out; 12,500 homes totally destroyed and 4,500 heavily damaged; and the great port destroyed.[16]

French critics of the air attacks during September 5–6 called them an unnecessary massacre of innocent French civilians. In defense of the bombing, Sir Arthur Harris, Marshal of the RAF, noted that "in past wars, without the heavy bombers, these ports (along the French coast) could only have been captured after prolonged siege." [17]

With headlights on, our trucks took us out of Le Havre into the blackness of the Normandy countryside. The trucks finally stopped at 5 A.M. "Out! Line up!" the sergeants yelled. Half asleep, we walked a couple hundred feet and found ourselves in a wet cow pasture (near a Normandy village called La Feuillie). Sergeant Thompson, one of the few with a flashlight, yelled, "Pitch tents for the night in a straight line. Here! Here! Here!" He pointed with his flashlight.

In the dark, my buddy John Karchner and I erected our pup tent and crawled into our sleeping bags, fully dressed except for shoes and leggings. We fell asleep almost instantly. We had had no sleep for twenty-three hours. Fortunately, we escaped sentry duty.

Harry S. Arnold's 393rd Regiment arrived in a nearby pasture the night before we arrived. He described the difficulty he had in setting up pup tents in the slippery dark. "Into these we crawled," he said. "We lay looking sightlessly into the black, contemplating our plight." Restful contemplation didn't last long. "The words, first muffled, then louder, penetrated our ears and brought our sought-after oblivion to sickening awareness. 'Cow shit. Goddamn cow shit. We're in the middle of a bunch of cow shit!'" [18]

And so it was—an apple orchard inhabited by cattle. "We were forced to reflect on the lot of the infantry. To die in an air-plane, whirling, aflame, breaking apart thousands of feet above the earth is terrible. To be incinerated or ripped apart in a tank is conclusively violent. But to die amidst the slime of animal droppings is ignominiously improper," Arnold concluded.

Karchner and I missed the cow droppings and awoke to the clatter of mess gear, after only two hours of sleep. We put on our shoes and leggings, headed for the outdoor latrine, then back for mess gear and breakfast. We had our first view of the Normandy countryside, mostly grassy fields and a few rows of apple trees. The apples from this area were made into a strong brandy called Calvados. We were near Rouen—famous for its cathedral, site of the burning of Joan of Arc, and a principal supply base for the British Army during World War I.

Sergeant Thompson told us to check and clean our weapons—again. I broke down my BAR, cleaned and oiled its parts, and reassembled it. Others sharpened knives and bayonets.

When some natives in wooden shoes approached our encampment fence, several of us rushed over to try out our high school and college French. I greeted a healthy looking young man (army age) named Bernard with a solid "bonjour," but our conversation went downhill from there. I barely understood him, and he barely understood me—after three years of high school French.

My friends—and I—were quickly unimpressed with my linguistic talents. But I struggled on. At this point, another GI beside me entered the conversation with fluent French. I remember his well-known name: Rothschild (John A.). Originally from St. Louis, he was enrolled in ASTP with me at Tarleton College. He and Bernard engaged in an animated conversation. For one thing, Bernard said he hated the "Boche." (That's what most French called the Germans. We called them "Krauts" or "Jerries.") After talking awhile, we parted. An hour later, however, Bernard brought back his wife, mother, and children to meet me. I had made a better impression than I thought.

When I got back to our tent area, I ran into my friend Louis Pedrotti. Usually unruffled, Louis was in a state of utter amazement. "Bet you can't imagine what happened to me at the straddle trench," he declared. He had just pulled down his pants and drawers when a French girl appeared in front of him. To Louis's amazement, she pulled up her skirt, pulled down her panties, and squatted just in front of him. Louis couldn't get his pants up fast enough. "Can you imagine that!" he exclaimed. This was our first introduction to the less inhibited life of the earthy, peasant French. We never figured out how she got by our perimeter guards.

Another night in the field. My buddy and I again escaped night guard duty.

☆ 3rd Battalion Morning Report to the 395th Regiment

November 4, 1944—

Moved by truck (285 miles) to Aubel, Belgium, by the way of Cournay, Amiens, Cambrai, Valenciennes (France), and Mons, Charleroi, Namur, Huy, Liege (Belgium), and then to bivouac area near Aubel.

At 6 A.M., L Company's field kitchen served a hot breakfast and handed out brown bag lunches for a roadside "picnic" at midday. The chaplains gave special field services that sounded to me like last rites. They said such things as: "Whatever happens, God will be with you." We checked our weapons with more urgency. Then Colonel Butler gave a pep talk on how we would honor the 3rd Battalion and show the Germans a well-trained American infantry outfit.

To us, Butler's talk was not just rhetoric. We believed strongly that we were an excellent infantry battalion. Although we griped all the time, we were truly proud of our unit. We had confidence in our officers and noncoms (for the most part), and we believed we knew our jobs well. These views spoke well for Colonel Butler.

The rift between the ASTP men and the old-timers had mostly ended in mutual respect for each other as soldiers. We knew we could count on most of our buddies in life-or-death situations. After six months of tough training, we knew each other well. Many of us ASTPers had been together an additional three months in basic training and nine months at ASTP colleges. We were like brothers. This was good because it helped us work well as a team, bad because severe wounds and deaths of friends would hurt so much. We felt particularly sorry for the few replacements who joined us just before we left Texas. Most came from the Army Air Corps (flying cadets and ground crews no longer needed) and replacement depots. They were lost souls who knew no one.

Sergeant Mysliewiec told us our duffel bags, containing nonessentials and our gas masks, would be picked up and stored for us. Anything left out of the duffel bag went on our backs—a powerful incentive to lighten up. Then we climbed into the back of a two-and-a-half ton truck, one of a long line of similar trucks (about 250 just for our regiment). The army called this huge formation a truck convoy or truck march. Each truck carried fourteen men in the back and one officer or noncommissioned officer up front with the driver.

The day was clear and sunny, about fifty-five degrees. The pleasant weather was deceptive. The Allied armies now had two enemies, the Germans and the weather. Autumn floods broke another meteorological record extending back over decades. By November 1, many rivers were out of their banks, slowing down our attacks.

Our truck convoy finally got under way—destination unknown. The trucks had two benches running lengthwise on each side of the back section where we sat, packed together tightly with our packs and weapons on the floor between the benches. We had to sit up straight all the time. Most men could not see much of anything because our sitting area was enclosed on the sides and top by olive-drab canvas. Fortunately, I sat on my pack next to the opening at the rear with my good friends Bill Parmelee and Gene Oxford, both from California.

The trucks were barely under way when we began seeing by the roadside wrecked and burned German Army vehicles, tanks, and artillery. This devastation, caused by U.S. air attacks on flee-ing German road convoys, continued for about ten miles. We concluded that the German Army could not have much bite left. Most of its vital equipment seemed to be sitting here, on this most direct road from Normandy back into Germany. (We did not know that German war production had reached its peak, de-spite two years of bombing, during this very month of Novem-ber 1944.)

As we passed through the towns and villages of northern France on this beautiful Saturday, locals turned out to greet us. French, American, and British flags waved from some homes in every community. Many houses and walls were pockmarked with bullets, evidence of recent skirmishes. We were following the German Army's escape back to the Fatherland. Amid the modest cheers and flag waving, I had an unhappy thought: our endless line of trucks filled with men made me think of cattle headed for the slaughterhouse.

Approximately every two hours our convoy stopped for "piss call" in discreetly unpopulated rural areas. As in Dorset, we made quite a sight. This time, however, more than three thou-sand men turned their backs to the road and urinated at the same time.

I sensed that we were moving north. This was confirmed by a sign announcing Amiens, a city on the Somme River vital to the British in World War I. I envisioned trenches, poison gas, and endless slaughter as the British and German armies slugged it out here from 1915 to 1917.

Near Albert, twenty miles north of Amiens, we sighted nu-merous signs pointing to the World War I front line and ceme-teries for the armies of the United Kingdom, Australia, New Zealand, South Africa, and Canada. We could not help but think of the supreme irony of our trip on this day, almost twenty-six years after the end of the "War to End All Wars."

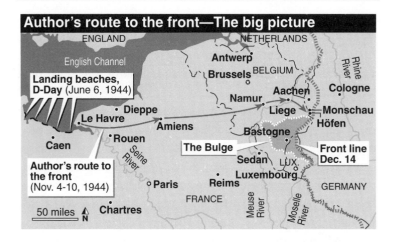

Author's route to the front—The big picture

From Albert, our route continued north through Cambrai, also of World War I fame. I concluded that we were headed to join either the U.S. Ninth Army in the Netherlands or the U.S. First Army in Germany and eastern Belgium.

In Belgium, the people welcomed us more warmly than they had in France. More American, British, and Belgian flags greeted us as our convoy moved noisily through Mons, Charleroi, and Chatelet. Belgians gave the victory sign and thrust wine, fruit, and bread into our waving hands. Our mood improved in the face of such generosity and cheerfulness. About ten miles south-west of Namur, we spotted, for the first time, a U.S. World War II military cemetery. That sight, and knowing we were near Flanders, triggered for me a memory of the famous World War I poem, *In Flanders Field*. Required to memorize the poem in junior high school, I remembered that it brought tears to my eyes. Written in 1915 by John McCrae, a Canadian medical officer, the poem began: "In Flanders Fields, the poppies blow between the crosses, row on row."

We noticed that fresh graves were being dug to take care of expected new arrivals. We knew who the new dead would be—

mostly infantry riflemen like ourselves. No one said anything. We saw occasional evidence of recent fighting in towns along our route. Apparently the Germans were moving north so fast they didn't have time to make stands against the onrushing American tide.

At noon, we stopped in a village. As soon as we sat down on low walls to eat our sack lunches, kids swarmed around us begging for candy and gum. They said they hated the "Boche." I almost forgot I was on my way to the front. I was a happy tourist traveling at no expense to myself. I was impressed with the density of population in the towns and small cities we passed through. They were so close together that the streetcar tracks in one town continued through several more towns. (I learned later that Belgium is one of the most densely populated countries in the world.) At Namur, an important German breakthrough point in August 1914, the road followed the Meuse River through Belgium on its way to the North Sea. Growing weary and reflective, we ceased talking. We knew we were getting closer to the front line and the confrontation we had dreaded for more than twenty months.

What we had seen and experienced during the previous three days led us to believe we were arriving too late to be part of the greatest war in history. But our optimism faded when Gene Oxford reminded us what had happened just a hundred miles north of us at Arnhem in the Netherlands only five weeks earlier. The Germans had clobbered an ambitious British-American parachute/glider attack intended to capture a Rhine bridge crossing and then make a fast end run to Berlin. Optimism faded even more when talk turned to what life would be like on the front line.

Large numbers of people were outside enjoying the sunny day. They waved and cheered. Others waved flags from windows. During brief stops in towns, we had several chances to talk from the trucks to people on the streets. Both adults and children could not say enough bad things to us about the "Boche." Some of our more cynical men wondered if these Belgians expressed friendly feelings toward the Germans when they marched victoriously down this same road toward France in 1940. I said I didn't think so. The Belgians' feelings about our arrival were too exuberant to be phony, and the emotions they expressed about the Germans were too angry not to be real. These people were friends of the United States and enemies of Germany.

We followed the Meuse River toward the only real city on our route, Liege, the first Belgian city of any size west of the German border (population 162,000 in 1944, 196,000 in 1994). It was about 2 P.M. The convoy slowed as it wound through the central area of the flag-decked city. We saw only a few signs of war damage. People cheered and talked to us whenever our convoy stopped. Undoubtedly, they had a much better idea of where we were going than we did.

Liege served as the first major objective of German invasions in 1914 and 1940. We were another of many foreign armies to pass through this gateway into either Germany or France, depending on your direction. For us, this road was a gateway into Germany. Only twenty-three miles to the east lay the German border, protected by four hundred miles of reinforced steel fortifications manned by German troops similar to us in many ways. They were waiting for us, and we were on our way to confront them. Other German troops were heading west in truck convoys similar to ours. We were all caught in inexorable tides. These thoughts tumbled through my mind as our convoy left Liege. We lost sight of the Meuse River, which turned north toward the Netherlands.

Out in the country again, we continued our journey to the east. Bill, Gene, and I sat in the back of the truck describing especially interesting sights for others who couldn't see. I spotted one sight I'll never forget. To the north, an especially long train was moving in the opposite direction from us. It was a U.S. Army hospital train marked with red crosses in large white circles. En route from Aachen, Germany, it was loaded with wounded men, just part of a day's cost from the front lines east of Aachen and in the notoriously bloody Hürtgen (formerly Huertgen) Forest. Innocent us. "That train is a bad omen," I declared after a few moments of silence. "Only a few days or months ago, those poor guys were going to Germany on this same road in the same kind of trucks."

That late afternoon sighting of the hospital train still gives me chills. We all felt sorry for the wounded on the train. But, as it turned out, most of those battered soldiers were vastly luckier than some of us. We would have been shocked if we had known the fate awaiting our group. At the time, however, we still thought the war would end in a month or two. But it didn't look so easy, after we saw the long hospital train and remembered the recent British-American fiasco at Arnhem.

Our convoy climbed slowly to higher ground east of Liege, then stopped in heavy woods near Aubel, Belgium. We had reached the end of our 285-mile day's journey. As we jumped out of the trucks into the darkness, we quickly learned why we had stopped. Off to the east, inside Germany, we heard the distant thunder of artillery and its nighttime accompaniment, a line of off-and-on gun flashes that extended as far as we could see, north and south. On the east side of the line were the Germans; on the west side, the Americans.

I stood in awe of the meaning of this sight: the armies of the United States and Germany locked in mortal combat. Here was the big picture the combat infantryman almost never gets to see. The U.S. First Army, which we had just joined, was on the offensive. We were trying to break through German defenses east of Aachen, to cross the Cologne Plain and reach the Rhine River before the worst of winter arrived.

On the German side, similar events were taking place. Hospital trains were crossing the Rhine heading east, new graves were being dug in German military cemeteries, and newly formed divisions and replacements of men and equipment were moving west. We, the new infantrymen, were the fresh cannon fodder required daily by the gigantic "meat grinding operation," a term coined by the GIs. It had a horrendous appetite. The same dramatic show, at a less intensive pace, was going on all along the entire five hundred-mile front.

Platoon leaders and squad leaders began ordering us to move to our bivouac areas deep inside nearby dark woods. As soon as the tents were up, we assembled for dinner. It included hot coffee and C rations, consisting of canned meat loaf or spaghetti and meatballs.

We dug shallow foxholes. Cold, heavy rainfall pounded our tent canvas. Some of it leaked onto our sleeping bags, clothing, and equipment. Having avoided the straddle-trench detail, John Karchner and I stretched out in our half-wet clothes in our half-wet sleeping bags. I was given an assignment for guard duty. We had barely drifted to sleep when we heard overhead the noise of a V-1 buzz bomb. We crawled out of our tent in time to see the flame from its jet engine disappear to the west. "Headed for Antwerp or Liege," Lieutenant Goss said.

When we bedded down for our first night near the front line, our 395th Regiment consisted of 153 officers, 5 warrant officers, and 3,041 enlisted men, of whom 1,080 were in rifle platoons. We were part of a new wave of infantry divisions moving into front-line positions on the Western Front in the fall of 1944. The official U.S. Army history of the Siegfried Line campaign says these new divisions tended to perform better than the divisions that fought in Normandy for two reasons: their training was better and more realistic, and their bottom ranks contained a high percentage of ASTPers—"men of proved intelligence." [19]

At 1 A.M., the retiring guard shook my shoes to wake me for my shift. (We slept fully clothed, including shoes and leggings.) It was still raining. I grabbed John's wet rifle and followed the retiring guard to our squad's portion of the perimeter, a lonely forest area five hundred feet from our encampment. After giving me the password and pointing out my area of responsibility, he departed into the night. It was chilly, but not bitterly cold—mid to high thirties. Being wet made it seem colder. To keep myself alert, I kept reminding myself of Sergeant Thompson's claim that enemy patrols sometimes got this far back. (This was a big exaggeration.) All was quiet except for the sounds of distant artillery exchanges, buzz bombs going west every twenty minutes, and an army train several miles away.

At 3 A.M., I went back to the pup tents to waken my replacement. I gave him my watch with luminous hands and then took him out to our guard site. I slipped into my sleeping bag at 3:10 A.M.—wet and miserable. Reveille came at 6 A.M. Then a welcome hot breakfast.

We cleaned and dried our weapons and maintained guard around our bivouac area twenty-four hours a day. We held in this position, approximately forty miles west of Cologne and the Rhine River, for four often-rainy days, continuing the routine of the first night and day. Each night the V-1s came down "buzz bomb alley" on their rumbling flights to the west. (One of them got confused and crashed into nearby woods, too far away to cause any damage to us.)

ON THE OTHER SIDE. On November 7, the German Army estimated the following strength available for its planned Ardennes offensive: thirty-eight panzer and infantry divisions, nine corps of artillery, seven Werfer (rocket) brigades. (These estimates of strength were overly optimistic.)[20]

☆ **3rd Battalion Morning Report to the 395th Regiment**
November 8, 1944—
Battalion commanding officer and staff went on reconnaissance of front-line area to be occupied by unit.

On November 8, Lieutenant Goss ordered us to have every-thing ready in the morning to move closer to the front. While we waited in our muddy bivouac area, Colonel Butler left, un-beknownst to us, on the trip reported in the battalion's "Morn-ing Report." He quickly discovered that the defensive line as-signed to our battalion in and around Höfen, a German village in the Eifel/Ardennes area, was six thousand yards long. "That," Butler explained, "is three to four times wider than recom-mended by army textbooks. I never dreamed that we would have a defensive position of this size without any backup or help from our division or regiment. When I got to Höfen," he added, "I found the area too big to cover in one afternoon. So I stayed in the village overnight."[21]

"My first battle experience," Butler said, "came that first night. I shared a room [no heat and no light] with the chaplain of the battalion we were relieving. Just after I got into my bedroll, the enemy started shelling the area around our build-ing. Six to eight shells landed in the yard outside the room. The impact shook the structure. I sat straight up in bed and looked over at the chaplain. He was still snoring. I figured that if a chap-lain could sleep through an artillery barrage, I could, too. So I went back to sleep. The Germans," he continued, "were mov-ing up artillery pieces in the area after it got dark, and the Amer-icans couldn't use counter-battery fire. Each night, the Germans were registering in their artillery on our positions in Höfen, one gun at a time."

Thirty-eight days later, a tremendous amount of artillery thrown on our positions benefited from this registering exercise.

☆ 3rd Battalion Morning Report to 395th Regiment
November 9, 1944—

Unit moved by truck to assembly area in vicinity of Kalterher-berg, Germany, by way of Aubel, Eupen, Elsenborn, Kalter-herberg. I Company moved into position on our left flank . . .

relieving part of the 15th Armored Infantry, 5th Armored Division. Change completed 1700 hours (5 P.M.).

When Sergeant Mysliewiec yelled, "Wake up," it seemed like the middle of the night. We crawled from our rain-soaked tents to face a soggy, cold world—on a day that would bring us within two miles of the front line. There was no time for griping. We had to move quickly to get ready for our next "truck march." At daylight, we gulped down a hot breakfast of powdered eggs, powdered potatoes, a biscuit, and coffee as we stood near L Company's field kitchen. After washing our mess gear in a tub of hot, soapy water and running quickly to the straddle trench, we broke down our tents, rolled up our sleeping bags on the muddy ground, and strapped it all on our packs. All the while, Sergeant Mysliewiec was barking, "Hurry it up! On the double!" The men on the last guard shift didn't have time to eat. They barely had time to pack before we marched to a large clearing in the forest to await the arrival of trucks. The operating mode was "hurry up and wait."

After the first half-hour of waiting in our still-wet clothing, I spotted something I didn't recognize floating down through the tall evergreen trees. I yelled to the others, "What's that coming down through the trees?" Those from the northern states knew right away. "My God, it's snow!" they chorused. Snow on the ninth of November! The winter of 1944–45 had arrived on the very day we were moving up to the front line. Unfortunately for us, we were arriving just before the coldest part of the year in this notoriously cold part of Europe.

That first snow ushered in a condition of extreme discomfort that was to plague the infantry on the Western Front for the next four months. And, as Siegfried Sassoon noted under similar conditions in World War I, "social incompatibilities were now merged in communal discomfort."[22]

The light flakes turned into a heavy snowstorm by the time the trucks arrived. They were similar to the trucks we had ridden from Normandy with one major difference: they didn't have canvas tops! We climbed aboard, squeezing together on the two side-benches with loaded rifles upright between our knees and packs on the floor. We sat there waiting for the trucks to move out. Sitting out in the open, convertible-style, with snow falling on us was not too bad at first. But our discomfort level quickly escalated as snow began to accumulate on our necks, shoulders, and legs and on the heavy packs piled at our feet. Cold water from melting snow trickled down my back.

Most of us felt that the officer responsible for sending us these uncovered trucks deserved at least a one-rank demotion for gross incompetence. A noncom said the officer ordered the tops taken off the trucks so we could get out of them quicker in case of strafing by German planes. We were too numb and too miserable for vigorous complaint. *Stars and Stripes,* the official U.S. Army newspaper, had complained bitterly in an editorial a week earlier about the thoughtless treatment given to front-line infantry replacements transported from the French coast to the Aachen front. It said the troops sat in the uncovered backs of two-and-a-half ton trucks with the rain pouring on them all the way. That sounded familiar.

Life for us went from bad to terrible. Someone ordered, "Let's go!" The trucks moved out, traveling slowly on the slippery road. Considering the wind-chill factor (something you didn't hear about in those days), the temperature dropped to five-to-ten degrees above zero. Sitting in wet clothes and shoes made matters even worse. So off we went, in the blowing snow, with our faces, necks, and ears about to freeze. We hunched over our super-clean rifles to keep them dry.

For the most part, everyone was quiet except for the occasional four-letter expletive that seemed to best describe our situation. We traveled like livestock instead of human beings.

A song from Gilbert and Sullivan's "Mikado" kept going through my mind. It recalls the "poor little dickey bird" that committed suicide by plunging himself "into the billowy wave," singing "willow, tit-willow, tit-willow." I hummed it to myself as the trucks wove through the ghostly forests and fields of the Ardennes.

The convoy sloshed its way south on the snow-covered, two-lane road. We were approximately fifteen miles behind the front line. Traffic was light. The only vehicles we encountered were occasional U. S. Army ambulances, Jeeps, or trucks carrying supplies, ammunition, or soldiers, or pulling 105-mm or 155-mm howitzers. Welded to the front bumper of most Jeeps and some trucks was a vertical steel bar that extended slightly higher than the front windshields. Its purpose was to cut wires extended across roads at night by German infiltrators with the intention of decapitating motorcyclists as well as drivers and passengers in Jeeps.

A road sign indicated that we were entering the town of Verviers. As in all the other Belgian towns we had passed through on November 4, the people displayed American, British, and Belgian flags. They cheered with enthusiasm as we passed by. Their messages: "bon chance" (good luck) and "beat the Boche." Most of us couldn't wave back because of our jammed, half-frozen condition in the truck. In a few minutes, we were out in the countryside again, following an indirect route to our destination. The torture of the biting cold wind and heavy snowfall continued. Conversation was virtually nonexistent. Facial expressions told the story.

We soon found ourselves in an entirely different environment. The convoy approached the next town east. The road sign, in ominous old German script, said "Eupen," an un-Belgian sounding name. We got a feeling as cold as the weather when we entered the gray, rundown town. No flags, no people cheering—in fact, few people! No one waved or acknowledged us. Most windows were shuttered. "Whoever lives here is making it very clear they don't like us," I commented to my companions.

We thought we had arrived in Hitler's Germany, but we were

wrong. Eupen is in the German-speaking part of Belgium. This land belonged to Germany until the Versailles Treaty gave it to Belgium at the end of World War I. These people were of German descent, ethnic Germans. Their mayors were called burgermeisters, and they spoke German in their schools and in their everyday life. The area gave many of us a feeling of foreboding. Perhaps, because of our nearness to the Germany of Adolph Hitler, it seemed sinister to me.

When Hitler invaded Belgium in 1940, he annexed this German-speaking part of Belgium. To him, the inhabitants were Germans, not Belgians. Overnight, they became part of the Third Reich. Most homes had photos of a father and/or son in a German military uniform. Military historian Charles MacDonald noted that "few American soldiers bothered to reason that ethnic Germans in regions conquered by the German Army had no choice but to serve the Fatherland." [23]

After we left Eupen, civilians disappeared from the landscape. The snow kept falling, and the convoy moved slowly to the southeast. Signs of battle began to appear: a shelled farmhouse, a battered German or American tank pushed off to the side of the road. Occasionally, we noticed long-range U.S. artillery positions in forest clearings. "Looks like we're getting near the war," I said to myself.

We drove for miles through a thick, empty forest. We sat in a half-frozen stupor, waiting silently for our torture to end. Finally, our truck convoy rolled into a village identified in old German script as Elsenborn. We were still in German-speaking Belgium. (Nearby Camp Elsenborn became 99th Division Headquarters in December.) At this point, our convoy turned directly north. Three miles farther, we entered Germany. There were no signs saying, "You Are Now Leaving Belgium" or "Welcome to Germany." Nothing indicated the frontier—only snow-covered fields. We were now part of the only Allied force—east, south, or west—that was fighting inside Germany in November 1944.

Fortunately, our trip for the day was about over. In another half-hour, many of us would have been on our way to hospitals with frozen ears and faces. The trucks slowed down as we drove into Kalterherberg. The village looked grim, old, and nearly deserted. As in Eupen and Elsenborn, signs were painted in old German script. No U.S. flags and welcoming people here. The three or four civilians I saw kept their heads down. A couple of old men with black caps drove horse-drawn wagons. (The 9th Infantry Division, the unit that had captured Kalterherberg in September 1944, ordered all civilians out of their homes in early October and relocated them in a camp at Malmedy, Belgium, thirteen miles to the west. They would not be able to return until the spring of 1945. A few old men remained to take care of livestock.)

Kalterherberg's landmark structure was a twin-steepled Catholic church that looked larger than one might expect in such a small community. Some of our group expressed surprise that the "evil Germans" had churches. The trucks eased on through the village and out the other side. Finally, we stopped by the side of a snow-covered field. Officers and sergeants passed the order down the line: "Everyone out!" We were stiff from the freezing ride, which had taken approximately two and a half hours. When I jumped from the truck to the ground, my legs felt like I was landing on numb, anesthetized stumps.

At the 99th Division convention in Denver in 1993, Paul Putty, ASTP friend from the University of Texas and a noted Dallas architect in his later professional life, told me he believed this trip in open trucks caused many trench-foot and frostbite casualties in the 3rd Battalion. Three or four days later, he added, several of the men in his I Company platoon had black toes.

My platoon moved into a snowy field for the night; set up our pup tents in a spread-out, tactical arrangement; dug shallow holes nearby in case of German artillery; dug straddle trenches; cleaned our weapons; and tried to thaw out by moving around quickly. Almost as soon as we got off the trucks, Captain Price called for ubiquitous day and night guard duty to protect our perimeter.

This was the first night we slept outside in the snow in below-freezing weather. With our tent and clothing wet and half-frozen, I felt numb to the point of almost not caring what happened to me.

5 • End of the Line in the "Quiet" Ardennes

A great feeling of awe came over me as I looked across at that dark, foreboding forest. For the first time, I was at the center of world history.
—The Author

November 10–22, 1944

☆ 3rd Battalion Morning Report to 395th Regiment
November 10, 1944—

K Company moved up into Höfen, Germany, *and occupied a position to the right of I Company. L Company moved up and occupied the position right of K Company. M Company moved up and attached weapons to I Company—one section of heavy machine guns; to K Company—one platoon of machine guns; to L Company—one section of heavy machine guns. All companies will be supported with 81-mm mortars. Adjacent units: Right flank [south]—2nd Battalion, 395th Infantry Regiment. Left flank [north in Monschau]—38th Cavalry Squadron [similar to a battalion, about eight hundred men], 102nd Cavalry Group. The 3rd Battalion front covers more than six thousand yards.*

"Speed it up! Our transportation is about to arrive," our sergeants yelled. Sergeant Mysliewiec passed out three hand grenades and extra ammunition. I placed one hand grenade in each of the two pockets of my field jacket and hung the third on an upper outside pocket of my jacket.

When the vehicles arrived, late as usual, we got a surprise. Instead of trucks, they were low profile, armor-plated personnel carriers called half-tracks. Instead of two wheels in the back they had tanklike treads; in front, they had normal wheels with heavy-duty truck tires. We crawled into a dark compartment with benches for six men on each side. Steel armor surrounded us. We sat in total darkness. We began moving slowly, with the tracks clanking on the semi-frozen road. Fifteen minutes later we stopped on a steep country road. "From this point you're on your own," the driver yelled. "Good luck!"

The countryside had an ominous, ghostly look on this crisp morning. Thick clouds blocked any sign of the sun. We could see clearly to the top of a north-south ridge. Out of sight, over the ridge, lay the main German front line, ensconced in the mostly undamaged fortifications of the Siegfried Line (known as the West Wall by the Germans). Visibility was excellent. Snow was everywhere, except for the black splotches where artillery shells had recently exploded.

We were in the Eifel highlands—known as the Ardennes on the Belgian side of the border—an area noted for dark, thick forests; mountainous terrain; heavy rainfall; and gloomy, bitterly cold winters. Freezing winds blew across its high plateaus and numerous deep-gorge streams and small rivers. Gloom prevailed in long sixteen-hour nights—dark at 4:30 P.M. and daylight at 8:30 A.M. To the north and south stretched more of the Siegfried Line—four hundred miles of it, along the German border from Kleve, north of Aachen, to Lorrach, near Basle, Switzerland. Often several miles deep, in two belts, the Siegfried

Line consisted of more than three thousand concrete pillboxes, bunkers, and observation posts. They averaged nearly eight per mile. Mostly hidden by five years of growth, the Siegfried Line also consisted of trenches, foxholes, barbed wire in all forms, and deadly antipersonnel mines.[1]

This complicated, ingenious network of interlocking defenses waited quietly for someone to trip a wire. A trespasser would set off warning flares, booby traps, and mines. It reminded me of a huge series of spider webs woven to ensnare prey. The Germans, of course, were the spiders. Occasional artillery, mortar, and rifle sounds echoed through the snow-covered hills and valleys. None of the shells landed near us.

"Spread out!" Mysliewiec ordered. "Don't bunch up!" The reason for these orders, and for armored half-tracks, was quickly evident. Artillery fire from German guns to the east and American guns behind us conversed in a slow exchange of shells. Our artillery was attempting to cover up the noise of our arrival. Nothing dropped near us. No sign of movement on the German side. Fortunately, enemy observers to the east of us couldn't see our side of the hill and the long line of vehicles carrying an entire company of infantry. We of the 3rd Battalion, 395th Regiment, were relieving a battalion of the 5th Armored Division.

We headed rapidly east up the hill in two columns. We were on our way to foxholes facing the enemy. From now on, our role was to kill men whose purpose in life was to kill us.

In a small pasture near the top of the hill, I spotted a damaged German Panther Mark V tank (forty-three tons) facing west, its long-barreled 75-mm cannon pointing at the ground and its hatch open. On the low side of the pasture sat a knocked-out U.S. Sherman tank (thirty-three tons) facing east, its short-barreled 75-mm cannon pointing off to the side at a crazy angle. Its turret had two holes, and its hatch was open. Two dead tanks facing each other, four hundred feet apart—a poignant scene if ever I saw one. The American trying to move east; the German trying to stop him. There they sat—like smashed watches with hands stopped at the moment of impact—just as when they knocked each other out during the American 9th Infantry Division's September 15–17 attack to capture Höfen. Surrounding this scene lay numerous expended and live 75-mm shells, debris from the two combatants. Some were live Panzerfaust rockets used by the Germans to knock out our tanks.

At the top of the ridge (elevation eighteen hundred feet), another scene of war presented itself. A battered German antitank gun was pointed down the road we had just climbed. A direct hit must have obliterated the German gun crew. A U.S. Army sign at an intersection named "88 Corner" warned: UNDER ENEMY OBSERVATION—MOVE FAST—ZEROED IN BY ENEMY. We ran until we passed an ALL CLEAR sign. No shells from a German 88 cannon followed us.

With his first sight of the front line, a good friend of mine—one of the platoon's best soldiers—fainted, falling headfirst into the snow. (It took him twenty years to admit this to anyone. He saw numerous other front lines after this with no fainting problems. In fact, he served so well that he was promoted to rifle squad leader. He stayed with the platoon until April, when he received multiple wounds from shell fragments.)

We were now moving south into Höfen (population 1,200 in 1944, 2,000 in 1998), a snow-covered village of scattered, mostly one- and two-story homes set in yards with trimmed hedges and fruit trees. Some had thatched roofs and attached barns. They sat perched on a long north-south ridge, surrounded by deep ravines on the north, east, and west sides. Without running water, the residents had to rely on wells and outdoor privies. Most of the homes were empty. Just a few were occupied by lucky American soldiers who used them to sleep in when they were relieved from their front-line foxholes.[2]

On the main street (Hauptstrasse), we passed the village landmarks—a gray Catholic church with a tall, single steeple and a solid building that looked like a school. Sandbags stacked against thick stone walls protected the school's front entrance, and a soldier stood guard. A Jeep and a staff vehicle hugged the front of the school building. (This, I learned a few weeks later, was Colonel Butler's 3rd Battalion command post.) We saw no one but a few U.S. soldiers, all carrying rifles. All civilians had fled.

One of my platoon's three squads left us in Höfen to bolster K Company's positions on the east edge of the village. Sgt. Bill Parmelee, ASTP friend who rode with me on the truck from Normandy, was a member of this squad.

We passed out of the village near its south end and followed a steep trail down an open slope for more than a half mile. At the bottom, we found ourselves in a small, snow-covered valley, completely cleared of trees but surrounded by hills covered with thick evergreen forests. Ahead, we could see a two-story farmhouse with a barn and a mill on a nearby stream. (The site was known as Höfener Mühle.) The rest of the valley was a cleared pasture, a perfect Old World scene for a Christmas card.

As we approached the house, we crossed a bridge over a small, sparkling river, the Perlenbach, a tributary of the Roer River. We did not know it at the time, but when we crossed the river we walked into what our opposing German unit considered its side of the front line.

We were getting increasingly wary of the entire setting with its spooky, lonely look. We were at an outpost. L Company's line was a quarter of a mile behind us. The cautious, quiet way everyone acted revealed our nervous feelings about the place. The front door of the house stood open. We found the downstairs rooms empty. Then, just as we sat down on the floor to rest, we heard what sounded like footsteps upstairs. We all looked at each other in tense disbelief. Lieutenant Goss quietly ordered someone to check it out. The "chosen one" tiptoed up the stairs with a bayonet fixed at the end of his rifle and disappeared down a hall. The tension ended as quickly as it began. "Relax," he said.

"No big deal." The next moment he appeared at the top of the stairs herding a goat. Our first scare became a hilarious joke.

"Where's the bathroom?" one of our men asked. Not inside. A look outside revealed a snow-covered bench attached to the front of the house where it joined the barn. It had two holes. "There's your bathroom, men," Sergeant Mysliewiec declared. "Right out in front for all to see. Better use it now while you have a chance. Won't be so easy where you're going." Someone warned us that our bare bottoms would freeze to the snow- and ice-covered bench on contact. I thought they were joking, but we Californians weren't sure. So we took no chances. We didn't want to sit on the snow, anyway. It's a hard job to sit down halfway. Before everyone took advantage of this facility, a lieu-tenant from the 5th Armored Division appeared. He pointed to foxhole locations—dark splotches in the snow located about eighty feet apart—off to the front and sides of the house.

As Cates, Karchner, and I approached our designated new home, we spotted three men in a larger-than-usual foxhole—a big dark spot in the middle of a snow-covered meadow. The trio manned a machine gun pointed south across the meadow. Un-shaven for three or four days, they looked cold, wet, dirty, and extremely fatigued—the unforgettable blank look, I quickly learned, of infantrymen manning the front line. This was the end of the line, the point beyond which one could not move without running into the German Army.

"Hi. Our platoon sergeant sent us to relieve you," I said as we approached the hole. "About time. What's your division?" the gunner asked. "The 99th," I replied. With no further talk, they started to pull out. They removed the machine gun from its placement and suggested I replace it with my BAR. (Since we didn't have enough machine guns to replace all 5th Armored machine guns, we substituted the BAR in several instances.) Just as they were leaving, I asked, "Where are the Germans?" "In the forest on that steep slope across the meadow," said the gunner curtly. "They are looking down at us. Your BAR gun is pointing in their direction." After that meager bit of helpful information, they left. In full view of the enemy, they wanted to leave as quickly as possible. We wanted to talk; they didn't. They knew that six men, three in the hole and three standing outside, made a tempting target for a mortar. They also knew that when one outfit relieves another, the opposing side usually increases its mortar and artillery fire.

I looked across six hundred feet of a flat, snow-covered field to a tree line at the south end of the valley. The thick Christmas-tree-like forest behind it covered a sharply rising hillside, about two hundred feet from the valley floor to the top. Fresh snow weighed down the trees. It was about one foot deep on the valley floor.

Our job, a company officer declared, "is to reduce the numerical strength of the enemy," which is a nice way of saying "to kill as many as possible." German officers probably told their riflemen the same thing.

We strained our eyes trying to spot German soldiers peering out from or moving behind the trees. We couldn't see any. The distance and trees, thankfully just beyond accurate rifle range, made it extremely difficult to see anyone. Binoculars would have helped, but only officers and a few top sergeants had them.[3]

As Cates and Karchner tried to deepen our hole and make it safer and more comfortable, I manned the BAR, looking across an excellent field of fire. Our foxholes were spaced so far apart we could not see any of our own men.

A great feeling of awe came over me as I looked across at that dark, foreboding forest. For the first time, I was at the center of world history. Many thoughts tumbled around in my head. But they centered on the huge effort going on behind us—war factories, training camps, great ship convoys—all to support this long thin bastion of front-line holes. So many of them, but so few of us!

General Bradley figured that there were six hundred American military personnel in the European Theater of Operations (ETO) behind every forty-man rifle platoon standing on the front line.[4]

We were in a lonely, rarefied position. Only 3,240 men of the infantry rifle platoons out of the 14,253 men of the 99th Division (same in all infantry divisions) actually manned the division's twenty miles of front-line foxholes twenty-four hours a day, seven days a week. More than half were the college "boys" from the ASTP. (We remained on the front until we were killed, captured, or wounded or injured seriously enough to be hospitalized, or until our unit was pulled back for rare and brief rest.) Men of the infantry weapons companies (one per battalion) and the weapons platoons (one per company) also served on the line, but usually just behind the rifle platoons. Others came up to the line for a day or two, but they did not live there all the time. Of course, there were always exceptions to this general rule.

Actually, we had a good reason to feel lonely. We of the infantry rifle platoons represented only 6 percent of the total U.S. Army military personnel in the ETO in November 1944.[5] We, of course, did not know that figure at the time. We also did not know, thankfully, that this small percentage of men to which we belonged took most of the casualties. We 6 percent who were in the rifle platoons carried an overwhelmingly lopsided share of the burden of the war![6]

I was terribly impressed with where we were—the end of the line. I felt very important, very lonely, and very cold. This is where we would apply the "kill or be killed" training we received over and over in Texas. With no one in sight, neither friend nor foe, our situation gave us the impression that we were the only ones on our side in the war. We realized that no matter how many supplies we had or how clever our generals' strategy, the final job of defeating the enemy was ours. If we failed, they failed. While complaining bitterly, I was proud to be part of our unequal burden.

After realizing our predicament, I became aware of the miserable conditions we had inherited. The bottom of our three-man machine-gun foxhole was slush—half-frozen mud and water. We wore nonwaterproof high-top shoes. (Some would call them boots today, since they covered our ankles, but we called them shoes.) The insides were almost as wet as the outsides. (In contrast, German soldiers claimed that their boots were remarkably resistant to water.)

Our hole was dug in the shape of a crude seven-by-seven-foot square. Cates and Karchner dug the front part deeper (to about five feet beside the BAR) and shoveled out slush in the center and rear. Unfortunately, the new bottom quickly became as slushy as the old one.

The mud reminded me of stories about World War I trenches in France more than twenty-five years earlier. Foxholes, however, were more disconnected and much lonelier. Information in trenches could spread quickly. Communications between foxholes was much more difficult. Only a rare foxhole had a wire-connected field telephone or a radio phone.

Sergeant Mysliewiec came out from the house to check our position. "We want as little movement as possible around the house and the foxholes," he informed us. Then he gave us the bad news. "You will stay in these outdoor positions all night." He told us to take turns on guard, with two hours on duty and four hours off. "Don't forget that going to sleep while on guard duty is a major offense on the front line, punishable by court martial and possible firing squad. One man sleeping on guard could be the death of us all." Then he added: "Our battalion captured its first German soldier today. Not bad for our first day on the line."

He returned to the dry, partially heated house that Goss and the sergeants had made their CP and sleeping quarters. Their heat came from a small stove with smoke-free briquettes the German inhabitants of the house had stored for winter.

While our leaders made themselves comfortable, we ate a

K-ration dinner. (These K-ration boxes contained canned meat or a meat substitute, canned fruit, biscuits, coffee powder, lemon powder, sugar tablets, and cigarettes.) As darkness descended, the temperature moved well below freezing. The half-frozen slush in the bottom of the hole froze solid. The whole scene was crunchy-crisp. The temperature in Höfen ranged from a high of approximately thirty-seven degrees Fahrenheit to a low of five degrees Fahrenheit, several degrees colder than Rhine River cities because of its eighteen hundred-foot elevation.

Cates took the first night shift in manning the BAR. Standing at the deep, front end of our hole, he raised and lowered one foot at a time, trying to keep blood circulating in his feet. "Can't see nothing," he said. "Just snow and darkness. No sounds."

Karchner and I tried to sleep. We took the canvas each of us carried for one-half of a pup tent and laid it out on the icy bottom of the hole. Then we placed our unzipped sleeping bags (wet from previous nights) on top of the canvas for use as a wrap-around blanket. I tucked my two wool blankets inside the bag as extra lining. We took off our ammunition belts and placed them beside our rifles, both within easy reach. As a final touch, we covered our sleeping bags with our soggy overcoats.

We crawled out the backside of the hole to urinate nearby. Then we tried to slip into our open sleeping bags fully dressed, in leggings, combat jackets, and muddy shoes. We left the bags unzipped because the zippers often stuck, and we had to be able to get out of them in seconds if a German patrol sneaked up on us. For the same reason, we always slept fully dressed. Our feet were within reach of Cates so he could shake them to alert us without talking.

We covered our heads with the sleeping bag's hood, which made us look like mummies. Despite our efforts, the cold went right through to our bodies, making us much too uncomfortable to really sleep. We just lay there in a fetal position and shivered and swore to ourselves. The clothing I wore (all partially wet) consisted of one pair of two-piece "long johns," one pair of woolen pants, one woolen shirt, a field jacket, a pair of wool socks, a pair of cheap cloth and leather gloves, canvas leggings, and high-top shoes. None of us had galoshes. I put my hands between my legs to keep them fairly warm. I didn't use the one pair of dry socks I had because they would quickly become as wet as the ones I would take off. Cates's rifle leaned against the side of the hole next to me; its barrel was protected with a condom as a cover.

To the accompaniment of occasional firing of distant artillery and a far-off rifle shot, Karchner and I kept turning, trying to find relief from the overwhelming discomfort. I promised that I would write a detailed account of this suffering after the war. The public and the rest of the army should know what this is really like, I told myself.

Our misery in this foxhole reminded me of a World War I story told by Field Marshal Montgomery. It illustrated how little some high-ranking officers, who decide the fate of armies, knew about the life of their men at the front. Montgomery said that when Sir Douglas Haig's chief of staff saw the mud and the ghastly conditions under which the soldiers had fought and died at Passchendaele during the winter of 1917–18, he said: "Why was I never told about this before?"[7]

When Cates's two-hour watch was up, he shook Karchner's foot. Karchner, of course, was not asleep. (We kept track of our time with my luminous-dial watch, a present from my parents. In Desert Storm in 1991, the army issued luminous watches to all front-line infantry.) Karchner put on his overcoat and steel helmet and moved over to the BAR. Cates, after a series of mumbled oaths, slipped partially into his sleeping bag. He did not want to put his muddy shoes into the bag because of the mess it would make.

After what seemed like several days, Karchner shook my foot. "It's your turn, Neill." He gave me my watch. I crawled out of my "sleeping" position of misery into a standing version and put on my soggy overcoat, ammunition belt, and steel helmet. I had a terrible time fastening my buttons because my fingers were so numb. I could do only half of them. I kept thinking of Palm Springs and people swimming in warm swimming pools or basking in the sun on this very same November 10–11. I told myself I would go there and never leave if I ever got out of here.

I moved in behind my BAR and looked for real, live Germans. It made my job exciting and scary to think that a German with a loaded rifle and a hand grenade could be out there just beyond my sight, looking for Americans like me. Despite a heavily overcast sky, I could see about seventy-five feet out into the darkness, thanks to the heavy white layer of snow. I strained my eyes trying to spot anything unusual. I soon found something to worry about. It was a raised dark spot off to the right side of my range of vision. I continued to watch the whole area but kept coming back to the same dark spot. It moved, ever so slightly, or so I thought. It was about the size of a man prone in the snow. Was it a German crawling slowly nearer to toss a grenade into our hole? I wasn't sure enough to alert Cates or Karchner. And I wasn't sure enough to fire at it. So I kept an anxious watch until Cates's second tour began. He wasn't sure, either. We continued watching the spot until daylight, when we learned it was a log. How glad I was that I didn't stir up the platoon and the Germans with a burst or two from my BAR!

Our first night on the front had ended with no incidents. I was surprised we did not freeze to death and amazed at the treatment the human body could survive. (Words cannot convey the awfulness of this ordeal to the reader. My buddies and I agreed it would be impossible to exaggerate how hopeless, miserable, and depressed we felt.)

During these first hours on the front, the Jewish soldiers in L Company began worrying about their dog tags. "Should I take them off?" they asked. If captured wearing them, the Germans would know they were Jews.

While we were replacing the 5th Armored Division's machine gun team, Warner Anthony, our platoon medic, replaced a 5th Armored Division medic in another area of Höfen. "When I got over to him," Anthony said, "he was wandering around outside his foxhole. I introduced myself, but he never told me his name. Since this wasn't too uncommon, I didn't pay any attention to it.

"In a few minutes," Anthony continued, "he got into his foxhole and sat at one end. I sat at the other. Then I asked, 'Why are we getting in here?' His answer: 'German artillery is going to start in a little while, simply because there is so much activity here.'

"The 5th Armored medic was whistling some dumb song that had no tune to it at all. In a little while, the artillery started. I thought it was quite intense," Anthony said. "It wasn't long before someone called out 'medic.' Without saying a word, he crawled out of the foxhole. He came back twenty minutes later, sat down, and started whistling the same dumb song.

"This was our first day on the line, and I had absolutely no experience," Anthony continued. "I had tied pressure bandages on perfectly good arms and legs. But I had no experience with the real thing, and I was sure this guy was going to give me some great wisdom. I asked about what to do, but I never got an intelligent answer. We didn't wait long for a second call. This time he said: 'That's one of your people.' When I asked what I should do, he said, 'I don't know. Tell me about it when you get back.' Someone was hit with a superficial wound on the back of his hand. When I came back and told him what I'd done, he said, 'Did you put any sulfa on it?' I said, 'No, I'd completely forgotten it.'

"Another person called for a medic. 'That's one of your men,' he informed me. I fixed up someone who'd been shot in the shoulder. When I got back to the hole, he was gone. So the advice I got was 'don't forget the sulfa, and from now on you're strictly on your own,'" Anthony concluded. The men we relieved had one excuse for the way they treated us. They were exhausted and demoralized.

While we were moving into positions around Höfen, our buddies in the 393rd Regiment of the 99th also were moving into front-line positions in woods about ten miles to the south of us. When they arrived by truck at Krinkelt, Belgium, E Company's Pfc. Harry S. Arnold said there were no civilians to be seen. Marching up snow-concealed roads, they passed scattered groups of 9th Division troops, the men they were relieving. "These seasoned men looked at us and asked with derision: 'Is this what the War Department is using for soldiers?' Laden with all the paraphernalia of the brand new soldier we, no doubt, were proper objects of derision," Arnold continued.[8]

Arnold's squad was halted. A 9th Division sergeant told the BAR gunner, assistant gunner, and Arnold to follow him. The sergeant guided them to an opening in the forest about sixty feet across (probably a firebreak) and stopped by two foxholes assigned to Arnold's squad. When Arnold asked the sergeant where the front line was, the sergeant answered, "The line is behind us. This is your observation post." He told Arnold that the sixty-foot swath through the forest was the border between Belgium and Germany, and that the woods on the other side of the swath were full of mines and booby traps. In addition, he warned Arnold about a BAR lying on the snow-covered ground in the woods. "Leave it alone. It's booby trapped." With that, he turned and left Arnold and the others in his squad to take over their new positions.

"It was prudent to toss a grenade silently from our hole in the direction of suspicious sounds," Arnold continued. "But, it was hard to determine where the noise came from in the dark. One fellow pulled the pin and prepared to toss a grenade, then was uncertain about what he had heard, and waited. When no further sound came, he found that he had thrown the pin aside and was unable to find it in the dark. He spent the rest of the night anxiously holding the grenade so it would not explode in his hole."[9]

Arnold described several incidents that show what it was like to live so near the German line. Captain Miller, E Company commander, and another officer visited the outpost to investigate the German side. The officers borrowed trench knives and began probing for mines along both sides of the road. Satisfied, they continued into the woods (nearer the Germans). A few minutes later, a muffled explosion and a cry came from the woods. Arnold alerted the squad, and a German machine gun began firing. Arnold said his squad "hit a German" during the shooting exchange. The squad found Miller lying in the snow. His face and side were bloody and blackened from the mine or booby trap blast. When the medics arrived, there was a discussion of how best to get him on the stretcher. "Lay the goddamn thing down," Miller grimaced, "and I'll roll over on it." The medics evacuated Miller to the rear, and Arnold never saw him again.[10]

ON THE OTHER SIDE. On November 11, Hitler, in an official directive, set November 25 for launching his big winter offensive.[11]

☆ **3rd Battalion Morning Report to the 395th Regiment**
November 11, 1944—
Battalion remains in defensive positions.

We spent November 11 (twenty-six years to the day after the end of World War I) in our little valley outpost at Höfener Mühle. Early the next day, Lieutenant Goss sent the sergeants out to the holes to notify us that we were moving out immediately. A captured German soldier told an interrogator that his unit considered us easy pickings since we were so far away from the rest of our battalion. Its plan was to cut us off and capture or kill us. Knowing our vulnerability, our leaders decided to pull

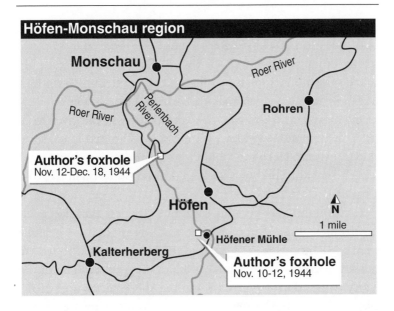

Höfen-Monschau region

Monschau

Roer River

Roer River

Perlenbach River

Rohren

Author's foxhole
Nov. 12-Dec. 18, 1944

Höfen

N

1 mile

☐● Höfener Mühle

Kalterherberg

Author's foxhole
Nov. 10-12, 1944

back to a safer position. We tossed everything into our wet packs and gladly abandoned the farmhouse and its spooky little valley. (A few weeks later, the Germans reoccupied the site.)

Moving at double time with our heavy loads, we climbed the steep, slippery trail back into Höfen. Now more secure in the environs of the battalion, we slowed to regular infantry pace. Artillery on both sides was mostly quiet except for the distant thunder from the bitter Hürtgen Forest fighting twelve miles to the northeast. We followed in reverse the same route we used on November 10 when the half-tracks dropped us at the north end of Höfen.

This time, we headed down into a deep ravine. At its bottom, a wooden bridge crossed the Perlenbach River, the same tributary of the Roer River we had crossed two miles upstream at Höfener Mühle. A heavy mantle of snow weighed down the tree branches and covered the ground to the icy water's edge, creating a beautiful winter scene.

My platoon (still consisting of two squads instead of the usual three) crunched its way through the snow into woods along both sides of the white-water stream. "We'll dig in a defensive strong point here around our two BARs," Goss declared. My squad spread out along the Höfen side of the stream. Sgt. Bruce Mather's squad, which included friend George Kelly's BAR team, moved into the tree line directly across the river from us. This was my new home, on the side of an extremely steep slope. It was so steep we couldn't go up or down without grabbing branches to pull ourselves up or hold on to them to avoid a bad fall.

As soon as Goss and his sergeants decided the placement of foxholes, dugouts for sleeping, and the ubiquitous straddle trench, each of us started digging the holes assigned to us. We quickly discovered that this location for digging could hardly be worse with so many big rocks and big roots in our way. However, we could not change the foxhole location for easier digging. Tactically, it had to be where our leaders marked it.

The purpose of our new assignment in the ravine was: (a) to block the enemy from moving freely behind Höfen, (b) to prevent him from capturing or destroying the 3rd Battalion's lifeline bridge over the Perlenbach River immediately north of us on the Höfen-Kalterherberg road, and (c) to deter the enemy from walking into the village on a good road from its unprotected west side.

Although the 3rd Battalion's main line of resistance (MLR) faced the enemy's Siegfried Line pillboxes to the east of Höfen, the Germans also had at least two strong points in an otherwise no man's land directly south and southwest of Höfen, between Höfen and Kalterherberg. They also had roving observers at unknown locations on the west side to watch traffic crossing the bridge and our activities in the ravine. Thus, thanks to gaps in our front line, the 3rd Battalion faced the German Army on its east, south, and west sides. I and K Companies confronted the enemy on the east, and L Company faced the enemy on the south, the southwest, and the west.

Two gaps, undefended by U.S. positions, existed in the front line on Höfen's southern and northern flanks—a two-mile gap immediately south of L Company and a six hundred-foot gap between us and the 102nd U.S. Cavalry Group defending Monschau. The south gap widened dramatically after December 11 to approximately five miles. Through these gaps, the enemy could move behind the west side of Höfen without meeting American defensive positions. In other words, Höfen was really a defensive island open to attack from all sides. That is why we built our strong point in the ravine beside the bridge on the west side of the village. (Later, Lieutenant Goss set up a barbed wire barricade on the bridge to halt vehicles for an identification check.)

To summarize, the 3rd Battalion held a large strong point made up of a series of small strong points on high ground blocking German access to two key roads. One led directly west to Eupen, headquarters of the U.S. Army V Corps; Verviers, a supply base; and Liege, a major supply base and transportation center for the U.S. First Army. The second road led directly south to Elsenborn and Camp Elsenborn, which, in a crisis, became 99th Division Headquarters on December 17.

Since I carried the BAR, I got the foxhole location with the best lines of fire. We located three other holes on both sides of my position to protect and enhance the BAR. With two riflemen per hole, this gave our side of the river a total strength of seven rifles and one BAR. The positions were spread about twenty feet apart. George Kelly's BAR position directly across the river from me had similar support, plus a bazooka-rocket man to kill tanks or armored vehicles. "Open fire on any movement spotted upstream," Goss declared. "That is our front line. But don't fire the two BARs unless the rifles can't do the job. We don't want to give away our BAR positions without good reason." Before we went to work, we pulled out a K ration for a late breakfast. We remained spread out. We couldn't sit down because deep snow covered the ground and nearby rocks.

This time our position was hidden just inside a tree line about twenty feet away from the river's edge. We looked out toward the walking trails that paralleled both sides of the river. From these positions, I had a clear line of fire for about five hundred feet along the trail on the other side of the river. But we could see little to nothing of the trail along our side. The same was true in reverse for George Kelly's squad on the other bank. Each squad could slow or hopefully stop an enemy thrust coming downstream on the opposite side of the river. Using the two squads as a symbiotic team represented a neat bit of strategy so long as the enemy came from the south. Our leaders (mistakenly) assumed little threat existed to our north.

"Let's get going on the foxholes," Mysliewiec declared. "Until we make them, we have no protection against a ground attack or from artillery." He "volunteered" two of us—fortunately neither Karchner nor me—to start digging the straddle trench three feet deep and eight feet long. Only after finishing that tough job could the "volunteers" get at their own foxholes.

We always carried our rifles, whether to the straddle trench or to pick up a meal at the CP. If I didn't have my BAR, I had the rifle of the man taking my place with the BAR.

At about 10 A.M., we started to dig with our twenty-eight-inch shovels through tree roots, rocks, and half-frozen ground. I would dig three or four inches, sometimes only an inch, then rest while Karchner dug a similar depth. Progress was slow, only eighteen inches by 2 P.M. Since we needed to prepare a level area to sleep before dark, we turned to the location marked for our dugout. It was about thirty feet up the icy slope that began at the foxhole and rose sharply four hundred feet to the top of the small, rugged mountain.

Mature Christmas-tree-like firs, planted in straight horizontal lines across the incline, covered the slope. In addition to the snow, the trees had a heavy sprinkling of silver strips, similar to the "icicles" used to decorate indoor Christmas trees. We figured these were dropped from planes, but we had no idea of their purpose. (The mysterious "decoration" was an important Allied weapon in the air war. British and American bombers dropped the tinfoil strips, called either "window" or "chaff," to confuse German radar. This perplexing new defensive weapon consisted of pieces of reflective tinfoil that, when dropped, produced a mass of "echoes," thus confusing the picture on German radar screens and making ground-controlled interceptions by night fighters almost impossible.) With both snow and chaff on the trees around us, we lived in a winter wonderland. The in-line trees illustrated the German penchant for order, even in forests. All the trees looked alike, and they made navigation through them at night by combat patrols extremely difficult.

We did not have time to build an acceptable dugout, so we concentrated on digging a shelf into the hillside for our pup tent. By sleeping with our heads into the hillside, we could at least partially protect our upper bodies from ground-exploding shells. But we were totally unprotected from our real danger— shells exploding in trees overhead (called "tree bursts").

We set up our tents on our new, still-sloping "shelf" with the closed end of the tent into the hillside and the entrance/exit on the open end. This enabled our buddies to easily reach our feet to wake us for night sentinel vigils. Inside the small tents, hidden from view outside the forest tree line and camouflaged by snow cover, we spread our two sleeping bags and placed our other things on the seven-foot by five-foot floor space. By 3:15 P.M., we had finished our first effort at making a place to sleep. We could now go back to our top priority—the fighting hole—and dig deeper.

At about 4 P.M., with daylight almost gone, a runner from our platoon's CP told us our first hot meal in three days had arrived in a Jeep trailer. Two of us at a time (not buddies) were permitted to get our mess gear and go back to the Jeep. When we got back, two more could go. To get to the CP, we followed an icy trail for about four hundred feet. A slip, which happened often, could mean the loss of one of our precious two meals a day. With our rifles hanging from our shoulders, we carried a big tin cup of hot coffee in one hand and our open tin mess gear containing our food in the other. We wolfed down dinner. By the time we had finished and rinsed out our mess gear in the icy river, it was dark. Incidentally, the cold water did not remove the grease left from the dinner. (When not on alert, we received just two "hot"—actually warm to cool—meals a day, breakfast and dinner. Occasionally, we had a K ration for lunch. Mostly, however, we lived on two meals a day.)

Night sentinel stands in the 3rd Battalion usually ran two hours on duty and four hours off for "sleeping" in a foxhole, dugout, or cellar, if one were lucky. My BAR team used two schedules—two hours in the foxhole awake listening and watching and four trying to sleep in the bitter cold, or three hours on guard in a foxhole and three hours off. The three hour "stands" were particularly tough. Time passed in slow motion.

The night's schedule began immediately (about 4:15 P.M.), and Karchner and I agreed that he would take over the BAR hole for the first shift. I took his rifle (leaving him with the BAR) and crawled and slipped up the steep slope in the darkness in search of our open pup tent. It was not easy in the blackness of the forest. When I finally found our tent, I crawled inside and, surrounded by total darkness, took off my steel helmet and wet gloves and stretched out, shivering, on my back. No reading or letter writing here. My fingers were so cold I continued having great difficulty unbuttoning my overcoat.

There was no place we could go to get warm during the twenty-four-hour day, even for a few minutes. No house, no cellar, no dry bed. The cold caused sharp pains in my face and ears, as if they were burned. The unremitting enemy—the demoralizing torture of extreme cold—surrounded us every minute, both night and day. It was an enemy we could not escape. Ernie Pyle was right when he declared that "nothing can touch the infantry for rough, and horrible living. . . . They lived like men of prehistoric times." [12]

Good God, I thought, we knew it would be tough, but in no way could we imagine the discomfort we were now experiencing. With the entry end of our tent wide open to the elements, it was just as cold inside as outside, about twenty-six degrees. Having had little sleep for three days and overcome by the cold, I drifted into a shivering sleep.

When Karchner's three-hour guard period was up, he crawled, slipped, and groped until he found our tent. He shook my foot to wake me up, gave me my watch, and crawled in. "Nothing going on," he said as he collapsed on his sleeping bag. I groped for tree branches and stepped cautiously down the slippery, unseen trail. A branch almost knocked off my steel helmet. I stumbled and fell a couple of times before I reached our shallow foxhole and started my first three-hour night vigil at our new ravine location.

Standing beside our foxhole-to-be, I tried to peer through the inky blackness to see the river and the path on the other side, and especially any Germans moving toward us. I put my hand up to my face, but I couldn't see it. How was I going to see any Germans? At least there was a positive flip side: How were the Germans going to spot me? The only thing I could see was the luminous dial on my watch. Fearing that the enemy might spot the dial, I turned it to the inside of my wrist. To prevent any noise from the jostling of the two metal dog tags hanging around our necks, we had placed specially made rubber frames around them.

With nothing to look at but the watch, I kept checking the time. When I thought fifteen minutes had passed I would look, only to be disappointed that just five minutes had gone by. An hour seemed like an entire night! Considering the wind-chill factor, a moderate wind brought the temperature down to near zero. It seemed as if my vigil would never end. Again, I cursed the army for not providing us with effective winter clothing and waterproof boots or galoshes. (Each of us fought the cold in his own way. The more layers of clothing the better. Some, who had good connections, simultaneously wore three or four sets of long johns, two pairs of wool pants, and two wool shirts. Most of us, myself included, apparently did not know the right people. I had only one set of everything.)

I kept looking at my watch. My feet were getting numb, despite constant stomping. I also found that we had another problem. The fast-moving river right next to us made so much noise that we wouldn't hear a German patrol crunching in the snow until it was right on top of us. We had no trouble hearing the noisy V-1 buzz bombs as they passed directly overhead on their way to Liege or Antwerp. They became part of the ceaseless symphony of battle.

Division artillery reported that approximately six hundred V-1s rumbled across the skies over the division during three weeks in November and December. Seventy-four either exploded in the air or fell from the air and exploded on the ground in 99th Division areas. Some crashed near infantry foxholes. The 99th Division artillery in Wirtzfeld, eight air miles south of Höfen, reported that as many as ten V-1s passed overhead in one hour. In our area, one V-1 turned in circles and then buzzed back in the direction from which it came. That must have caused some cursing on the German side.

Before the night was over I had completed two shifts (six hours) and Karchner had completed three (nine hours). In between, we were supposed to sleep. We reversed the schedule each night so that we each had longer nights in our holes followed by shorter ones. But the extreme discomfort and listening for strange sounds kept me awake at least half of my three-hour "breaks."

While my BAR team began digging foxholes on our sector of the front, our 99th Division buddies in the 1st Battalion, 394th Infantry, approached their assigned portion of the front near Losheimergraben, Belgium, eleven air miles south of Höfen. BAR gunner John E. Mellin told what happened after trucks dropped off his 1st Platoon, A Company, about six miles behind the line. "We spent the night of November 11 under our shelter halves, trying to keep warm. A friend had a small gasoline stove about the size of a one-quart thermos bottle, but it didn't help much.

"The next day," Mellin continued, "we marched to the unit we were replacing. It was part of the veteran 9th Infantry Division of North Africa, Normandy, and Hürtgen Forest fame. As we passed some of them on their way to the rear, they taunted us with comments about our 'nice, clean uniforms.' They looked like Willie and Joe in Bill Mauldin's cartoons—unshaven and deadly tired. When we reached our destination, the 9th Division men had huge bonfires going in the woods to keep warm. This surprised me," Mellin said, "because fires told the enemy our location.

"We dug foxholes and constructed log cabins for sleeping. Our cabin had no heat, but it was much drier than foxholes. Our feet, however, were wet all the time. A sad but humorous incident occurred," Mellin said, "that showed how our illustrious officer corps was going to solve the trench-foot problem. My platoon leader came to each of us, made us heat water in our steel helmets, wash our feet in warm water, dry them, and then put on a pair of new socks. Then we put on our wet shoes. We were back where we started. Officer intelligence did not win the war."

I had a "dry socks" experience similar to Mellin's. With the arrival of daylight just before 9 A.M., our night guard schedule ended. Our wet, half-frozen feet were bothering us, so our leaders told us to take advantage of the light to find our one pair of dry socks. We exchanged them for the wet ones we'd been wearing for a week. As expected, the dry ones soon became wet in our wet shoes.

Sergeant Mysliewiec ordered us to keep one man in each foxhole throughout the day, with shifts changing every hour or two. One man dug while his "buddy" kept an eye out for Germans. The one who was digging always had his rifle within quick reach. Our job focused on a single goal—to complete the foxholes as quickly as possible.

Our first full day in the ravine had begun. I started the first daylight shift on guard at our still partially dug BAR foxhole, but I wasn't in the hole. It was too shallow, so I stood outside with the gun, hidden just inside the tree line. George Kelly's BAR team watched the blind spot on our side of the river. Kelly and I were both out of our holes so our buddies could dig deeper.

Breakfast arrived by Jeep trailer at the platoon CP. As the men came back with their food in their greasy mess gear, they passed on a message from General Lauer. He wanted us to look smart by shaving every day. Mysliewiec confirmed the order a short time later. He set a good example by being clean-shaven himself. So, after much grumbling and a few "choice" words, we slipped out of the tree line to the river to fill our steel helmets with ice water. We slipped back into the trees to shave off a nearly four-day growth of beard, a painful job with frigid water and no mirror. We didn't plan to pay much attention to General Lauer's desire for daily shaving, because we didn't expect to see him this far forward. As it turned out, we never saw him. In fact, I rarely saw any officer other than Lieutenant Goss. I never saw our company commander or our battalion commander.

Lauer's directive about shaving set off a startling (and eloquent) reaction from one of his men in the 394th Regiment. Percy J. Pace, at the time an artillery forward observer, told me about it. It was told to him by an eyewitness right after it happened in late December 1944.[13]

The eyewitness, an assistant BAR gunner in the 394th Regiment, told Pace that General Lauer was on an inspection tour. He rode standing in an armored car, with his head and chest sticking out of the turret. Freshly shaved, he wore a tanker's hat with two stars and a tanker's jacket—nice and warm. As he drove on a snow-covered road between Elsenborn and the front, he spotted a dirty looking BAR gunner and his assistant gunner (Pace's eyewitness) controlling traffic. Lauer ordered his driver to stop. Looking down on the forlorn BAR gunner, Lauer yelled: "Soldier, why don't you have a shave?" The soldier, who had just spent the night on a combat patrol, didn't respond. Lauer then asked him why his face and clothes were so dirty. At this point, the BAR gunner aimed his rifle at the general. "Don't move a muscle, sir, or you're dead," he responded. Then he added: "You don't know what questions to ask. Ask me why I don't have overshoes and an overcoat, if my feet are frostbitten, how long it's been since I've had any rest or sleep, how long it's been since I had a hot meal, and why I don't have dry shoes."

The demoralized BAR gunner then told the general that he didn't have a razor, a pack, or an overcoat. He explained that he had nothing except what he was wearing and that he had lost everything during the Battle of the Bulge. "If you came here to find out how morale is, you already know. It's real bad." Still pointing his BAR, the gunner told Lauer to turn his vehicle around and go back the way he came. "When you have better questions, come back and I'll let you pass." Lauer followed the gunner's instructions and disappeared. Pace, a lieutenant at the time, occupied a foxhole fifteen feet in front of the BAR team's position. He said he knew of no disciplinary action ever taken against the soldier. "It was obvious," Pace said, "that the general had no idea of the problems faced by the men on the front line."

Following my platoon's attempt to wash and shave with cold water, as ordered by Lauer, we returned to our top priority of finishing our foxholes. Unfortunately, some of the larger tree roots were impossible to cut out with our tiny shovels. In desperation, I went to our platoon's CP to explain our predicament to Lieutenant Goss. He had a crew building a room for his new

CP. Dug into the side of a hill, it was deep enough to stand up straight. Substantial logs formed the sides and roof. It was a well-protected front-line dugout.

I noticed that Goss's construction team had the kind of saw we needed. "We're stymied unless we have something better than the entrenching tool," I complained. "We need two small saws as soon as possible." Squeaky wheels sometimes pay off, but not this time. I returned empty-handed, but with a promise that within a day we would have the two saws.

We were getting into a pattern: breakfast arrived with daylight (about 8:30 A.M.) and dinner near dusk (4 P.M.). By the time dinner arrived, we felt half-starved. (This feeling continued for our entire five weeks in the ravine, with two exceptions.) We had an additional problem with eating. Since we rarely had hot water and soap for cleaning our mess gear, we used snow and ice water from the river. This did nothing to eliminate the grease accumulating after each meal, which set us up for chronic diarrhea.

After eating and "cleaning" our mess gear, we started the morale-breaking schedule of the night before. We dreaded these nights because we didn't know which would kill or drive us mad first: the cold, the long periods of boredom, or the lack of sleep. We nearly forgot about the ever-lurking enemy prowling around us during night patrols. The subject of sex, usually ubiquitous among young soldiers, seemed almost completely forgotten.

Diarrhea added greatly to our torture and fatigue. I had just fallen into another shivering sleep when I awoke with an urgent call of nature. With no time for procrastination, I pushed my overcoat off my sleeping bag and groped for toilet paper. I got on my hands and knees and backed out of the tent into the wind and blowing snow. I had to do all of this silently because any sound of movement was asking for a blast of bullets from our sentinels. I crawled a satisfactory distance from the tent, unbuttoned my field jacket with great difficulty, and pulled down my wool pants and long johns. When I crawled back into the tent I lay shaking, trying to put my wet clothes back together. I had to repeat this demeaning, but necessary, act twice more during that night (as well as several other nights).

An hour or two later, we had a quick reminder that we were not in just any snow-covered forest. Those on sentinel duty were jolted to sudden alert when a rifle fired several times in our immediate area. It was easily heard over the river noises. I missed the excitement because I had slipped into a rare deep sleep in my tent. Safety switches on the rifles and the BAR were clicked off by those who were awake. They peered more intently than ever into the inky blackness, but they could hear or see nothing. After those first shots, which came from one of our M1 rifles, silence returned. The enemy did not respond.

Intense alert continued until daylight when we found the "probing German." "He" was only a soaked overcoat hung in a tree before nightfall. I was glad I didn't do the shooting. The embarrassed rifleman had one consolation: he hit the coat. In addition to the lesson it taught about moving around at night, the "shooting" gave us a good laugh—something we desperately needed.

On the day following my request for saws, Lieutenant Goss kept his promise. We received saws, hatchets, and two picks to finish our foxholes. Digging, although still difficult, went much faster. The two-man holes—each about five feet deep, three feet wide, and six feet long—were finally finished by the end of the day. Before darkness, we began cutting some of the more solid branches from the trees around us to make small logs for forming the foxhole's protective roof.

While my 2nd Platoon lived a life of misery in the snowy forest, Roger J. Moore, a radio operator who lived close to our battalion's CP in Höfen, admitted he was lucky to be living and working in a house. "Not only did we have rugs and beds," he said, "but also we had china and silverware, a water pump, stoves, electric lights, and a phonograph. We used German sta-

tionery, German ink, German clocks, and German coal." The radio operators stood guard about one night out of three.[14]

Despite the better living conditions in Höfen, all was not
quiet. Colonel Butler had his first encounter with a German
fighter plane and one of his first experiences of being shot at. "I
was standing out on the main street in Höfen watching the
plane go by," Butler said. "It circled and came back. Our antiaircraft guns and machine guns were shooting at it. I thought
they must have hit it," he continued, "because it started smok-
ing." Wrong conclusion. "It wasn't hit at all," the surprised
colonel discovered. "It was firing at us. I got the message when
bullets came down the street towards me. The smoke came from
the plane's machine guns. I jumped down behind a building just
in time to keep from getting hit. From then on, I knew smoke
trailing behind a plane didn't necessarily mean it had been hit
and was on its way to a fiery crash."[15]

On November 14, Butler held a meeting of staff and company
commanders at his headquarters in Höfen "to outline the priority of work at hand." He emphasized the difficulty of defending a six thousand-yard front with only an infantry battalion of
836 men and officers. "Each staff officer and company commander must do his utmost to strengthen the battalion's position," Butler declared. He pointed out that since the 99th Division was spread so thinly over a twenty-mile front and our
3rd Battalion was located farthest north of the front, we could
expect little or no help in case of an attack.

Butler and his officers decided to replace a thin line of riflemen
with a series of strong points. Capt. (later Maj.) Keith Fabianich,
commander of K Company, said each strong point would con-
sist of a machine gun or a BAR, protected by riflemen. My position in the ravine, which we had started digging two days
before the meeting, served as one of these strong points. In
other action, the battalion reinforced its 81-mm mortar platoon
with four additional mortars, raising the total from six to ten.

Fabianich said the battalion made extensive use of antitank and antipersonnel mines to cover all routes approaching Höfen. Placing barbed-wire entanglements in front of the battalion's defensive position also strengthened our front. To give flexibility to the defense, the battalion held in reserve one rifle platoon— L Company's 1st Platoon—in the center of Höfen. Phones were installed in every strong point (including mine) and every observation point. In addition, the battalion provided each of its companies with extra radios. The effort to strengthen the battalion began immediately after Butler's meeting. It was completed on December 15, a fortunate bit of timing.[16]

On the day following Butler's meeting, we finished the log overheads for our foxholes and spread a piece of canvas over the logs to keep out rain and melting snow. On top of the canvas we placed some pine-needle branches for camouflage. We left about two feet of open space between the log overhead and the foxhole, giving us an embrasure with plenty of room to observe and fire from the sides and front. The rear of the hole was closed by the overhead logs that lay on the steep slope behind us. Thus, we were blind if attacked from the rear. We aimed the BAR upstream (south). Our orders were to fire on anyone on the trail upstream.

We were now ready for the Germans. Or, were we? Not quite. When I tried to get into my hole, I discovered entry was almost impossible. A slight miscalculation. Not enough space between the logs and the ground. Since we had never built foxholes with overhead tree-burst protection in all of our months of training, we had to improvise. My solution called for digging the hole two feet longer, beyond the overhead, with three steps leading out of the hole. In addition, we cleared a shelf behind the hole for our ammunition belts, hand grenades, and emergency food supply of K rations. These simple adjustments did the job.

There was, however, one big catch. We could not get out of the hole without making ourselves easy targets for the enemy. A rear exit was impossible because of the steep slope behind us and because of the log overhead sealing off the back. In a very real sense, our foxhole could easily trap us if we were caught in a firefight with an advancing force. In this situation, we would have to climb out in front of the enemy, making ourselves easy targets. We would have to fight in place to the death. No chance for a withdrawal to fight another day. Thus, we could end up having dug our own graves. (A grave and a good foxhole have similar dimensions.)

Still, despite the inherent hazards of this more elaborate foxhole, we now had a defensive fighting position that cost virtually nothing but three days of time and the wear and tear to our bodies. Quite a contrast to the hugely expensive Siegfried Line built by German fortification experts. American taxpayers got a much better "buy" than German taxpayers.

My BAR team constructed four solid foxhole positions in three days, not bad considering the roots, rocks, and semifrozen ground. But that did not alleviate the problem we had with the cold and the slushy bottoms of the holes, and thus, with our constantly wet feet. Every night was a tormenting struggle, with temperatures five to twenty degrees below freezing. The weather warmed slightly, with daytime high temperatures in the mid-thirties. The sky never cleared. The last time we had seen the sun was on that bright, brisk day we left Normandy on trucks bound for the German border—so long ago, or so it seemed.

German cooperation was crucial during our first three days as we constructed our fortified positions. A volley of 105-mm howitzer shells would have wiped us out. Other areas of the Höfen front received sporadic incoming shells, but nothing came close to us. Now, we were 50 percent safer. Sleeping in the pup tents, however, left us totally unprotected from tree bursts. Our misery with the cold and wet continued unabated. Since light from a candle could be seen through our tents, we lay trapped in darkness until daylight. Nothing exciting happened during the night, just the cold and the occasional artillery going both ways.

The primitive fortifications we constructed, mostly with our small entrenching tools, made a stark contrast to the sophisticated emplacements used by our nearby enemy. Since our front line ran through the middle of the Siegfried Line, the German Army used these facilities all along its line opposing us.

Construction of the Siegfried Line began in 1936. Its purpose was to protect Germany's western border with France and Belgium. The task went to Dr. Fritz Todt, the engineer who supervised the construction of Germany's superhighways. The giant project was nearly finished by the time Hitler invaded Poland in 1939. Employing half a million military engineers and workers and many thousands of German boys and girls who, at age seventeen, served for six months in public works programs, the project helped solve the unemployment problem in Germany during the worldwide economic depression.[17]

Siegfried Line pillboxes usually, but not always, had:

- two efficient machine guns aimed across clear fields of fire;
- barbed wire and antipersonnel mines blocking an enemy's approach;
- trenches leading to outpost foxholes and neighboring pillboxes;
- carefully prepared fields of fire, but limited to fifty-degree angles;
- no weapon larger than a 37-mm gun;
- support by artillery and mortar fire from positions to their rear;
- three to eight feet of reinforced concrete overhead, and a similar amount on the sides and underground;
- good camouflage concealment;
- sleeping quarters for five to eight soldiers;

- electricity and telephone wires installed underground;
- a small fireplace equipped with a tin chimney, which could be closed off by a heavy steel door. Smokeless coal briquettes usually served as fuel.

The size of the typical pillbox was twenty to thirty feet in width and approximately twenty feet in depth. At least half of the structure was underground. Most were constructed so that they could support each other if under attack. They rarely provided sanitary facilities.[18]

With the expert guidance of Will Cavanagh, a Battle of the Bulge authority, my wife and I inspected one of the few remaining Siegfried Line pillboxes in the Höfen area during a visit in July 1993. Entirely concealed by large bushes, it sat in partial ruin caused by demolition efforts. The intact portion was splattered with the marks of small arms fire caused by attacking American forces.

The pillbox's walls of concrete and steel were four feet thick. Cavanagh said the pillbox contained two heavy machine guns, one aimed toward Monschau and one pointing toward the foxhole area that I occupied in the ravine, less than a quarter-mile to the southwest. In addition to the fighting room with a wide embrasure for firing, the pillbox had a sleeping room with four or five double-decker bunks. It also had a steel escape door at the back. In the 1960s, Cavanagh told us, German writing on one of the interior walls said: "You give us the orders, and we will follow." As Cavanagh went on to explain, "Riflemen in foxholes protecting and supporting the pillbox tried to fight off the approaching Americans." They also alerted the men in the pillbox and supporting mortar teams and artillery of the approaching enemy.

German Army maps identified the pillboxes so their artillery and mortars could support them during an attack. Not on the maps were fortification bunkers built under or inside houses in

Höfen. These bunkers were so well disguised even the Germans had trouble finding them. I spotted one of these so-called houses during a visit to Höfen in 1977. Other bunkers were hidden inside large haystacks. (In contrast to pillboxes, which served as fighting positions, concrete bunkers were usually designed to house local reserve troops and CPs. They had no firing embrasure except for small rifle ports to cover the entrance.)[19]

While we were finishing our foxholes in the ravine, General Lauer (commanding officer of the 99th Division, and Colonel Butler's boss) came to visit the 3rd Battalion. "He wanted to see the front line," Butler asserted. "Lauer arrived with several vehicles and was 'hot to trot,' as far as I was concerned," Butler added. "He wanted a look at our area. So I took him down to the three-story building in I Company sector where a forward observer directed artillery fire. There was a good view of the German positions on our left flank." Butler said General Lauer pulled out his field glasses, walked up to a window, and looked over no man's land and the German line. At this point Butler said, "General, do you see that hole in the window in front of you? Well, that was shot out yesterday. The bullet killed the artillery observer who was directing fire. Now, if you keep standing there you're going to get shot, too." Butler said the general put his field glasses in their case, turned to his staff, and left immediately. Butler and his staff had a good chuckle. "That was General Lauer's first and last visit to the 3rd Battalion in Höfen," Butler said.[20]

Dawn on November 15 introduced the usual dreary day. As the men began stirring after another miserable night, I offered them some sick humor by singing "Oh, What a Beautiful Morning" from the new musical "Oklahoma." Two or three threw snowballs at me as I sang, "I have a wonderful feeling everything's going my way."

I think I kept my voice low enough so the sound wouldn't carry beyond our immediate confines. Too often, however, we became careless and talked back and forth too loudly. Since we spaced foxholes so far apart, we had to speak louder to communicate. Fortunately, the rushing river drowned out most of our thoughtless noise. (We also did not realize the Germans operated so close to us. Because of the thick forest, they could approach within a hundred feet of our foxholes without our seeing them, as long as they came through the forest and not along the two river trails we watched so closely.)

We now started work on our dugout—where we would sleep—about thirty feet up the slope from our foxhole. We were in a hurry because of the dangers of tent living, a practice rarely found on the front line. While Karchner stood daytime guard in the BAR foxhole, I moved our pup tent to another shelf I had dug as a temporary home site. With more time now available, we dug farther into the slope so that all of our bodies could lie below ground level while we slept. The dugout floor now had a nine-foot-long flat space. Our other buddy teams were doing the same thing.

I spotted a German-built wooden guard shelter near the bridge and broke it into usable pieces. In this business of dugout building a carpenter had a big advantage, but none of us was a carpenter. Pieces of wood from the German shelter gave us material for the sides and back of the dugout and for roof support. For the roof itself, we decided to find two inside doors from an empty house in Höfen.

About this time, we heard a report about one of our men sleeping on guard duty. The soldier, Pvt. John Brown—the man who stole ice cream from the officers' mess on the *Marine Devil* and who got into trouble in Dorchester—was sent by his platoon sergeant to a forward foxhole at night to watch and listen for enemy activity and report back regularly by phone. After the first hour, Brown failed to call in. More time passed with no call. The platoon sergeant sent two men out to find him. When they reached his foxhole, he was enjoying a nap. The enemy could have walked right by him without his knowing, or without L Company and the 3rd Battalion knowing. Captain Price, our company commander, threatened to have Brown shot by a firing squad. Our officers and noncoms told us numerous times that this offense called for a death sentence. Our front was depending on Brown and others at various forward spots. If they did not perform their jobs properly, they would jeopardize the entire battalion. This time Brown's indiscretion was neither cute nor funny. Price finally relented, however, and decided not to press charges.[21]

Although many men committed dishonorable acts in the U.S. Army during World War II, only one man was actually executed. His crime: fleeing when confronted by the enemy.

The first man killed in the 3rd Battalion was Samuel B. Gibney, Jr., an L Company runner. The incident occurred shortly after midnight, November 16, at battalion headquarters, of all places. It was just five days after we arrived on the Höfen front. A married man with no children, Gibney was one of eight battalion runners who slept in a large first-floor room.

An eyewitness, William H. (Bill) Huffman, an I Company runner sleeping in the room with Gibney, described what happened. At about 6 P.M., Gibney finished a cup of coffee, took off his shoes, and climbed between the blankets that formed his bed on the wood floor.[22] Foxy, his buddy, said, "Gibney, you're going to sleep your life away." In five minutes, Gibney's heavy breathing indicated he was sleeping soundly. The rest of the guys talked, cleaned carbines, smoked, and drank coffee and bouillon. Soon everyone was bedding down.

Around midnight, a shattering explosion in the midst of the sleeping runners shocked them awake. "The noise was deafening," Huffman said. "A second shell struck just outside, and the flash revealed that most of our outside wall had disappeared." An acrid stench and choking dust filled the room as the men checked to see if all their buddies were alive. They heard a gurgling groan, and someone cried out that Gibney was hit. Huffman made his way to Gibney across the turned-over stove and fallen stovepipe. A medic sleeping with the runners tried to find Gibney's wound by feel, since he had no flashlight. A third shell shook the building.

The medic cursed the blackout. He cut away the shirt and undershirt from Gibney's back. He found a deep hole as big as a man's fist next to his spine. Huffman grabbed a towel and tried to keep the blood sopped up as it gushed and gurgled from Gibney's mouth and nose. Then he discovered that Gibney's left arm was nearly severed above the elbow. The medic told Huffman to stop the bleeding. He had his hands full stuffing bandages from his medic's kit into the gaping hole in Gibney's back.

Huffman cut away the shirt sleeve and undershirt with his trench knife as blood spurted from the shattered arm. He grasped it above the wound and squeezed as hard as he could. The blood spurt slowed. Someone produced a heavy cord, wound it above the cut, and pulled. The gush slowed to an ooze. Blood continued to bubble from Gibney's mouth and nose.

At this point Capt. Herbert S. Orr (M.D.), the battalion's chief medical officer, arrived with one of his medics from the battalion medical aid station across the street. "Clear out men," Orr declared. "We'll take over." The runners moved into the officer's room across the hall.

Gibney's buddy, Foxy, had been asleep on his side or stomach when the shell struck. A shell fragment embedded itself in his posterior, and the wound was extremely painful even though it was not serious.

The uncertainty about Gibney's fate was quickly settled when Dr. Orr declared that Gibney was dead. Dr. Orr's Jeep took his body to the battalion aid station. Huffman and the other runners slept fitfully for the rest of the night. Huffman said he woke with a jerk every few minutes. "I couldn't erase the vision of Gibney's bloody face from my mind. I kept thinking of his last words when he went to bed, 'Got to keep up with my sleep. May not have a chance much longer.'"

At dawn, the runners were up, poking about their old room. "Only now were we impressed by the fact that of the eight men in the room, seven had lived, and six had escaped injury altogether," Huffman said. The runners surmised that a shell from a German 88-mm gun struck the stone wall just above the windows. The lower part of the inside walls was pocked with holes, and the door to the hall was splintered beyond repair.

The runners performed the "saddest task of all"—gathering Gibney's personal effects and taking them to battalion headquarters. They cleaned everything stained with blood. "There isn't much left to send home when an infantryman is killed," Huffman continued. "I looked at the pitiful little array of possessions: the wrist watch, a billfold, nail clippers, a pocket knife, pen and pencil set, comb, razor, and other toilet articles. I thought of Mrs. Gibney and what she would think when the effects of her husband eventually arrived at her home in Paris, Texas. She would receive a War Department telegram and, later, this little bag of articles." [23]

Gibney's death taught us about the wicked wounds caused by fragments from bursting shells, the number one killer of front-line infantry. We learned about the random way shell fragments pick their victims and the dangers of living above ground level in a building. Cellars were almost always safer. A well-dug but miserable foxhole with solid logs overhead provided the best defense. But the foxhole presented other problems for its inhabitants, like freezing bodies or the difficulty of reaching and evacuating the wounded from remote locations. Gibney's death shocked us because he spent most of his time in battalion headquarters, one of the sturdiest structures in Höfen.

In this case, the tragedy also took place under especially good conditions. There was a medic in the room, a heater for warmth, dry blankets, a phone, a real doctor, and an aid station across the street. In most cases, the wounded were at remote foxholes or on patrols one to three miles from help. Often, the difficulty of moving a seriously wounded man over rough, icy terrain without a litter was formidable.

Later in the day, during daylight hours, battalion headquarters in Höfen had some more excitement. Cpl. Harvey Lipshitz, a member of the headquarters staff, went outside to relieve himself at the straddle trench. While he was in the squat position, an artillery shell landed near him and exploded. Lipshitz hit the ground quickly. Thanks to his fast reaction, and a pile of lumber between him and the explosion, he didn't get killed. As soon as the shell fragments stopped flying, he grabbed his rifle by the barrel, partially pulled up his pants, and ran quickly back into the building. "The goddamn shell blinded me," Lipshitz told a friend. "You damn fool," the friend replied, "open your eyes!" Lipshitz opened his eyes and said, "By God, I can see better now." Colonel Butler said the incident was funny, "until we discovered he was wounded in an armpit and had to be evacuated." Lipshitz never returned to the battalion.[24]

A couple of weeks later, Lieutenant Le Buff, battalion supply officer, was squatting at the same straddle trench when the Germans fired a twelve-inch railroad gun. One of its shells landed about five hundred feet away, throwing a piece of shrapnel nearly two feet long and an inch wide into the ground between his feet. When the big piece of shrapnel cooled off, Le Buff pulled it out of the ground. He ran back to the command post to show off his souvenir. Although untouched by the shrapnel, he was unable to have a bowel movement for two days.[25]

ON OUR SIDE. On November 16, a heavy U.S.-British air bombardment involving twenty-four hundred bombers preceded a massive American ground attack just east of nearby Aachen, Germany. It was aimed at reaching the Roer River and pushing on to the Rhine after capturing the Roer River dams.

Unseen planes flew over our 99th Division positions for several hours. Participating in the raid were twelve hundred U.S. Eighth Air Force heavy bombers and twelve hundred RAF heavy bombers. When the bombing stopped, the First and Ninth Armies launched a massive ground attack that failed to achieve a breakthrough. It took two weeks to advance only seven miles. By the time the attack reached the Roer River, General Omar Bradley declared that "it was apparent that we had become engaged in a costly war of attrition."[26]

On November 17, L Company installed a field telephone in my newly-completed foxhole. It provided a wire-connected communications link to the platoon CP and, through the platoon, to the L Company CP. This one phone served the BAR foxhole and the four support rifle foxholes. I did not feel so isolated now.

With approval of Sergeant Mysliewiec, Karchner and I took off after breakfast with rifles slung over our shoulders and walked up the steep hill into Höfen. We were shopping for materials to finish our dugout. With help from I and K Companies, we identified several empty houses. All were observable from the main German line. Entering these empty houses was scary business. Although no German civilians remained in the village, enemy patrols came in and out of the town fairly often without being spotted by 3rd Battalion defensive positions. Usually, but not always, they came in at night, hid in empty houses all day observing our activities and defensive positions, and then slipped back to German-held Rohren the next night to report their findings. Our front line was loose—with too many gaps in it—and the Germans knew it.

Because of the danger of German infiltrators hiding inside empty houses, we entered each house cautiously, investigating every room before checking out what we could use. Desperate for safer and more comfortable sleeping quarters, we were willing to take risks. The first house we entered looked as if no one had been in it since its owners had fled eight weeks earlier. Partially eaten meals lay on a breakfast-room table. In the living room we got a surprise—a miniature Catholic altar depicting Mary holding the infant Jesus. How out-of-place it looked to us in the middle of the Siegfried Line. Neither of us, both Protestants, had ever seen such a display of religion in a home. This spartan, neat home had two bedrooms. One had several toys, a crib, and a single bed. Beds in both rooms were neatly made. "Wonder what happened to these people?" I asked.

Curious to know more about a German family, I opened a drawer in the kitchen area. Much to my surprise, it was full of paper money. "Hey, Karchner," I called, "we're rich!" Then, after remembering German inflation in the 1920s, we decided it was probably worthless and put it back in the drawer. Besides, we were reluctant to take anything from this apparently respectable family, even though it proudly displayed the photo of a German soldier (who was not a member of the SS) in the living room.

We carefully ventured into another empty house nearby. Stacked carefully in the cellar were about twenty jars of preserved cherries, a large heap of coal briquettes, and a small wagon. Despite its altar, similar to the first house, and the appearance of another good family, we decided we had to drop our qualms about taking things that weren't ours. Our survival and comfort came far ahead of feelings about the people who lived in these homes before we arrived. So we unhinged two wooden doors and placed them on the wagon we found in the cellar. On top of the doors we set about ten jars of preserved cherries. I pulled the wagon slowly, and Karchner kept things from falling off. When we came to "88 Corner" and the sign warning about enemy observation, we started running. The doors stayed on the wagon, but we lost several jars of cherries. When we arrived at our platoon CP, we showed off our "finds" to Goss and Thompson. "Those cherries look great," Thompson said, "but how do you know they haven't been poisoned?" With that worrisome thought, Karchner and I lost interest and left them at the CP. Later, some hungry soul opened a jar and tasted them. "Excellent," he said. After that, at least six jars were consumed in two days. Several men became sick, not from poisoning but from gluttony. The less glamorous part of our booty, the two doors, provided us with an excellent dugout roof.

We mentioned our surprise at the displays of the strong Catholic influence in the two homes. Several other members of our squad said they had seen similar signs of religious devotion in numerous other homes. They noted that some of the 3rd Battalion's Catholics had bragged about stealing some religious items, such as rosary beads. The fact that some American Catholics would steal religious items from German Catholics bothered me.

I learned what happened to the people of Höfen during a visit I made to the area in 1993. All 330 residents of the northern half of Höfen abandoned their homes and livestock on September 15 when the American 9th Infantry Division captured Monschau and prepared to drive German defenders out of Höfen the next day. The American commander wanted German civilians removed from Höfen because of fear for their safety and because the town was the perfect location for German spies. The residents packed a few essentials and walked into an unoccupied, heavily forested ravine between Monschau and Rohren. When the Americans captured Höfen on September 17, they decided to return home. At noon three days later, American soldiers told them to prepare to leave for Monschau. "You'll probably be gone for only three days," the Americans told them. (They could not return until May 1945.) When they left their homes they were still wearing summer clothing. In Monschau, they had to find shelter from residents of the community. They left their livestock—mostly cows—to fend for themselves. In a half-hour, all 330 Höfen refugees were taken in, mostly by people they knew.[27]

Residents in the south part of Höfen also fled their homes on September 16, but they could not return until 1947. They left their homes for empty forests south and southeast of Höfen. With no protection from heavy rain in late September and October, they were forced to leave their miserable forest hideaway and cross into the German side of the front. They were sent to east Germany. Many were overrun later by Russians and held prisoner for two years after the war ended. One, five-year-old Karin Uhl, went with her parents to Dresden just in time to experience one of the worst air raids of World War II.[28]

While we relieved Höfen homes of helpful materials, my friend Louis Pedrotti, bazooka man for L Company's 1st Platoon, observed a humorous happening shortly after the 1st Platoon settled down in Höfen as the battalion's only reserve unit. "When we arrived in Höfen, we occupied several houses in the village," Pedrotti said. "We were making ourselves right at home when we noticed German helmets passing by the high windows of our house. Naturally, we all thought it was the guys of K Company cutting up again. Only later did we find out that the helmets were really and truly worn by Wehrmacht heads. The saving grace," he added, "was that the Germans had about the same quality of reconnaissance as we did."[29]

My BAR team and support group continued its regular schedule of nighttime guard duty. Our only movement was between foxhole and dugout. Unless notified otherwise, we considered any other movement hostile during the long nights. At about this time, thanks to some group ingenuity, we found a partial solution to the difficulty in navigating down the steep, slippery slope from dugouts to foxholes. The answer was plenty of new rope, which we had found in one of the houses in Höfen. We tied it to trees leading down to the foxholes.

Our debilitating routine continued unchanged. Dysentery,

lack of food and sleep, and shoes and feet that were perpetually cold and wet took their toll. The excellent physical conditioning we enjoyed when we arrived continued to erode. Every few days, we heard reports of 3rd Battalion men being killed and wounded, some of whom we knew well.

One of our men learned an important lesson on how to conduct himself if captured and interrogated by the enemy. His insight came as he watched an intelligence officer (not from the 3rd Battalion) interrogate a German prisoner. The officer asked the prisoner for information about his unit. The German replied, just as the U.S. Army taught us, with name, rank, and serial number. That is all a prisoner of war is required by international law to tell his interrogator. Nothing more. After several attempts to obtain useful information with the same result, the infuriated American yelled at the enemy soldier and smashed his face with the butt of his hand pistol. When the German recovered from the blow, he spat out several bloody front teeth. When the American returned to questioning, the prisoner cooperated.

The observer, of course, learned that the "name, rank, and serial number" rule was sometimes more an ideal than a reality. Smashing a prisoner's face with a pistol butt was not the only way some of our interrogators got German prisoners to talk. Snow provided the raw material for a less violent approach used by some U.S. intelligence officers. They asked recalcitrant prisoners to remove their boots and socks and stand outside in the snow in their bare feet until they became cooperative. How commonly U.S. infantry used torture in interrogation is unknown. We knew it happened, but I find it hard to believe it was widespread.

Lt. Paul Fussell, an infantry platoon leader in the 103rd Division, said he discovered a productive way to deal with prisoner interrogation. "Treat them kindly," he advised. "It was not just fun to witness their astonishment at being offered a cigarette first thing, but such an act, if at all visible across the way, helped encourage others to give themselves up, too. They were often not unwilling to tell a bit about details on their side of the line."[30]

Combat with the Germans came quickly for some units of the 99th. After only four days on the front about eleven miles south of Höfen, a German machine gun killed Lt. Charles M. Miller of L Company, 394th Regiment. Battalion leaders wanted quick retaliation. Allen J. Ferguson, company commander of L Company, was assigned to lead a revenging patrol to knock out the machine gun nest. As Ferguson picked up his carbine, he declared, "Isn't this exercise [going on the patrol] silly?" The patrol moved across an open field of snow and toward enemy positions in the forest on the other side. "I could not help thinking how vulnerable we were," said Bob Mitsch, a member of the patrol and my basic training and ASTP buddy. "The enemy could easily spot us approaching. It was broad daylight!"[31]

Sergeant Tom Barr was guiding the captain up front because he knew the machine gun's location. Just as Barr said, "Here's where it happened," the machine gun blazed away at the patrol. Captain Ferguson was shot in the head. "We all hit the ground simultaneously. Pfc. Alfred Slaybaugh, our BAR man, immediately opened up on the Germans. We were all pinned down on the wet, slushy hillside with machine gun bullets cracking over our prone bodies," Mitsch said. "When the captain and others up front were hit, the call went out for one of our medics to move up and help the wounded. Since I was the last in the squad's line, I crawled backwards, feet first.

"As soon as a medic reached me," Mitsch continued, "a German sniper began to fire at the two of us. The bullets hit the slush next to my body. It seemed strange to me that the sniper waited until the medic arrived before firing. He could clearly see the medic's big red cross on a white background.

"For awhile," Mitsch said, "our pinned-down position looked hopeless." After much exchange of fire, the BAR finally knocked out the machine gun. That made it possible for the men to pull back across a firebreak, leaving the captain and Pfc. Clarence Robinson lying in the snow, both fatally wounded. A third man, Bob Cowden, was wounded but still alive. "He was pulled back across the snowy field and finally carried to our line. I said many prayers during this tense period," Mitch said. After the patrol returned to L Company's positions, field artillery fired a salvo of white phosphorous shells aimed at the area of the German machine gun nest. Mitsch said he didn't sleep much that night. He kept thinking of Captain Ferguson, Lieutenant Miller, and Private Robinson lying lifeless out on the snowfield.[32]

In my immediate area, our long nights on guard continued. We were even more alert, however, after we received intelligence reports of enemy activity. Captured enemy soldiers revealed that their patrols passed through our position at night without our knowing it. Some used the river trail, coming within fifteen feet of my BAR. I didn't hear a single suspicious sound, thanks to the noise of the river. That was scary. We might almost have touched them, but the total inky blackness made it impossible to see them. Thankfully, they could not see us, either. They passed in front of us like ghosts in the night.

On the lighter side, we now had something most front-line positions didn't have—a mascot. We spotted a rooster coming down the bridge road from Höfen. He had a strange jumpy walk. When he got closer, we discovered he had only one leg. The other leg was probably sliced off by shell fragments—another victim of the war. Since he looked so pathetic and since we saw a potential meal in the offing, we decided to adopt him. Anyone who looked worse off than we did deserved our attention. Besides, mascots are supposed to bring good luck. His condition was symbolic of the way we felt. We gave him scraps of food, which he ate with great relish. He recognized a good thing and decided he'd found a badly needed home.

During this so-called "quiet" period, Colonel Butler became fairly friendly with a German sniper. "Each morning," Butler said, "I'd walk the entire six thousand-yard front to talk to my men, see how things went the night before, and keep the situation in hand." (He didn't visit us because we were so isolated from the rest of the battalion.) "A sniper some distance away shot at me almost every day," Butler said. "He never hit me because it was a fairly long distance, and he couldn't get the exact range. He never knew how close he came to me. I was talking to one of our men on the line when the sniper, my German friend, fired and shot off a twig above my head. I reminded the man I was talking to that I had previously told him to get that S.O.B. He replied, 'You know, colonel, he is a very good soldier. We have done everything we could think of to get him. We set up ambushes and we tried to spot him by every means we could, but we have not been able to locate him.'" (Years later Butler said, "The sniper never got me, and we never got him.")[33]

On November 19, forty men from the 3rd Battalion attended their first religious service in Höfen. A Protestant chaplain conducted the service in the Catholic church—the only church in the village. As in all other group activities on the front, the men spread out inside the church, all with loaded rifles. They sang "Onward Christian Soldiers" in hushed voices because they did not want the nearby enemy to hear them. When the chaplain was halfway through the Twenty-third Psalm, a shell exploded near the back of the church. Plaster sprayed the men as they dived to the floor. In a calm voice, the chaplain said, "Gentlemen, I am certain the Lord is my shepherd. I suspect, however, that right now he desires to lead men to a more sheltered place. Do any of you have any suggestions?" The congregation moved into a nearby basement, where the service continued without further mishap.[34]

Our routine of misery in the 2nd Platoon continued, but with a new urgency. Because German patrols were passing by us undetected, Lieutenant Goss set up an arc of antipersonnel booby traps. They began along the river two hundred feet south of our most southerly foxhole, across the river trail, into the woods, curving around behind our dugouts, and ending up by the bridge road. Goss "volunteered" a team to install the booby traps—hand grenades, equipped with instantaneous fuses, that we taped to trees. A trip wire or white string ran from the pin of the fast-fused grenade to another tree. Anyone passing between the trees would trip the wire or string, pull the pin out of the grenade, and cause it to explode. At the river trail, we set up a double booby trap consisting of both a fragmentation grenade and a bouncing flare that would light up anyone who tripped the two wires at night. This would give us a clear nighttime target. We didn't know how many were set up or their exact locations. We just stayed away from the general area of our perimeter. (German observers apparently spotted us placing the booby traps because they never came through that way again. Instead, they moved through the unprotected area higher up the slope behind us.) The booby traps gave us a much stronger sense of security from a sneak attack to our rear or from a patrol moving down the river trail.

The booby traps endangered us as well as the Germans in some areas. Even Colonel Butler was tripping them. "Each time I tripped one," Butler said, "I would have to run and take a dive before it exploded. This happened to me several times." In one incident, which occurred at a battalion observation post, Butler spotted a booby trap wire he was about to trip. It was inches away when he stopped. He halted so suddenly that he was hit by Capt. Ernest Golden, commander of the battalion's M Company, who was following closely behind him. This jolt pushed Butler to the point where the wire and his chest touched, but it did not pull the wire. Butler survived by pure luck. The booby trap's grenade had a no-delay fuse, which meant it would explode at the moment the pin was pulled.

We received more reports of Germans moving even in daylight through our lines or through the undefended gaps between the 3rd Battalion and the cavalry unit defending Monschau. So battalion headquarters ordered us to dig a lookout foxhole at the top of the steep, three hundred-foot slope immediately behind our dugouts. Digging up there was vastly easier, and we completed the job by noon. The new foxhole, fitted with a field telephone, gave us a wide view of open fields rising to the northeast, including our I Company line facing east and the main German line a mile east of I Company. I manned the new position for the last three hours of daylight. I had Karchner's rifle and a pair of binoculars. My orders: "Watch that slope closely and report at once if you see anyone crossing those fields." I watched but saw no movement. I enjoyed the big view in contrast to the snail's view we had along the river. There was only one catch. I was nearly six hundred feet of thick woods away from the CP and the positions of the rest of my squad. No other American soldiers were within a half-mile of me. If Germans passed my way, I was easy pickings. They could come up behind me without my seeing them. Crunching footsteps in the snow would serve as my only warning. Every few minutes, I put the binoculars down and turned to check the woods behind me.

On this first lonely outing at the top of the mountain I carried a K-ration box inside my combat jacket. Always hungry, I opened the box and devoured the small helpings of biscuits, canned meat (Spam), and canned fruit. As a nonsmoker, I had always given the enclosed mini-pack of four cigarettes (with matches) to Karchner or other friends who smoked. But this time I took a second look at the bait the tobacco industry provided in all K rations—with the approval of the U.S. government. "What the hell!" I told myself. "I may be dead tomorrow. A cigarette may make me feel less hungry and give me a sense of warmth." I lit up. By now, after ten days on the line, almost everyone smoked. From my observation, the most popular brands were Camel and Lucky Strike; the least popular, Raleigh and Chesterfield.

After giving in to temptation, I smoked half a pack a day until I quit in 1954. Although no one knows the exact figure, the tobacco industry undoubtedly turned thousands of nonsmokers into addicted customers. After all, our commander in chief, President Roosevelt, made his cigarette holder affectation famous. His administration's decision to include free cigarettes in army food packets, as sought by congressional representatives from tobacco states, condemned thousands of young Americans to premature death. Even at that time cigarettes were known to be harmful, but doctors still lacked solid evidence that they caused cancer.

Noted war correspondent Quentin Reynolds declared that "there is no substitute for a cigarette" in war. He explained: "It may be mostly mental. When you smoke a cigarette you get an illusion of normalcy that helps you take the beating that you are taking. I can't rationalize it or explain it; I only know that things seem easier when you have cigarettes and matches." He added: "This isn't merely my own reaction; it's the reaction of every cigarette smoker I know. . . ."[35]

From our outpost foxhole on the mountain, we could alert our two squads in the ravine of approaching Germans, and they could alert the rest of the battalion. The view from this foxhole also clarified our position in relation to the battalion and to the enemy. Clearly, our positions in the ravine formed an island of defense, and the rest of the battalion, defending the village of Höfen, formed another much larger island of defense. Our positions were really strong points along a so-called "front line" surrounded by big areas of undefended woods. Thus, if the Germans knew the locations of the undefended areas, they could walk in behind us undetected. That is what happens when one division is stretched thinly across a twenty-mile front.

We kept making improvements in our foxholes in the ravine and cleaning out bottom mud and slush. We remained soaked and near frozen. In the midst of this gloom, we received a pleasant surprise: a chance to clean up and dry our equipment, to shave with hot water, and to dry our pants, shoes, and socks. Sergeant Mysliewiec and George Prager, our German-speaking platoon runner and bodyguard for Lieutenant Goss, took me and three other members of our platoon back to a small, rather spooky three-story hotel (about ten guest rooms). We hadn't known it existed. Hidden in thick woods about a half-mile behind us, it seemed like heaven. It was the first time I had been inside a building for more than twenty minutes in the last sixteen freezing days! A picture postcard of the place gave its address as Monschau, Germany, but we could not see any sign of village or town. A painted sign on the front of the building said "Hotel Perlenau, 1840." (I found out years after the war that the village of Monschau is a gem of undamaged medieval architecture two miles north of the Perlenau. In 1944, it had a population of 2,600; it had dropped to 2,140 by 1998. Hidden in a deep Roer River ravine, it is not visible from Höfen.)

The army allowed the Perlenau's owner Herr Carl Müller, his daughter-in-law, and an elderly male servant to live in the hotel as long as they followed orders and had no contact with enemy patrols. None of them spoke English. The daughter-in-law's husband was in an American POW camp in the United States. We assumed they passed a rigid interrogation by army intelligence to stay in an area so close to the front line. Actually, German patrols could reach the hotel without American interference through a six hundred-foot gap in our line at the south end of Monschau.

At Prager's order in German, Herr Müller let us hang our wet things to dry around his warm stove, and he got us some hot water to shave. We used our steel helmets as basins. While we waited for our shoes and clothes to dry, I had a chance to write my second letter from the front. I'm sure it gave my parents a jolt, because we now datelined our letters "Somewhere in Germany." They knew there weren't many Americans in Germany at this time. As usual, I asked them to send me any kind of food. A portion of the letter follows:

> Somewhere in Germany
> Nov. 20, 1944

Dear Mother and Dad,

As you can see, the Fuhrer's Fatherland is partially, at least, in our hands. I'm writing this from the dining room of a quaint hotel where we can clean up. . . . The proprietor is on the job for us now. He seems quite pleasant. What else could he do? We all have loaded rifles. . . .

Except for the wet, cold weather, I'm feeling fine and surviving nicely. . . . We are attempting to shoot a few deer for Thanksgiving, but so far we have failed. . . . Someday we may get to Paris or some large Belgian city. . . .

> Love, George

After ninety minutes of warmth, we returned to our foxholes with drier clothes, equipment, socks, and shoes for the first time in sixteen days. But how long would they stay dry? Two hours?

On the next day, November 21, I had my first and only encounter with a booby trap. Sergeant Mysliewiec had an interesting assignment for me and Pfc. Ivan Bull, also of our squad. Mysliewiec explained: "Go up to the top of the hill toward Höfen where the two wrecked tanks sit and capture one of the heifers wandering around there. It's near Thanksgiving, and everyone's hungry. If we don't get one now, I Company will." He reminded us that Germans in pillboxes to the east could observe our heifer roundup. "You don't need to worry about them because you'll be out of accurate rifle range, and they won't fire mortars or artillery at just two men," he assured us. This heifer expedition came shortly before Colonel Butler ordered all livestock in the area to be killed. His reasoning: as the animals roamed the area, they tripped booby traps and set off anti-personnel mines intended for the Germans. This meant 3rd Battalion units had many false alerts both day and night. It also meant the tripped devices required replacement.

Bull and I spotted the two heifers grazing among empty shell casings and some live shells half-covered with snow. To the east, we saw a couple of German pillboxes, verifying Mysliewiec's comment that the enemy could see us. We moved as fast as we could. Bull, a former farm boy from Iowa, thought he knew how to move livestock. We separated the heifer we wanted from her friend and waved our rifles to push her toward the road. Progress was slow. Bull yelled some commands in German. As we left the field, Bull noticed some German antipersonnel mines.

Once safely back on the road, the heifer waddled slowly down the steep hill. At the bottom, we directed our victim into our platoon CP area. Several of our men were out of their holes watching our arrival. Just as the heifer entered the tree line, I noticed a white string across her path. The heifer hit it. My eyes followed the string to a grenade tied to a tree. The fast-fused grenade exploded almost at the same moment I saw it, about fifteen feet from my head. I stood there frozen, surprised I was still standing. A quick check of my body revealed no wounds. My first comment: "Those things are no damn good!" The men who were watching the incident found my reaction hilarious. The heifer entered an open area near the CP where one of our men shot her. Fortunately, we had an experienced butcher. He took over. Before the end of the day, the heifer's carcass hung frozen from a tree. Mission accomplished.

After our comic experience with the heifer, another memorable incident took place in the same area on the German side of the line. It involved a playful German soldier who enjoyed taunting us. He smoked a cigarette outside his Siegfried Line pillbox every morning in plain view of I Company. "Each morning he would leave his bunker, seven hundred yards from our positions, lie on the ground or snow, and have a smoke," Colonel Butler reported. "Everyone shot at him with 30-caliber rifles. When he finished his cigarette, he would stand up and wave a red flag back and forth, showing that we had missed him. The distance was too far for accuracy."

One morning, when the soldier was inside his bunker, the 3rd Battalion registered an 81-mm mortar on his outdoor resting place. This meant the next shot would land on that spot. The next day he came out for his morning smoke and stretched out on the ground. While the German was enjoying his smoke, Butler ordered five rounds from the mortar. "The man never moved. Nor did he ever know what hit him," Butler said. "You can push your luck with the 3rd Battalion too far," he added.[36]

☆ 3rd Battalion Morning Report to the 395th Regiment
November 21, 1944—

First Platoon, L Company, went out on a (night) patrol with mission to take prisoners from pillboxes. Results: No POWs taken. Casualties inflicted on enemy. No casualties to our men.

6 • Ominous Signs

Our company received a big jolt with news of the death of Sgt. Charles M. Murray of Waycross, Georgia, a popular sergeant in our 1st Platoon. This tall, lean soldier was on one of the daily contact patrols L Company conducted from the south end of Höfen into a large, thick forest, partially an unoccupied area but also the site of several German strong points and observation posts. Since the forest included an undefended gap in the American line, we kept careful watch on German activity in the area.

These patrols departed between 10 and 11 P.M. and sometimes passed by Höfener Mühle, where I first went on the line. At a predetermined point, the patrols would connect with similar patrols from the 2nd Battalion, 395th Regiment, and then return to their starting points. German patrols also moved through the area looking for American activity. Sometimes daring German civilians living on the German or American side crossed the front line undetected to visit friends and relatives on the other side.

One of our riflemen shot Murray as the two American patrols approached each other in the dark. Apparently, the rifleman misunderstood the prearranged recognition signals. He hit Murray in the leg, normally not a fatal wound. The patrol carried Murray over two miles of rough, snow-covered terrain in darkness to the Höfen medical aid station. Carrying him without a litter was slow, and the patrol did not reach the aid station until the wee hours of the morning. By then Murray was dead. His body was transported to Henri-Chapelle American Cemetery where he was buried two days later. Murray's death hit us particularly hard because many of us rated him as the best soldier in L Company. Since we had trained together for nine months in Texas, we all knew him well. He was also my platoon sergeant in March for the refresher basic for ASTPers. We had often benefited from Murray's teaching and good example. He was the model of a good soldier and a man we would trust to lead us into battle. If he could be killed so easily, what about the rest of us? We no longer thought we were invincible. "Carry on, men" was one of Murray's favorite sayings. That's all we could do—mourn our loss for a few days and carry on.

During this period, Cates, Williamsen, Karchner, and I spotted several medic Jeeps carrying wounded 3rd Battalion men to the rear. We watched in silence. I figured that our future boiled down to one of four possibilities: (1) We get killed and go to the nearest military cemetery (Henri-Chapelle)—*fairly good chance*. (2) We get wounded/injured and go to a hospital—*very good chance*. (3) We get captured by the enemy and spend the rest of the war in a German prison camp—*fair chance*. (4) We stay with our platoon on the front until the war ends—*unlikely chance*. We talked about which outcome we preferred. I don't remember Ensign Williamsen's reaction, but the rest of us agreed the best alternative would be a disabling light wound or injury that would send us to a warm, dry hospital. No one now thought the war would end soon. We all agreed that being killed was preferable to being painfully maimed for life. (Within two months, one of us was killed and three were casualties in hospitals. Four out of four.)

On November 22, 3rd Battalion riflemen captured two Germans, one wounded and one not, in front of our front lines in Höfen. A 3rd Battalion sergeant motioned to the unwounded German to carry his wounded buddy into the village in a wheelbarrow. As he was moving the wounded man, shells from German artillery hit near them and killed both men.

"Pfc. Alfred, my driver and body guard, was with me watching this episode," Colonel Butler said. "The two Germans now lay there with their mouths open. One of them had teeth full of gold fillings. As we got closer, Alfred said, 'I'm going to get those teeth when we come back here.' When we returned," Butler continued, "the teeth were gone. Someone had gotten there ahead of him. Alfred was upset that we didn't get back sooner." [1]

On the following day, Thanksgiving, the L Company cooks in Kalterherberg promised us turkey and all the trimmings for dinner. All day, we worked on our dugouts—a slow, discouraging process. We spent the remainder of the daylight hours standing guard and shivering in the cold. What a contrast to the way we usually spent Thanksgiving at home. My thoughts drifted back to sunny Thanksgiving days in southern California with my family.

Our much anticipated turkey dinner finally arrived at dusk, and the pouring rain had turned to sleet and snow. Those on foxhole duty went with their greasy mess gear for their special dinner. The rest of us replaced them in the foxholes and waited. When they came back with full plates, we climbed out of our holes to get our dinners. They ate alone, standing in slush one to a hole, almost too far apart to talk to each other. We had high hopes for an enjoyable meal, something we had not had for weeks. Dinner included a generous helping of real turkey, mashed potatoes (made from dehydrated potatoes), gravy, and cranberry sauce. While the first group ate alone in the holes, the rest of us tried to eat together in a partial opening in the forest, inside the tree line. We sat, spread out, on pieces of a blown-up Siegfried Line pillbox. We ate mostly in silence. For once, even the artillery on both sides was quiet.

There we sat, wet, cold, and miserable. As we usually did when it was especially cold, we ate with our wet gloves on. I tried the turkey—which looked more like soup than the turkey dinner I imagined. It was already cold and tasteless. Even the coffee was cold. Nevertheless, we ate every scrap because it was food and we were hungry. As each man finished eating, he got up, brushed the snow from his pants, and disappeared quietly into the trees to begin the night guard vigil in the foxholes. Before I went to wash my mess gear at the CP—with warm water and soap for a change—I paused for a few moments. I wanted to remember this scene: four GIs—wet, shivering, dirty, unshaven, overly tired, depressed—sitting in a darkening, tree-surrounded snow scene, eating a cold turkey dinner in silence. This was my Thanksgiving 1944!

On another sector of the 99th's front, Edward E. Anderson, B Company, 393rd Infantry, said morale went up when he and his buddies heard they would get a hot meal for Thanksgiving. A chow line was set up a short distance behind their foxholes, and one squad went through at a time. "By the time my squad's turn came," Anderson said, "the Germans spotted the unusual activity of the chow line. Bullets began to ricochet in the trees over our heads. Some of the men fled for their foxholes, but several of us were so determined to get our first hot meal in a long time that we continued through the line on our knees, despite the flying bullets." Fortunately, no one got hit. (A few days earlier, Anderson had "celebrated" his nineteenth birthday. He was one of the few men in 99th Division rifle platoons who had arrived on the line before he reached age nineteen.)[2]

The day after Thanksgiving, my squad made up for the "bust" of the previous day. We had a wonderful treat at the

Hotel Perlenau. It was the most enjoyable meal I have ever eaten. It took our minds off our troubles for at least an hour and a half. The good feelings lasted for several more hours.

Following our orders, Herr Carl Müller, his daughter-in-law, and the elderly male servant cooked part of the heifer Ivan Bull and I had captured. George Prager, our platoon runner and interpreter (fluent in German), sat on the kitchen sink with his loaded rifle in hand, watching every move as our German hosts prepared the food. Besides the meat, Herr Müller had found some excellent potatoes. A couple of cellars in empty houses in Höfen provided cherry and peach preserves for dessert. Prager's job was to make sure they didn't try to poison us. It was an unforgettable scene.

When Lieutenant Goss received the "dinner's ready" signal, he divided each squad in half. One group walked three-quarters of a mile to the hotel for the first seating, while the other group remained in the foxholes. When the first group returned, the second group left for dinner. Being famished, most of us ate too much. Leo Wresinski, who occupied the pup tent next to mine, was so sick he vomited all night and some of the next morning. Several others got sick, too. We worried that a German night patrol might hear their agony. I decided the risks we had taken to capture the heifer were worth the dangers. Morale rose sharply. Most of us felt warmer and more comfortable than we had for a long time. Life seemed worth living again.

Two days later, our foxholes at the edge of Höfen spotted a German Army motorcycle with sidecar approaching on a road from the southeast. As it got nearer, our riflemen could see that the sidecar carried a passenger. To their disbelief, the motorcycle continued towards them with no reduction in speed. Safety latches clicked off rifles. When the motorcycle became an easy target, several rifles issued a simultaneous blaze of fire. The motorcycle skidded off the road, right in front of the American foxholes. Upon investigation, the riflemen found a dead driver and a dead officer wearing his dress uniform. He carried a suitcase, as if he were going home on leave. Unfortunately for him, his driver got onto the wrong road.

After twenty-two days of heavy fog, rain, sleet, and snow, the sky cleared. Blue sky lifted our spirits. For the first time, we glimpsed our air force in action. Previously, we had seen only German fighters and the 99th Division artillery observers in Piper Cubs behind our front line. The Luftwaffe made numerous appearances, usually one plane at a time. Clear skies brought the Eighth Air Force's B-17s (heavy four-engine bombers) out in large numbers. Formation after formation flew high over us on their way to German targets. As they were about to pass into German-held territory, enemy antiaircraft fire became fierce. I saw several B-17s (at least three) fall out of formation, leaving a trail of smoke as they drifted toward the ground. That gave us something to think about. We were not so sure about changing places with those flyers. We figured the planes were heading for Cologne to give that already battered city another drubbing.

ON OUR SIDE. On November 26, the American First Army and Ninth Army and British-Canadian forces took a major step forward as the first supply ships began unloading in Antwerp. Supply problems eased considerably. In anticipation of this event, the Germans began launching V-1 and V-2 weapons against the city in mid-October. One V-2 smashed into a jammed theater and killed hundreds of civilians and military personnel.

About this time, we heard a report that several German soldiers had approached our line in Höfen. They held up white sheets of paper dropped on them by our propaganda people to encourage surrender. Thinking this was another German trick, several of our riflemen clicked off safety switches and let them approach within easy range. Then they opened fire, killing all of them.

In a happier vein, our one-legged rooster remained with us, even with no fencing. Although he still looked pathetic, he started to put on some weight.

Lieutenant Goss installed a small, modern stove in his dugout. Liberated from a home in Höfen, it burned smokeless coal briquettes. With hopes of installing similar stoves in our new dugouts, we collected a supply of briquettes from Höfen cellars. Relief from the cold was urgent. We now thought it would get us before the Germans did. We continued to pick up food and useful utensils from Höfen homes for our almost-finished dugouts. We decided that Höfen residents would have little left if we remained in the area much longer. We had already killed most of the livestock for food and for military necessity, and some of our men had collected furniture, doors, or anything else that could be burned for heat. Pfc. Don Stafford of I Company said he found a fox fur neckpiece and a rabbit fur vest in a house attic. He wore them for warmth.

We were getting increasingly angry about the poor quality of our so-called winter equipment. With no help from our leaders, we continued to improvise to save our toes and feet. Paul Putty of I Company started using the toilet paper that came with C rations to wrap around his toes. "I would save the wax paper from packages of food my folks sent me to wrap around my feet. Then I'd put my socks and shoes back on. I think that's what kept me from getting trench foot," he declared. "Every time I wrote home," he continued, "I asked for socks and a toothbrush. I never had a chance to brush my teeth. I used the toothbrush to clean my rifle."[3]

Even in January, the lack of good winter equipment was severe all along the front. Showing surprising frankness, *Yank* magazine, an official army publication, published the findings of its investigation into the problem. The investigator reported troops' complaints about how many "Blue Star commandos" (rear echelon) wore new combat and paratrooper boots and new combat jackets. *Yank* disclosed that the sleeping bags weren't warm enough for outdoor-living infantry; the wool gloves with leather palms were not warm enough; the improved combat boots were in short supply (only forty men out of a company of two hundred had them); the new, warmer field jackets were in short supply; and the socks were rough-ribbed and hard on infantry feet. *Yank* also reported that infantrymen on rest passes to the rear strongly resented the fur-lined jackets they saw on Army Air Corps personnel. Since infantrymen were often out in the cold twenty-four hours a day, they felt they rated at least similar protection.

Two days after our first heifer feast, we had a second meal with the remainder of the carcass. George Prager, with his loaded M1 rifle, again sat on the kitchen counter in the Perlenau Hotel kitchen overseeing the preparations of our meal. I was part of the second shift in late afternoon, as soon as members of the first shift returned to their holes in a state of ecstasy. We were about halfway through the main course when a messenger arrived from the platoon CP ordering immediate return to our foxholes. Apparently the "powers that be" had received a warning about a possible enemy attack. Our meal was rudely interrupted. We grabbed our rifles and ran back to the holes. This was the second best dinner I have ever eaten in my life. The special alert kept the entire squad awake all night. It was another false alarm.

Although no one spoke about it, I sensed growing unease among both the men and our leaders. My uneasiness gained more credibility when Goss took us in shifts to visit the 395th Cannon Company, which had lined up short-barreled 105-mm cannons on the vital Monschau-Kalterherberg-Elsenborn road high up behind George Kelley's BAR position.

At first, I could not understand why we were making this visit. I soon found out. When I looked down the barrel of one of the guns, I was surprised to see it aimed at my BAR team's foxholes. "Hey," I said, "how come you're aiming at us?" The answer really got my attention. "If the Germans break into your area," a cannon company sergeant said, "you get down into the bottom of your holes and we'll fire directly on you. You're in your holes, and the Germans are outside. Our victims will be mostly Germans. We will not hit many of you," he promised, "and we will wipe out the invading Germans." We returned to our positions feeling more uneasy. Our so-called "quiet" front might not be so quiet in the near future.

About this time, twenty-eight-year-old 1st Lt. Seymour Saffer received what he called "a chilling assignment" to lead his first combat patrol into enemy territory in a heavily forested area a few miles south of Höfen. Saffer's patrol was the first of the daily morning patrols ordered by the 99th Division. Each platoon officer in B Company (395th Regiment) was responsible for taking out a patrol every third day. "Division told us the purpose of these forays was to let the Germans know we're out here, to take prisoners if possible, and to mark German road and trail blocks on our maps," Saffer explained.[4]

Capt. Hugh Gettys, twenty-six years old, commander of B Company, presented Saffer with a neatly folded map of the area. It was encased in a celluloid overlay and showed firebreaks and intersections. An artillery forward observer with a radio was assigned to the patrol, and Saffer was ordered to call headquarters at every intersection to give his location. The patrol consisted of one squad (twelve men) and two BAR teams. Counting the artillery observer and Saffer, the patrol totaled twenty men. The patrol gathered at dawn and took off into no man's land in single file. The forest was dense but the patrol maintained a diamond formation, with the BAR teams at left and right points. Two scouts were out front. The artillery observer and Saffer walked in the center. "The silence was eerie," Saffer said. "My heart was pounding. I found out quickly that it was one thing to go out on a patrol; it was something quite different to lead one."

Within six hundred yards, the patrol was in trouble. The fire-breaks so clearly defined on the patrol's map were concealed by many years' growth of underbrush and trees. Saffer had to resort to using a compass. He opened it and aimed for an azimuth. The arrow quivered. To steady it, he placed it on the map on top of the snowy ground. It still quivered but finally gave him the direction he needed. (He found out later that the compass was a World War I model.) The patrol relayed hand signals from man to man and proceeded. Two explosions blasted the silence. "We hit the ground and waited for more, but none came," Saffer said.

Cpl. Ray Enoch staggered in from the right point, bleeding profusely from his upper left arm. "Mines!" Enoch blurted out. "York is dead!" Saffer stopped the bleeding with a tight bandage. Following Enoch's footprints in the snow, he went in search of York. "I found him, but I was not prepared for the sight that greeted me." Quiet, dependable Truman York, at thirty-two the oldest man in the platoon, had taken the full brunt of a German antipersonnel mine. The blast dismembered his body and blew away his rifle, helmet, ammunition belt, and even his dog tags. Beside him, still emitting smoke, was the empty mine canister. "Kneeling beside him, I could no longer control my tears," Saffer said. When he returned to the squad, he called battalion to say that his group was returning with a walking wounded. They slowly retraced their footsteps in the snow. A medical Jeep was waiting to take Enoch to the battalion aid station. The following morning, a detail returned with York's remains.

"This account is just one example of what was happening on our so-called 'quiet' front more than two weeks before the Battle of the Bulge," Saffer said. "Men wounded on a quiet front bled and died just the same as if they were hit in a large-scale offensive."[5]

ON THE OTHER SIDE. On November 29, the German high command delayed the launching of its Ardennes offensive until December 10, due to Allied pressure on other sectors of the Western Front.[6]

On the same day the Germans postponed their attack, Karchner and I completed our dugout—our new, "elegant" living quarters. Three of the four two-man dugouts that made up our BAR position were ready for occupancy by nightfall. This was cause for celebration because our quality of living improved immeasurably. We slept in the dugout and commuted about sixty feet to our foxhole.

We lengthened the dugout at the last minute to make room for a tiny, modern-looking stove that we pulled out of a Höfen house. Although the dugout leaked in several places, we could keep our sleeping bags, blankets, and clothes drier than before. But everything remained at least partially wet. The layer of logs overhead made the dugout vastly safer from tree bursts. It was now wide enough (about six feet) for two men to sleep in parallel sleeping bags and for storage of rifles, ammunition belts, and entrenching tools. It was high enough (about thirty-two inches) to raise up on one elbow to write letters. It was long enough for my six-foot-one body to lie straight without my feet sticking outside our "door," an army blanket hanging down from the dugout's roof to about one inch above ground level. We figured we were now about 80 percent safer than we were in the pup tents and much more comfortable with some warmth from the stove. Just as important, we could use a candle to read and write.

The division received its first casualty report on November 30. The 324th Medical Battalion, the medical unit that served the 99th, reported that it evacuated 959 men from the 14,253-man division between November 13 and November 30. Only 100 returned to duty. Trench foot accounted for 423 casualties, 44 percent of the total. My regiment (the 395th) blamed the trench foot losses on lack of overshoes. Battle casualties, caused mainly by antipersonnel mines and booby traps, totaled 134, or 14 percent; combat exhaustion totaled 15, or 1.6 percent. Most of the 959 evacuees came from the 3,240 men in the division's rifle platoons. Put another way, in seventeen days during a "quiet" period, the 99th Division's rifle platoons lost approximately 30 percent of their total force. However, losses from the original roster of the entire division totaled approximately one out of every fifty men. We in the rifle platoons were about fifteen times more likely to become casualties than others in the division. In fact, General Eisenhower said that all along the Western Front during this period, the infantry was taking "almost all" of the casualties in "the dirtiest kind of infantry slugging." Gains were measured in yards instead of miles.[7]

Gen. Omar N. Bradley accepted partial blame for trench foot casualties. He said the lack of winter clothing in November was traceable in part to the September crisis in supplies during the race to the Rhine. "I had deliberately bypassed shipments of winter clothing in favor of ammunition and gasoline. As a consequence, we now found ourselves caught short, particularly in bad-weather footwear. We gambled in our choice and now were paying for the bad guess," Bradley said.[8]

Eisenhower blamed the trench foot problem on the miserable conditions along the front. "Cure is difficult," he wrote, and "sometimes almost impossible." He said "effective prevention was *merely* [emphasis added] a matter of discipline—making sure that no one neglected the prescribed procedure. This was to remove the shoes and socks at least once daily and massage the feet for five minutes."[9] He made it sound easy. Few of us knew about Eisenhower's magic five-minutes-per-day recipe for prevention. He failed to mention the faulty shoes issued to us by the army and the effects of constantly wet socks. He also failed to mention what happens to feet with prolonged exposure to sub-freezing temperatures.

Thanks mostly to inferior shoes, trench foot and frostbite had reached crisis stage by the end of November. The two afflictions are similar. Cold, accompanied by moisture in the case of trench foot, plus slow circulation in the foot kills tissue. Sometimes gangrene sets in and forces amputation of toes or possibly even feet. Although the army developed preventive new footgear—the insulated shoe pack—it was not available to us. (A friend in the 10th Mountain Division at Camp Hale, Colorado, had shoe packs in early 1943.) The after-effects of trench foot lingered for years for many victims. I met two of them at the 1993 annual convention of the 99th Infantry Division Association. One said his toes still go numb. He had to have an operation to improve blood circulation in his feet. The other veteran said he also had undergone the operation.

On December 1, two cooks from a replacement center in Kalterherberg decided they wanted to know what it was like on the front line. They had never seen one. During a slow period, they took off on an unauthorized three-mile walk to Höfen. Their adventure was reported to Colonel Butler, who related it to me. "In the movies," Butler explained, "the front line is well defined. In actual combat conditions, no one puts up a sign that says, 'Here's the front line. If you move forward from here you are going to get shot; if you stay behind this line you won't get shot.'" The cooks strolled to Höfen and then kept walking east, apparently looking for a sign announcing the front line. They walked fifty-five yards in front of our front line to a German pill-box in no man's land—fortunately evacuated by the Germans. It was not occupied by the 3rd Battalion, either, for two good reasons. It was too far forward, and it had a massive German mine field in front of it. The two serene cooks walked right through the hidden mine field—and even farther east. It was awfully quiet. They knew something must be wrong. So they turned around and walked back through the same mine field.

When they got behind a building, a GI grabbed them, told them what they had done, and started bawling them out. A sergeant showed up, and he bawled then out again. Finally, the company commander appeared, and he lectured them. On the previous day, two of three men who were trying to clear the mines (the commander of an engineering company, a first lieutenant, and the first sergeant) had been killed in the same field. The commander missed a mine. The lieutenant following him missed the same mine. But the sergeant behind him hit it. The blast blew his arm off and tossed him onto a second mine, which also exploded. This second mine killed both the lieutenant and the commander. The sergeant lost his eyes and both arms. "This was the same mine field the two cooks had walked through twice, following different routes each time," Butler noted.[10]

On December 2, my twenty-third birthday came and went. I didn't realize it was my birthday until a day or two later. Days ran together. Most of us did not know the date, or whether it was Saturday or Wednesday. We were on duty seven days a week, so we did not keep track of weekends. We barely knew the month.

The day following my birthday, combat engineers began reinforcing our bridge over the small, noisy Perlenbach River. The reason, our leaders told us, was to enable heavier equipment such as larger guns and tanks to cross. This sounded ominous, like the advance groundwork for an American attack to the east. We did not look forward to that. Figuring the lag in sending mail, I wrote a note home wishing my parents a happy Christmas. I could hardly have been briefer, but we had rushed all day trying to keep up with everything we had to do.

One of our men got a glimpse of the future early in the morning of December 4. Pfc. Harry Arnold, E Company, 393rd Infantry Regiment (located ten miles south of Höfen), ran up a hill to his platoon's observation post and then returned to his foxhole. "I wanted to get my circulation warmed up," he explained. A rushing sound came from behind just as he reached the halfway point. He hit the ground and looked up. A small, fast, black plane with no propeller flashed low overhead speeding toward Germany. It had German markings. "I had seen my first jet airplane. It was probably doing reconnaissance," Arnold surmised.[11]

An important German secret weapon, the new jets could fly one hundred miles per hour faster than anything the Allies had. Fortunately for his enemies, Hitler gave much higher priority to the V-1 flying bomb and the V-2 rocket. Neither of these spectacular weapons threatened to change the course of the war. The jet fighter did. If available in significant numbers, it could have made Allied air attacks over Germany too costly. But, by the time enough of the jets were available, Germany had little fuel to fly them.

Only five days after we completed our new dugout, my buddy John Karchner disappeared. Despite frequent rubbing, Karchner's feet had reached crisis proportions. His toes became seriously discolored and numb, signs of trench foot and frostbite. Warner Anthony, our platoon's medic, called for a Jeep to take Karchner to the medical aid station in Höfen. The medics there decided to send him to medical facilities behind the front. (He ended up in an army hospital in England.) Since Karchner and I slept in the same tent, stood in the same foxhole, did almost all the same things, I wondered why I didn't have trench foot or frostbite. I checked my feet. My toes were moderately numb, but they were only slightly discolored. I think my circulation must have been better than Karchner's. With him gone, I no longer had a foxhole buddy. This made me much more vulnerable. Cates, my "elderly" (twenty-seven-year-old) assistant BAR gunner, became both assistant gunner and ammunition bearer.

I was alone in my foxhole for two days when I had a bit of good luck. Lieutenant Goss said two men in the platoon could leave their foxholes and dugouts and get some warmth and uninterrupted sleep at the Hotel Perlenau. The idea was to keep us from going stark raving mad. Goss picked Pfc. Willie Shipp, a rifleman in my squad, and me. Before darkness descended,

Shipp and I found our rarely used toothbrushes. Cates and I traded weapons. He took my BAR, and I carried his rifle. I promised I would clean it in a room with a roof that didn't leak.

"Carl Müller, the owner, expects you," Goss said, as we walked out to the empty, darkening road leading to the hotel. We wore our steel helmets and ammunition belts. The hotel was empty except for Müller, his daughter-in-law, and the elderly male helper. The surrounding forests were notorious for probing German combat patrols. Parts of the area were undefended. In fifteen minutes we arrived, and Müller's daughter-in-law took us to a room with twin beds on the second floor. To our amazement, it even had the incredible luxury of an electric light, thanks to a generator on the nearby river. A blackout drape was drawn to prevent light from showing outside.

In our feeling of good fortune, we forgot where we were and let down our guard. We placed our steel helmets on the floor and stood the rifles against the wall. After removing our leggings, wet shoes and socks, rifle ammunition belts, soaked overcoats, and combat jackets, we sat down on real beds with sheets and a mattress. We stretched out, luxuriating in our good fortune. We wanted to enjoy every moment. The hotel had only limited heat, and our room was cold. We did not even think of complaining; we thought we had arrived in heaven. Müller's daughter-in-law brought us another unheard-of luxury—hot water with which to shave and wash our hands and faces. There was no hot water, however, for a bath or shower. Unshaven for days, Willie looked extremely tired and haggard. So did I. We desperately needed this short respite. After we shaved, we lay down on the beds and talked about home, school, and what we hoped to do with our lives.[12]

We enjoyed talking but quickly decided that we couldn't just bask in the delight of clean, dry beds. Our rifles needed cleaning, and we needed as much sleep as we could get. We put some papers across our beds and broke down our rifles. Just as we had both guns completely broken down, we heard a knock on the door. "Come in," I yelled. In came Carl Müller. In a second, I realized our stupidity. Here we were in an empty hotel—alone with the enemy—and both of our rifles were torn apart. Müller viewed our situation. He saw we had no weapons to defend ourselves. For seconds, as if pondering our predicament, he paused. Then, much to our relief, he asked if we wanted more blankets. I have rarely felt so stupid. Shipp told me he felt the same way. How could we be so dumb? I would hate to explain that to our officers. As soon as Müller disappeared, we scrambled to get the rifles back together. We locked our door, placed our rifles beside our beds, and pulled up the blankets. We stopped talking, and overwhelming fatigue quickly conquered worries. We slept until daylight—the first full night's sleep in five weeks. Our one-night respite from the war was over.

The next day, by some strange quirk of army thinking, trucks came up near our platoon CP and dumped the big barracks bags we had left in Normandy. They contained all of the possessions we thought we would not need on the front. "Come to the CP to pick them up," Sergeant Mysliewiec ordered. We wondered what to do with all this stuff. The decision was easy. We would throw most of it in the river. I did not find a thing in my bag to eat or anything that would keep me warmer, but I did find my Kodak box camera loaded with a partial roll of film.

After four weeks of no relief from the cold (except for that one night at the Perlenau), I could keep my dugout fairly warm for a couple of hours each night with my supply of coal briquettes. Now that my dugout was finished and my tiny German stove was installed, I could also heat water to make cocoa and bouillon. But I did not have either. We were frantic for food packages. Some of our men burned oil- or gasoline-soaked rags in tin cans to warm their dugouts at night when the smoke would not be visible. When they emerged in the morning, their faces were black from soot. Most of the fumes from my stove escaped through a camouflaged short-tin chimney. Fortunately for us, we found a crop of potatoes on an open slope near Höfen. To harvest our bonanza, we sent three men to dig up as many as they could in an hour and share them with each dugout. They used their bayonets for digging in the half-frozen ground. (British soldiers did the same thing during their bloody stay in the Somme sector during World War I.) We were lucky that our diggers didn't hit any of the antitank or antipersonnel mines the Germans had laid in mid-September to defend Höfen. I filled an empty tin can with water from the river, dropped four potatoes in it, placed it on my dugout stove, and soon had four boiled potatoes. What a gourmet feast! They tasted wonderful, dirt and all, and helped solve our food shortage. For the remainder of our time in the ravine, we ate boiled potatoes at least three days a week. I never tired of them. We were too hungry to be fussy. After more than fifty years, I still have a special fondness for boiled potatoes.

Another lucky break brought me light. Someone gave me a candle. The prowling enemy could not see it because light did not show through my new windowless, half-underground dugout. It enabled me to read and write during the seven to ten hours of darkness I spent inside my lonely "home" each day. I felt like a prehistoric man who had discovered how to make fire and overnight had light and some warmth in his cave.

I wrote the following letter home:

Somewhere in Germany
December 9, 1944

Dear Mother and Dad,

I haven't been good on writing, but I assure you I have been well occupied. For those not on daytime guard, we have work parties constantly improving our defensive positions.

We've been paid in Belgian francs, so if passes start coming through, I'll have plenty of money.

Today, we had an extra treat. Our platoon leader was able to secure, through the officers' PX, a Hershey bar for each of us. The last such treat came three weeks ago. Oh, how good it tasted!

It appears improbable that we'll knock out Germany by the end of this year. My guess is February or March—but who really knows?

You should get this by Dec. 25. . . .

I have my camera, and tomorrow I will finish up the first film you sent. I'll send copies as soon as possible.

Merry Christmas to you all. The new year should be a great one because our war should end.

Love, George

On the same day I wrote the letter, Sgt. Richard Byers, 99th Division artillery, began observing substantially increased German activity overlooking Losheim, Germany. Did this have ominous implications? "Our OP [observation post] and every other OP along the nearby line," he said, "began turning in intelligence by the reams. We described German working parties repairing roads, reinforcing bridges, and just generally crawling over the landscape like industrious ants." Since all had been quiet along this front for weeks, Byers and his fellow observers began to wonder why the Germans suddenly became so busy. Were they planning to attack us, or were they expecting us to attack them?[13]

The following day, I set off a flurry of activity that ended with the probable death of three German soldiers. For the previous couple of days, I had waited for possible sunlight so we could take pictures before I threw my box camera into the river. I decided to use up the rest of my film without waiting any longer.

For the first picture, taken by Williamsen, I squatted in the snow near my foxhole. I wanted to hold my BAR, but we decided against it for security reasons. Instead, I posed with my entrenching tool. Next, the six of us at my BAR position stepped out of the tree line for better light. We considered it safe from enemy observation. Williamsen took my picture in a squatting position, in much better light. Then I lined up the group at the same spot. I was taking the picture this time. "Get closer together," I asked, "and I'll get a quick picture." My subjects moved closer together as I suggested, two men kneeling in front and three standing behind. I was about to click the picture when a shell whined our way. We raced toward our foxholes like a family of marmots running from a hawk. During this scramble, I dropped my camera and the back burst open, exposing the film. (Only one shot was not ruined by exposure. It was one of me posing with an entrenching tool.) I kept running. The first shell landed with a thud nearby, but it failed to explode. No one was hit, but we received a good scare. Another shell whistled in. It hit closer with another thud, but no explosion. After a third shell landed, also a dud or delayed action, we decided by their sound that they came from a larger mortar (perhaps 81-mm) and not artillery.

I reported the attack to the platoon CP on my foxhole phone. Sergeant Thompson, who was nearby, also heard the shells, but he couldn't see where they were landing. While we were talking, another shell whistled over my head. I could see exactly where it landed because it shook snow off the tree it hit. Again, no explosion. By keeping my head above ground level, I could pinpoint where most of the shells landed. Thompson connected my phone line with our artillery. "We have your foxhole plotted on our map, so if you tell us where they land in relation to you, we can project where the shells are coming from," an authoritative voice at artillery said.

The shelling kept up for ten more minutes. Altogether, about fifteen shells landed in our area. I continued to expose my head to get a clear view. I was so eager to do a good reporting job that it never entered my mind that I could be hit by shrapnel. After fifteen minutes of playing artillery observer in reverse, I heard our 105-mm howitzers open up behind us. In a complicated mathematical exercise, the artillery men plotted backwards from the shell landings I reported to the approximate location of the unfortunate German mortar team. The shells whistled over our heads toward the enemy. The artillery unit kept this up for two or three minutes. Then silence. I put down the phone, wondering what had happened. A few minutes later, an artillery guy called me. "Good job of observing, Neill. We knocked them out. That three-man mortar team won't bother you any more. Our shells landed right on top of them. We have confirmed the knockout." Then he added: "We should recruit you as an artillery observer."

I was elated. I felt sorry for the three dead Germans, but they were trying to kill us. "Kill or Be Killed," the theme of our training at Camp Wolters and Camp Maxey, was fulfilled in my favor. Next time? Instead of just digging fortifications and almost freezing to death in a foxhole, I had clearly earned my pay. I didn't tell Sergeants Mysliewiec or Thompson what started the shelling in the first place. The less said about that, the better. Our picture-taking episode and the results were not something to brag about. But we learned something important, fortunately without a casualty on our side. We now knew the enemy had observers watching us, and they were probably nearby, hidden in the trees.

Two men in my squad checked out the supposedly uninhabited woods on the steep mountain overlooking the Hotel Perlenau. They found no signs of enemy activity, but they spotted what they thought was a pigeon flying away from the hotel. The bird disappeared to the north toward Monschau. The men immediately suspected spying activities. After watching the hotel for ten more minutes, they thought they saw another pigeon flying from the hotel area. Convinced they had uncovered a nest of German spies, they raced back to our positions to report their finding. They wanted a couple more men to join them and "kill the bastards." That would be Carl Müller, his daughter-in-law, the servant, and any other Germans found there. "How do you know they were pigeons?" I asked. They were "almost" sure. "How do you know positively they came from the hotel?" "It sure looked like it," one of them replied. "They came from trees near the hotel." I suggested we call company headquarters and have them alert battalion headquarters to the possible danger. "A quick inspection would uncover whether they had pigeon lofts or not," I added.

But the two men wanted to "shoot the Germans before they do any harm." Fortunately, Sergeant Thompson refused to panic. A quick investigation revealed no evidence of carrier pigeons. With so much hatred and suspicion around, the situation could have easily gone the other way. The value of a human life on the front got cheaper every day.

The next day, Lieutenant Goss came over from his CP to visit us. He brought a blunt message. "If any of you get an idea to re-treat across the river, I will have a message for you." Slapping his M3 grease gun, a light submachine gun that sprays 45-caliber bullets, he warned: "I'll save one clip [with twenty bullets] for those of you who try to flee to the other side." He attributed the following order to General Lauer: "We make our stand right where we are. No one moves back from these foxholes." My first thought: What made General Lauer think we might retreat? Had anyone voiced the possibility? The warning gave me the impression he did not trust us. Was he expecting a major attack? We did not think the German Army capable of such a thing. I, for one, believed we would never need to pull back. But I wasn't sure how we could go forward either. The Siegfried Line seemed extremely tough. Safe in his headquarters in Butgenbach, Belgium, several miles behind the front, General Lauer did not have the slightest idea of the situation confronted by squads and platoons. (Hitler accelerated German defeats in many battles because of his "no pullback" decisions, which were made many miles from the battlefield. Hundreds of thousands—no exaggeration—of young Germans lost their lives needlessly to the whims of his megalomania. Three examples: Normandy, Moscow, and Stalingrad.)

ON THE OTHER SIDE. On December 12, Hitler again delayed launching his planned offensive against the Americans in the Ardennes. He set the new date for December 16.[14]

Word came down the grapevine on December 13 that my good friend, Gene Oxford, had been killed by a German antipersonnel mine. The news left me extremely upset—almost sick. Oxford, a BAR gunner for L Company's 3rd Platoon, had been on a combat patrol. The explosion shattered both legs and both hands. Douglas Packard, medic extraordinary and close friend of Oxford's, did everything he could to ease the pain and make him comfortable, but he could not save him. Packard tried to give him a transfusion, but he couldn't find any place to do it. They talked, friend to friend, as Oxford died. Packard was shattered.

Packard, Oxford, and I had been in ASTP at Tarleton College, and Oxford had also taken basic infantry training with me at Camp Wolters. After being together so long, we had become as close as brothers. Oxford had sat next to me in the truck from Normandy to the Belgian frontier on November 4. We wondered then what was going to happen to us. Oxford was one of our most competent soldiers. He was a thoughtful, vigorous, athletic type and an excellent student. His hometown was Taft, California. He had planned to enter the University of California, Berkeley, after the war.

With Murray's death, and now Oxford's, it seemed to me that fate picked our best men to die. Alone in the darkness of my fox-hole, I prayed with a fervor I had never experienced before. "If I get out of this alive," I swore to myself, "I will dedicate my life to helping prevent another catastrophic war." (I tried to follow that vow for the next twenty years, and I quickly learned that one individual can't do much. Reality taught me that the best most of us can do is to make life a little better for others.)

On the same day as Oxford's death, December 13, the U.S. First Army launched (unknown to us) another of several attempts to capture the Roer River dams, nine air miles northeast of Höfen.

Capture of the dams was vital because whoever controlled them also controlled the river's flow across the thirty-mile-wide Cologne Plain, the First Army's path to the Rhine River. Thus, if the First Army tried to cross the Roer River east of Aachen with the Germans controlling the dams fifteen miles up-stream, the enemy could release a destructive flood on the crossing troops. Or they could let the troops cross the river, and then cut off the spearhead from its source of supply. If successful, the new American offensive would also wipe out the enemy around Höfen. Our front line would then move about ten miles deeper into Germany—to us, an incredible achievement.

The north prong of the two-pronged offensive, led by the 78th Infantry Division, attacked from north of Monschau. The south prong jumped off from the middle of the 99th Division's front line north of Krinkelt and only eight air miles south of Höfen. The attacking units consisted of the 2nd Infantry Division (which led the attack), the 1st and 2nd Battalions of our 395th Regiment, and the 2nd Battalion of our 393rd Regiment. Both battalions of the 395th were removed from the front line south of Höfen, leaving a big undefended gap. The attack began at 8:30 A.M. The riflemen spearheading the attack started off cautiously toward the Siegfried Line's barbed wire, hidden mine fields, foxholes, and concrete and log pillboxes. They moved slowly through deep snow, over rough terrain, and against stiff resistance.

The troop movements made to carry out this American offensive could prove decisive to us in the days ahead for two reasons:

1. Removal of two battalions of the 395th Regiment (1,672 men) out of the American line south of Höfen widened a mostly undefended gap on our south flank from two miles to about five miles. The gap was only partially filled by 312 men, half from the 99th Division's Reconnaissance Troop and half from the 2nd Division's Reconnaissance Troop. If we in Höfen ran into trouble, no one was nearby to help us. Fortunately, the Germans were unaware of this dangerous gap.

2. The second troop movement brought A Company of the 612th Tank Destroyer Battalion into Höfen on December 13–14. They moved their guns into preselected positions so quietly that most of our 3rd Battalion riflemen did not hear them. The 612th's new job was to provide support from its twelve three-inch guns when the American offensive on the dams reached Rohren, only three miles northeast of Höfen. (This move substantially strengthened our 3rd Battalion's position at Höfen—just in time for an unforeseen challenge.)

At the same time as the Americans prepared to launch their offensive, the Germans were also preparing an attack. German armies with twenty-four divisions and 970 tanks and self-propelled guns moved up quietly into next-to-last pre-attack positions during that same night of December 13–14. They were now about 2.5 miles behind the German front line. Because of unusually tight security, German field officers learned of their mission barely a day earlier. They had no time to reconnoiter the terrain in front of them or to plan their attack with accurate information.[15]

Several days earlier, outposts along the entire Ardennes Front had begun reporting ominous sounds emanating from behind the German lines. The strange noises, they suggested, came from tanks and other heavy equipment. Higher commands discounted these reports from the 99th and other divisions along the Ardennes Front. Some forward observers said they could see lights behind the German line. Similar reports had been passed on to higher commands for several of the previous nights. General Lauer said he asked several times during this period, and earlier, for air reconnaissance over German territory across from the 99th's front, but his requests were denied.

Very different thoughts were on the minds of local residents of Monschau. They were planning to celebrate Christmas. The American military government had approved their modest program. It included a Christmas concert on December 23 in the Aukirche (church) featuring an American soldier as soloist and a choir from Eupen. Walter Scheibler, American-appointed burgermeister (mayor) of Monschau, said the U.S. Army would provide transportation and food for the choir. "To provide a better Christmas for the children," Scheibler said, "the Americans gave us seventy pounds of flour and twenty-five pounds of sugar so we could make cookies." The American military government in Monschau canceled these happy Christmas plans two days later due to unexpected military activity.[16]

On December 15, the Americans in the newly arrived A Company, 612th Tank Destroyer Battalion, moved fast after their overnight arrival in Höfen. They dug in their guns, camouflaged the positions with white sheets, and built walls of sandbags for protection against shrapnel and small arms fire. Snow was falling, and the weather was bitterly cold. Before darkness, however, A Company's tank destroyers were ready for action.

They figured they did not have long to wait, maybe two days, because the 2nd Division-led attack captured Wahlerscheid—one-third of the way from the jump-off point to the Roer River dams. After taking Wahlerscheid, the 2nd Division's attack force prepared to move on to Rohren. But unexpected events the next day forced the division to give up the attack and return to its starting point of the offensive on December 13, thus giving up the hard-earned gains of the previous three days. Another costly effort to take the dams went for naught.

On the same day, December 15, an "American" lieutenant appeared at an artillery command post in the 99th Division area at Bullingen, Belgium. He walked up to a captain and asked him to point out on a map the locations of all the battalion's gun batteries. The captain obliged, and then took the lieutenant outside to show him more. Some of the captain's men, in the room at the time, thought he was making a mistake because no one recognized the lieutenant. After the lieutenant left, one of the captain's men told him in blunt words how stupid he had been. The next day, German artillery hit every one of the batteries.[17]

Unbeknownst to us, troops of three German armies crept forward at dusk on December 15 to predawn jump-off points along the Ardennes-Eifel front. The Sixth Panzer Army—by far the strongest of the three—faced the 99th Division.

Officers of the three German armies read their men inspirational pep talks from their generals. Two examples:

"Soldiers of the West Front!! Your great hour has arrived. Large attacking armies have started against the Anglo-Americans. . . . We gamble everything! You carry with you the holy obligation to give everything to achieve things beyond human possibilities for our Fatherland and our Fuhrer!"—Generalfeldmarschall Karl Gerd von Rundstedt, Commander-in-Chief, West.[18]

"Forward double time! Remember the heritage and the ardor of our dead comrades as well as the tradition of our proud

Wehrmacht."—General der Panzertruppen Hasso von Manteuffel, Fifth Panzer Army.[19]

To prevent detection, Hitler ordered the three armies to function under a total radio blackout as they tried to assemble twenty-four divisions. In another effort to maintain secrecy, Hitler ordered the assembling armies not to conduct reconnaissance patrols or registration of artillery. The movement of this great mass of German troops to the Ardennes sector required the use of 1,502 troop trains and 500 supply trains.[20]

In and around Höfen, the 3rd Battalion, 395th Regiment, prepared for night in its usual manner. Nothing happened during the early hours of darkness. At approximately 11 P.M., however, outposts and front-line positions along the entire battalion sector reported hearing unusual noises in the vicinity of Rohren. In Höfen, Pfc. Don Stafford of I Company heard loud noises of many engines coming from the forest south of Rohren for a half-hour. The 3rd Battalion fired artillery and mortar concentrations into the noise areas until 3 A.M., December 16. Subsequent reports from front-line units in the Höfen-Monschau area indicated nothing unusual.

7 • Battle of the Bulge: German Fury Hits U.S. Line

This time, the Kraut's stuck his head in a meat grinder.
—LT. GEN. GEORGE S. PATTON, JR.

DECEMBER 16, 1944

AT APPROXIMATELY 5:30 A.M., THE GERMAN ARMY launched the Battle of the Bulge, a no-holds-barred offensive against five American infantry divisions. Stretched thinly, they defended sixty miles of the so-called quiet Ardennes Front.[1]

The 99th was one of the five. From the American side, the first sign of the onslaught was a north-south line of strange pinpoints of light flickering on the eastern skyline. Seconds later, bursting shells from approximately one thousand artillery pieces—including rocket projectors—created a firestorm on American positions, shattering the predawn darkness. The flickers of light were flashes from German guns.[2]

Approximately half of the American forces asleep at the time were now wide awake and scared. They had just received the wake-up call of a lifetime. Those not in deep foxholes or strong cellars dashed for the nearest safety. The firestorm lifted, after thirty minutes in some parts of the line and after two hours in other parts. Then silence.

Approximately one quarter of a million Germans in twenty-four divisions started moving west, through snowy fields and forests.[3] An hour earlier, they had risen from fitful sleep in barns, cellars, and Siegfried Line bunkers. For many, it was their last walk. They outnumbered American infantry by at least three to one, or sometimes by many more than that. Approximately sixty-nine thousand Americans were now fully alert and waiting for a possible infantry attack.[4] Safety switches on rifles clicked off. Eyes and ears strained for any signs of the enemy. In most areas, they waited only ten to thirty minutes.

Waves of infantry began to attack the Americans from Höfen-Monschau in the north to Echternach, Luxembourg, fourteen air miles north of Trier, Germany, in the south. Ghostlike, they appeared in the foggy predawn darkness. The three attacking armies consisted of the Sixth Panzer on the north flank, by far the most powerful; the Fifth Panzer in the center; and the Seventh Army on the south flank. The size of German troop allocations revealed the enemy's priorities to the three sectors. The north was clearly top priority. Incredibly, this accumulation of massive force caught the American high command completely by surprise. Hitler wanted total surprise for his long-planned offensive, and he achieved it. With the arrival of daylight, the Luftwaffe came to life over the front. It committed nearly one thousand planes to the battle.[5]

Within a few hours, and after suffering staggering infantry losses, the determined Germans threatened to obliterate parts of the American line. The outnumbered and outgunned men of the 99th, 2nd, 106th, 4th, and 28th Divisions fought for their lives. They tried to accomplish the near impossible: to defend their too-thin line. To survive, many American platoons and companies, cut off from their battalions, fought back while withdrawing to better positions. Others managed to hold on, leaving the ground in front of their foxholes piled with German dead. Some were overrun and captured so quickly they did not know what happened.

General Bradley spent the morning driving to Paris from his headquarters in Luxembourg. He lunched in Paris at the Ritz Hotel and then drove to Versailles to meet with Eisenhower at his office in a small stone annex behind the elegant Trianon Palace Hotel. The hotel was just around the corner from the Palace of Versailles. Bradley wanted to impress on Eisenhower the urgent need for more riflemen to replace the heavy losses in his infantry divisions.

Despite the gravity of the situation at the front, Eisenhower and Bradley did not learn of the massive German attack until 4 P.M., an incredible ten and a half hours after it started. Bradley said Lt. Gen. Bedell Smith, SHAEF chief of staff, placed a hand on his shoulder and said, "Well, Brad, you've been wishing for a counterattack [to get the Germans out of their Siegfried Line bunkers]. Now it looks as though you've got it." Bradley smiled and said, "A counterattack, yes, but I'll be damned if I wanted one this big."[6]

Thus began the last large-scale German offensive of World War II and "the greatest battle ever fought by the U.S. Army."[7] Some, including the Germans, called it the Ardennes Offensive. With a bit of undeserved irreverence, American media dubbed it the Battle of the Bulge (named for the bulge the Germans created in the American line). The name stuck.

Hitler's timetable called for decisive German infantry penetrations of the American line on the first day, opening gaps for tank divisions to race through. His plan called for German armor to reach the Hohes Venn (near Malmedy) on the second day, the Meuse River on the third day, and to secure a crossing of the Meuse on the fourth day. The objective was to capture Antwerp, the vital Belgian port supplying the Allied armies (American, British, and Canadian) fighting in Belgium, the Netherlands, and Germany. If successful, Hitler would have achieved his second objective: to drive a wedge between the Americans in the south and the British and Canadians in the north.

Although Hitler's troops achieved some breakthroughs on the first and second days of the attack, fierce resistance by American rifle companies, mortar and machine gun teams, and division and corps artillery slowed down the German advance and threw it fatally behind schedule. As soon as advancing German infantry reached the foxholes of American rifle platoons, the battle turned into hundreds of small, separate firefights involving close-up contact. With communications cut and units often separated, most decisions were being made at the platoon, company, and battalion levels. Full colonels and generals often did not know where their men were or what they were doing. They had to hope that training, experience, and discipline would pay off in the confusion that reigned across the vast battlefield. It was as if the fighting men had disappeared in a thick fog. In other words, this was a time for self-starters and individual initiative, especially at the platoon and company levels.

The experiences described in this and the next four chapters provide a sampling of what it was like during the opening days of the Battle of the Bulge for the men on the front line.

DAY ONE IN HÖFEN

☆ **3rd Battalion Morning Report to the 395th Regiment**
December 16, 1944—
From 0525 to 0545 [5:25 to 5:45 A.M.], our positions in and around Höfen received a heavy barrage of artillery and rockets covering our entire front line. The heaviest concentration was in the center of our position. The enemy barrage severed all wire communications with subordinate units and rear headquarters. Radio communications were limited to the front line and to our heavy weapons company.

At 0555, enemy [infantry] attacked in strength at five different points. The main effort was located at the boundary between I and K Companies. Another force tried to penetrate the Monschau area, immediately north of our extreme left flank [I Company].

Since communications between our artillery liaison officer and 196 field artillery guns was out until 0650, the attack was repulsed by our own machine guns, small arms, mortars, and hand-to-hand fighting. By 0745 the enemy had withdrawn, with the exception of one penetration in the center of the battalion position [left flank I Company and right flank K Company]. This penetration was liquidated by personnel from the 612th Tank Destroyer Battalion [A Company] and members of our battalion's front line. The penetrating troops were forced into a building, and they were entirely surrounded by the above-named units.

The attack on our extreme left flank was repulsed by artillery and rifle fire.

The battalion did not commit its reserves [consisting of only one platoon of forty men from L Company].

At 1235, the enemy again launched an attack against our right front [K Company]. This attack was broken up by artillery and mortar fire.

Results of this day's fighting were as follows: The Germans lost 104 dead in an area fifty yards in front of our front line to one hundred yards behind the line, and another 160 wounded counted in front of battalion lines. The wounded could not be reached without endangering the lives of our men. We captured nineteen prisoners of war. The 3rd Battalion lost four killed, seven wounded, and four missing.

We learned from a prisoner of war that the enemy's mission was to take Höfen at all costs.

The German 751st Regiment of the 326th Volksgrenadier Division was identified as the unit that conducted the attack.

[The 326th was composed of approximately 11,000 men, com-
pared to 14,253 in an American infantry division.]
    Enemy artillery continued throughout the day, with heavy
concentrations from 1025 to 1033. All 3rd Battalion troops
were on the alert for the remainder of the day.

I woke up in my dugout at 5:25 A.M. to a thunderous storm
of shells bursting into and near our positions. The sound was
terrifying. I had never heard anything so much like the end of
the world—and of me. The earth trembled; so did I. I expected
to be crushed at any moment; I tried to get closer to the ground,
but couldn't—I was already there. I held my steel helmet over
my head, expecting my treasured dugout to blow into a thousand pieces. The shells falling around me were among the first
the Germans hurled in the Battle of the Bulge.

I lay there alone, trapped. I couldn't dash for my much-safer
foxhole. I'd be cut to ribbons before I got halfway. The only
thing to do was to lie still and pray that the logs over my head
were thick enough to stop the hail of shell fragments. Despite
my fear, I remained remarkably clearheaded.

The artillery frenzy on the Höfen area (from ten battalions of
German artillery) continued uninterrupted for five minutes, but
it seemed like an eternity.[8]

Then the storm eased, but did not stop. I made a split-second
decision to dash to my foxhole. I had been sleeping, as usual,
fully dressed with shoes on, ready for just such a moment. I
grabbed the M1 rifle and rifle belt of the man who was on guard
with my BAR in his foxhole and crawled backwards through my
hanging-blanket door. Grabbing the guide rope attached to the
trees, I slid down the icy hill to my empty foxhole. During those
few seconds, two shells landed in our area, but far enough away
to leave me unscathed.

The artillery storm returned to the intensity of the first five
minutes, accompanied by ear-splitting Nebelwerfer rockets, ap-

propriately named "screaming meemies." Some big shells going over our position, heading farther west, sounded like speeding trains, one after the other. After pummeling us for about thirty-five minutes (rated one of the heavier barrages of World War II), the apocalyptic bombardment of screaming, whistling, whining, and crashing ceased.

I stood up in my hole to look out into the inky blackness. The noise of the river prevented me from hearing anything but faint, sporadic small-arms fire and distant artillery. "Everyone OK?" I called to the foxhole downstream from me. No one answered. Then I called to Willie Cates and Ensign Williamsen in the next hole upstream. "We're OK," Williamsen answered. Then he added: "Harmon, McEwen, Shipp, and Corrigan are OK, too." They were in the next two holes upstream from Williamsen and Cates. I was worried because no one answered from the foxhole to my right. After waiting five to ten minutes in total darkness, I stepped out of my foxhole.

I felt surprisingly calm, but I wanted reassurance and someone to talk to. Thoughts raced through my mind. What was the meaning of such heavy shelling? Was I exaggerating its intensity? Was it the prelude to an infantry attack?

I heard muffled voices from Wresinski's dugout and moved up the slope to hear better. "What's going on?" I called. "Something's wrong with Wresinski," a voice answered. I slid back into my foxhole and tried to call the platoon CP on my field telephone. Silence. That was scary. Was the wire cut? Since I had heard two voices at Wresinski's dugout, I decided the best thing to do was to stay in my hole, ready to fend off a possible enemy infantry attack.

Sergeant Mysliewiec slipped and slid his way over the hill from the platoon CP to check on us. He said everyone except Wresinski was okay. He gave the impression that whatever was wrong with Wresinski wasn't serious. "Stay on the alert in your holes," Mysliewiec ordered as he climbed back over the hill.

Now, for the first time, our artillery back in Kalterherberg opened up on the Germans. Outgoing shells whined over our heads on their way east, in the direction of Höfen. The noise echoed eerily through the surrounding hills and mountainous ravines. Hearing our artillery raised my morale. Two artillery battalions with twenty-four 105-mm howitzers were located two miles directly behind us. Additionally, nearby 155-mm howitzers under V Corps assisted us, including seven battalions in the Hürtgen Forest. Especially effective was the use of massive TOT (time on target) when many guns at different locations timed their firing so that their shells would land on a single target simultaneously.

As soon as the faintest sign of daylight arrived, I went to Cates's hole to return his rifle and to pick up my BAR and my watch. After daylight, Wresinski's buddy slipped into the empty foxhole next to mine. "How's Wresinski?" I asked. "Don't you know?" he asked. "He's dead! They've taken him away." Then he explained: "When we tried to race from the dugout to our foxhole after the first big barrage, Wresinski said he felt too weak to get up. We looked for a wound and couldn't find anything. He felt no pain. So we didn't consider it a serious problem. He got weaker and weaker over a period of twenty minutes. The next thing we knew he was dead. We made another check of his body with a flashlight and found a tiny slit in his abdomen. A small piece of shrapnel had entered his body and cut an artery. There was no external bleeding. He quietly bled to death, internally." (Wresinski was one of the first American fatalities in the Battle of the Bulge.)

I was dumbfounded. Suddenly, I understood the cheapness of life on the front line. I had already lost friends in other units, but I didn't internalize the finality of death until someone physically next to me disappeared.

Wresinski's body was already on its way to an army morgue, which consisted of a shed and a garage at the Hotel Perlenau, and then to a newly-dug grave at the Henri-Chapelle American Cemetery. Three other 3rd Battalion men killed by German attacks during the day would accompany him.

The loss of only four killed in the 3rd Battalion was remarkably small, considering the intensity of the attack. It spoke well for all the work we did in November and early December to improve our foxholes and dugouts. It also spoke well for our leaders, who made certain we followed through with their orders.

Wresinski's dugout was only twenty feet from mine. Yet, he was dead and I was untouched. So were the other two men sleeping in his dugout. Wresinski and his buddy and Karchner and I had built our dugouts at the same time and, since they were "next door," we had compared notes. They had not dug as deeply into the hillside as we had. We were more protected against shrapnel. We now appreciated the need to dig too much, rather than too little. We all agreed that more than half of us would have been killed if the barrage had come two weeks earlier when we were still sleeping in canvas pup tents with no overhead protection.

I stood watch in the lookout foxhole at the top of our steep hill during the late morning. I could hear and see what was going on for two miles to the east and north. Off and on, the sounds of busy gunners drifted my way—much more activity than at any other time since we had arrived on the line. They were firing everything from rifles to heavy artillery. The sounds came from both sides of the front, but more from our side.

Before my three hours were up, I heard a low-flying fighter plane racing up our ravine. Fierce antiaircraft fire from the west side of the Perlenbach River followed its flight from north to south. Then, a mile beyond our position, it crashed into a tree-covered mountain. The show was over almost as quickly as it had begun. I saw only flashes of the plane through the trees, so I couldn't identify it as friend or foe. But, since our guns were firing at it, I assumed the crash meant one fewer Luftwaffe plane and pilot. When I got back to the platoon, Mysliewiec said the plane was so low that its German markings were clear. What the pilot achieved was beyond me. Maybe he'd had enough of war.

Earlier my phone line had been cut by shell fragments or by enemy infiltration between my position and the platoon CP. Now my phone worked.

In early afternoon we heard that large numbers of German infantry had attacked I and K Companies in the dark, beginning ten minutes after the first German artillery barrage lifted. According to a report from one of our runners, the Germans were beaten back by a sheet of machine gun and rifle fire and had suffered many killed and wounded. That's all we heard. Nothing official.

Throughout the day we continued on alert in our holes. We saw no signs of enemy troops. Before nightfall, someone noticed that our mascot, our one-legged rooster, had disappeared. With no foxhole to dive into, he was probably blown to pieces.

When the predawn barrage first fell in the center of Höfen, Colonel Butler had an entirely different view and experience from those of us in the ravine. "I had my moment of truth when I left 3rd Battalion Headquarters thirty minutes after the shelling began," Butler asserted. The barrage had knocked out all telephone communications at the CP, and Butler wanted to reach a radio located a block away. It still had contact with the division. "As I stepped out of the building," he said, "the scene was unbelievable. A huge rocket was stuck nose-down in the yard just outside headquarters. It was eight feet long and eighteen inches wide. Fortunately for us, it was a dud."[9]

Across the street, the school building that 3rd Battalion Headquarters had vacated the day before was in flames. All communications lines were down or hanging from their telephone poles like drooping ribbons. Butler later said, "The street had turned to dirty gray and smelled like death itself because of the heavy artillery thrown at us. I felt like I was in another world, and all by myself." As Butler reached his destination, M Company (heavy weapons company) opened up behind him with its 81-mm mortars. "They swished over my head, landing on German infantry approaching our forward foxholes," Butler said. At the same time, I, K, and L Companies opened up with small arms and machine gun fire on German soldiers attempting to overrun their foxholes.

The Germans aimed powerful Luftwaffe searchlights at low clouds, creating an eerie artificial moonlight to help their infantry see where they were going. "When our artillery people told me they could knock out the searchlights, I said no. That's the last thing I wanted," Butler declared. "Their men were easier targets for our gunners. Without that light, we wouldn't have been able to see them." Commanders of I and K Companies reported that the German lighting stunt increased visibility for their riflemen to about six hundred feet.

"From then on," Butler said, "I was just too busy to keep track of all the events. I didn't have time to get scared. What the men did was incredible." When the day was over, the battalion still held Höfen, and the Germans pulled back to recuperate. "Our side had to take desperate action to save the day," Butler explained. "It was not uncommon for BAR gunners to let Germans get within ten feet of their foxholes before they opened fire with a blast of twenty bullets. By letting attacking units get so close, our men were able to hit a much higher percentage of the Germans. In two cases, the enemy fell in the BAR gunners' foxholes."

During this attack, Butler asserted, "boys became men, tough guys turned yellow, and the squads, platoons, companies, and battalions either lived up to expectations and became fighting units, or they went to pieces.

"In addition to the effectiveness of the men in foxholes, another factor played an important role in our success." Butler was referring to a decision he made when the battalion first arrived in Höfen. Since he couldn't control the wide front with so few men, he decided that if an enemy attack got close or into American positions he would place artillery concentrations of fire on his own men and they would stay low in their foxholes. "This was one of the best decisions I ever made. On December 16 [and again on December 18], I had to fire five 5-minute concentrations of artillery on my men. And, when that fire was lifted, they came out of their holes and killed the Germans missed by the artillery. It was astonishing how effective this was!"

Another view of the scene in Höfen came from Capt. (later Major) Keith P. Fabianich, 3rd Battalion operations officer. "The shelling," he said, "produced an enormous amount of damage within the village. Fires raged everywhere, and the streets were choked with the debris of smashed buildings and fallen telephone poles. The battalion command post was hit repeatedly, and all sentries on outside duty were either killed or wounded. The Germans advanced with their characteristic slow walk toward the battalion's positions. When they got close, every weapon within range began firing at them. The sudden burst of fire surprised the enemy troops and practically swept them away," Fabianich declared. "Because of the visible success of the defense, the entire battalion was elated." [10]

On the I Company front, my good friend, Pfc. Don Stafford, former Berkeley student and ASTPer, was surprised that the Germans wore noisy hobnailed boots that alerted our men in houses of the Germans' presence on streets outside at night. "I thought it was nice of them to let us know they were coming. We shot several, thanks to the advance warning." [11]

Stafford was impressed with American artillery. In one case, he said, American shells exploded outside the house where he slept. "The blast of one shell tossed three German soldiers fifteen feet into the air like Raggedy Ann dolls. When they fell back on the road, they never moved." Stafford also noted that the American antipersonnel mines did not work. "The Germans walked or ran right through them and none exploded." The reason: ice jammed the triggers.

Also on I Company's front, Pfc. Paul Putty said he and others on the second floor of the house they occupied stayed busy shooting Germans from windows. "The BAR gunner on the first floor was mowing them down," Putty said. He added that so many German bodies were piled up that his group received an order the next day to get rid of them. The order didn't tell how to do it. "We threw a bunch down a well," Putty added. "I remember that." [12]

Pfc. Bruce Waterman had one of the best views of the German attack from the south end of the 3rd Battalion's front. He was on two-hour guard at a second-story window of L Company's CP (a house). He was looking out to the east and northeast toward the German lines. "Suddenly," he said, "as far as I could see, there was an instantaneous flash of artillery, mortar, and tank fire along the entire German line. In seconds, shells began exploding just to the north of us in Höfen and on 3rd Battalion foxholes defending the village along its eastern edge. No shells hit near us, so I could continue watching the fireworks without ducking. After a short pause, I heard lots of rifle and machine gun fire coming from our front foxholes." [13]

Warren Wilson, who was on I Company's line, said the opening German barrage sounded like a hundred freight trains hitting simultaneously. "All at once, the sky was filled with artillery, 'screaming meemies,' machine guns, and burp gun fire. Shells hit our house, but no one was hurt," Wilson wrote in his diary. "Nearby, Lt. Ernest J. Chiodi was hit and died of shock. Pfc. James Devereaux was killed when a shell hit another I Company house. Barr, Broadbent, Belefont, and Barnes were captured. Crist and Craft got away. Several of the fellows are breaking emotionally. . . . I shot at one German twenty times, and Davis kidded me because I missed him. I shot at stumps, trees, just anything." [14]

In a wonderful bit of good luck for our 3rd Battalion, all twelve of the three-inch guns that slipped into Höfen during the night of December 14–15 were ready for action—just in time. They came with A Company, 612th Tank Destroyer Battalion, a seasoned outfit from Normandy battles. The men moved quickly, digging in the guns, camouflaging them, and unloading plenty of ammunition by nightfall, December 15. After the German barrage ended, Maj. James B. Kemp, the battalion's executive officer, reported that shrapnel cut all communications lines between A Company's twelve gun sites. Telephone wire crews rushed out to repair the severed lines.

At 6 A.M., German infantry came into view, thanks to the "moonlight" produced by enemy searchlights. "The Germans seemed to rise from the haze in front of Höfen and slowly approached the village," Sgt. Sam Mestrezat wrote in his diary. "Our 3rd Platoon, A Company, answered enemy fire with its three-inch guns" and quickly "had a machine gun in operation. . . ." Another squad of the 3rd Platoon moved its machine gun out of a house to a road where it could provide supporting fire. The 3rd Platoon's outpost was soon under heavy small arms fire and was nearly surrounded. "There were so many enemy attacking that it seemed our thin infantry line must have broken or withdrawn." Mestrezat called the 3rd Battalion CP to make sure that the infantry line was still intact and would not withdraw. In the meantime, machine guns and rifles fired continuously.[15]

Mestrezat called the situation "extremely grave" not only for his hard-pressed outpost but also for the entire sector. He reasoned that if the Germans had succeeded in cracking into the town, their initial striking force could have swelled to a thousand or more men in a few minutes. Then, he said, all of his unit's defenses could have been flanked and attacked from the rear. "We could not have held the town, and it is doubtful any of us could have escaped." As the battle raged around the unit's outpost, American artillery poured shells into the draw from which the enemy was attacking. A tremendous deluge of American artillery now outnumbered the enemy artillery.

"While it was still pitch black, we received one of those rare breaks that turned the tide," Mestrezat said. He explained that an artillery shell set fire to the house directly in front of their besieged outpost. The flames that swept over the house illuminated the scene, which greatly aided the outpost's defenders. The attackers, forced to take cover, sought refuge in a house down the slope. Americans poured gunfire into the doors and windows, pinning down the Germans. "We all sweated out those incredibly long minutes until daylight," he added.

At daylight, a lieutenant and several of his men approached the house into which the enemy had fled. They dragged out eighteen German prisoners, six of whom were wounded. Inside, they found two Americans from the 3rd Battalion who had been taken prisoner when the Germans overran 3rd Battalion infantry positions. They also counted ten dead German soldiers lying in the immediate area. Mestrezat's unit suffered one man wounded by small arms fire. As darkness waned, the battle subsided then ceased entirely. The Germans' bid had failed, and the Americans still held the town.

One man volunteered to tour the front just after daylight, Mestrezat said. He returned with three German prisoners he had taken from a machine gun and mortar position. He compelled them to carry the mortar back to the American lines. He also reported that "no man's land" was littered with German dead and wounded. The entire area was completely torn up from artillery fire. "The morning's artillery barrage," Mestrezat declared, "was the heaviest we had ever undergone." (His unit had been in action since June 11, when it landed on Omaha Beach in Normandy.) During the late afternoon, enemy artillery shells landed in the area of the tank destroyers' command post. They knocked out two Jeeps and cut communications wires again.

As darkness descended on the Höfen front, the deafening

sounds of battle faded to near silence. American defenders in forward foxholes, however, could hear the weakening cries from the approximately 160 German wounded who fell during the day. Pfc. Don Stafford, a rifleman with I Company, described the scene from his foxhole. "The sounds," he said, "emanated from victims of our withering artillery, mortar, machine gun, and rifle fire. Forced to withdraw, the enemy left many dead and wounded lying where they fell. Some lay only two hundred feet in front of us." [16]

Stafford said they groaned and cried for water, medics, comrades, and their mothers. A few German medics tried to help those more distant from the American foxholes, but they could do little because their numbers were minuscule compared to the number of wounded. They moved cautiously because they feared being shot. Stafford said his platoon did not help the German wounded because of the intense danger involved. (By early morning all the wounded left on the field would be frozen.) "The cries became weaker as they went through the agonies of slow deaths," Stafford said. "Those heartbreaking sounds still haunt me fifty-five years later." Hundreds of similar sounds— from wounded Americans as well as Germans—faded to silence during the night all along the Ardennes Front.[17]

In a lucky break for our 3rd Battalion, we probably escaped annihilation. Walter Scheibler, burgermeister of Monschau, described what happened. "During the planning stage for the attack on our area, General von Gersdorff, chief of staff of the German Seventh Army, discovered that the Sixth Panzer Army was scheduled to fire on Monschau-Höfen with a battery of Germany's heaviest siege guns." The twenty-four-inch guns, eight inches larger than on the largest American battleships of World War II, were those of the Heavy Karl Battery. Since General von Gersdorff had a personal interest in medieval Monschau, he conducted a campaign to get the orders changed. Leaders of the Sixth Panzer Army finally agreed when they realized the big guns would fill the narrow streets of Monschau with so much debris that their tanks would not be able to get through. The fire plan was changed, and the Heavy Karl Battery fired on other targets. "If General von Gersdorff had not made his effort to save Monschau," Scheibler said, "the village would have been shot to pieces." Germany would have lost one of its most beautiful villages. In addition, the heavy guns could have blasted gaps in the 3rd Battalion's defense lines in Höfen, making a successful defense much more difficult.[18]

Day One in Other 99th Sectors

Near Losheimergraben, Belgium, fifteen miles south of Höfen, Pfc. John Mellin and his assistant BAR gunner woke up with a jolt at the bottom of their well-built foxhole. The German artillery barrage was engulfing the front-line position of his squad, A Company, 394th Infantry, 99th Division.

When the shelling stopped, thirty to forty German infantrymen appeared in a skirmish line on a hill in front of Mellin's foxhole. "They all wore their long, gray overcoats and were fairly close together, only five feet separating them, perfect for our gunners," Mellin said. "By the sound of rifle fire coming from both sides of the advancing Germans, we figured their skirmish line extended far beyond the men we could see moving toward us. At first, I wondered why they didn't turn around and go back. We didn't want to kill anyone. But they couldn't hear my thoughts. They kept moving toward our foxholes. We started firing, picking them off one by one. It wasn't long before the snowy hillside was covered with bodies. We watched the wounded crawl to each other for mutual assistance, helping to stop bleeding and fix bandages. We also saw some who never moved."[19]

Soon, a heavy firefight erupted on Mellin's left where B Company (1st Battalion, 394th Regiment) was dug in. "We found out that they had been overrun," Mellin said. A German machine gunner now occupied a B Company foxhole on a hill looking down on Mellin. "He began a tattoo on our log roof, but it held. All he did was knock a few splinters down on us. Unfortunately, our log roof prevented us from firing back at him. We couldn't aim high enough to reach him."

Mellin put his helmet on the end of his BAR barrel and stuck it out of the entrance to his hole. The German blasted away, but missed the helmet. About this time, Mellin's squad leader hollered for the men to leave. Mellin said he couldn't think of a worse thing to do because the Germans surrounded his regiment, and foxholes provided protection. "I ran over to his hole to get him to change his mind. I succeeded, but I nearly got killed in the process." The German machine gunner traced Mellin's run with a hail of bullets. Miraculously, he was not hit, even though twigs snapped off all around him.

When Mellin got back to his foxhole, the German machine gunner and his two assistants came up a draw at the bottom of the hill near the foxhole and set up their gun out in the open. Mellin swung his BAR around to his left to fire at them. At this instant, a movement on his right caught his attention. Another German had sneaked up in front of Mellin's hole behind a pine tree that German shelling had knocked down during the barrage. He stood up, lowered his gun, and fired a burst at the embrasure Mellin was firing through. One of his bullets caught Mellin along the side of his head and knocked him to the bottom of his foxhole. One bullet sliced off the top 20 percent of his right ear and another creased the right side of his head, fracturing his skull and causing brain damage.

"When I regained consciousness, I put my hand to my head and felt blood. I told my foxhole mate I was hit. He reminded me to take my wound pills, and he continued firing at the Germans." At this point, fortunately for Mellin, the firefight died down. A side of the foxhole caved in, and mud covered Mellin's wounds. His squad leader dug him out, bandaged him, and asked if he could walk. He said he could, took two steps, and fell flat on his face. A litter-bearing medic put Mellin in a nearby Jeep. "On the way to the road, I heard one of our machine gunners say, 'Who's that poor bastard?' I couldn't understand why he was saying that about me. I also remember someone at the battalion aid station taking off my overshoes and saying that I wouldn't need them any more." Mellin had just gotten them. They were size 13 and scarce.

When Mellin gained consciousness, he was on a hospital train headed for Paris. With each jerk of the train, he noted, wounded men moaned and groaned. This was the beginning of fifteen months of hospitalization for him. Doctors diagnosed his head wound as critical.

Mellin's 1st Battalion won the prestigious Presidential Citation for its performance during the first four days of the Battle of the Bulge in Belgium and Germany. Its colorful language reveals the frantic flavor of the fighting:

The German's Ardennes offensive was spearheaded directly at the 1st Battalion, 394th Regiment, 99th Division. It was defending a front of 3,500 yards, protecting the right flank of the 99th Division. The enemy [the Sixth Panzer Army] launched its initial attack against the battalion with an unprecedented artillery concentration lasting approximately two hours. The barrage was followed by an attack of six battalions of infantry, supported by tanks, dive bombers, flame throwers, and rockets. For two days and nights the battalion was under intense small-arms fire and continuous artillery concentrations, with little food and water, and no hope of replenishing a rapidly dwindling supply of ammunition. Knowing that reserves were unavailable, the men of the 1st Battalion . . . repeatedly beat back the superior numbers of the enemy forces coming at them from the front, flanks, and rear. . . . Outnumbered six to one, they inflicted extremely heavy casualties upon the enemy. By their tenacious stand, the 1st Battalion . . . permitted other friendly forces to reinforce the sector. . . .

South of Höfen, a squad leader displayed such extraordinary bravery that he was awarded the Congressional Medal of Honor. Although painfully wounded during the opening German artillery barrage, Sgt. Vernon McGarity, squad leader for L Company, 393rd Regiment, walked without help to an aid station. After being treated and refusing evacuation, he hobbled back to his hard-pressed men, who were under orders to stand firm at all costs.[20]

Throughout the night of December 16–17, he led his men's efforts to hold back the Germans. When morning came and the Germans attacked with tanks and infantry, McGarity braved heavy fire to immobilize the lead tank with a round from a rocket launcher. The fire from McGarity's squad drove German infantrymen back, and three supporting tanks withdrew. Then, under heavy fire, McGarity rescued a wounded American and directed devastating fire on a German light cannon. When ammunition began to run low, he remembered an old ammunition hole about a hundred yards distant. He braved hostile fire to replenish his unit's supply. Meanwhile, the Germans emplaced a machine gun to the rear and flank of McGarity's squad. Unhesitantly, McGarity destroyed it. He left cover and, under steady fire, killed or wounded all the hostile gunners and prevented all attempts to re-man the gun. Only when the squad ran out of ammunition could the enemy capture him and his men.

As soon as the early morning German artillery barrage ended, Lt. Eugene Kingsley left his command post in a forest area northeast of Krinkelt to see what was going on. Kingsley, executive officer of B Company, 1st Battalion, 393rd Infantry, heard the machine gun manned by his battalion's heavy weapons company for a few minutes. Then it stopped. "I went up the hill to the gun's emplacement," Kingsley said, "and I found our gunners dead." On the way, he was amazed to see German riflemen advancing through his company's line. He saw them; they didn't see him. An automatic gun started firing at him. "I ran back to my position and found my platoon sergeant and runner. I sent them back to the company command post to find out what the hell was going on. They never returned.[21]

"I started firing at the Germans I could see coming at our position, and I attracted a lot of inaccurate fire. I fired at a German officer who walked along the front with a riding crop. He seemed unconcerned about his safety and what was going on about him." As if things weren't already bad enough, "our own artillery started falling on us," Kingsley said. He learned later it was deliberately directed on them to stop the Germans. He agreed with the decision even though it threatened the lives of his men.

"I was firing in the kneeling position when I was hit in my right arm. It fractured a bone. Before I could get the rifle off my shoulder, I was hit again, this time in my left arm. I swore, 'OK, you bastards, I quit.' I fell into my dugout. Some of my men came in with me. I told them we would surrender. We were almost out of ammunition." Kingsley's men raised a white flag, and he walked with his men toward the Germans. Since he couldn't raise his arms because of his wounds, he feared the Germans might shoot him. But they held their fire and accepted the surrender. American artillery still fell on them while the surrender was taking place. One of Kingsley's men came up to him for help. "He had his entire lower jaw shot off," Kingsley said. "I asked one of the Germans to take the morphine shot out of my pack and give it to him. . . .

"A couple of stretcher bearers were carrying a wounded German captain. He was about twenty-six and a good looking man,"

Kingsley said. "He rose from the stretcher and the blood flowed out of him as though a hose had been turned on. He lay back and died. They rolled him off into the snow and went back to the front for another wounded comrade." After adding more American prisoners, two German guards marched the entire group through their forward positions and into the Siegfried Line. This walking was particularly painful for one of Kingsley's sergeants who had a bullet lodged in his ankle. "I had to urinate," Kingsley said. "But with both arms helpless I couldn't do it. My wounded sergeant offered to help. I was very grateful."

The Germans separated Kingsley (because he was an officer) from his men for interrogation. They gave him a tetanus shot and then drove him to a church where American wounded and German wounded were collected together. "One German soldier lying next to me gave me a cigarette and lit it for me," Kingsley said. The soldier said: "For us, the war is over. . . ." After a pause, the wounded German added: "Perhaps if we get better we will fight each other again." Someone started playing "Silent Night, Holy Night" on the church organ. "It was a moving experience lying there with the wounded of both sides as we listened to the familiar music," Kingsley said. "All of us had tears in our eyes."

Between November 10 and December 18, Kingsley's company of 193 men suffered 25 killed and 116 wounded, captured, and evacuated. That translates into a 74 percent loss in five weeks.[22]

8 • Battle of the Bulge: Last Stand at Lanzerath

The Americans couldn't believe what they were seeing: two columns of singing German parachutists walking close together with no flank protection.
—THE AUTHOR

DECEMBER 15–17, 1944

"WE HAD LITTLE SLEEP LAST NIGHT BECAUSE WE KEPT hearing rattling noises from the German side of the front." That's how twenty-year-old Lt. Lyle Bouck, Jr., leader of the Intelligence and Reconnaissance (I&R) Platoon of the 99th Division's 394th Infantry Regiment, described the ominous enemy activities during the night of December 15–16. (His position was on the 99th Division's most southern flank, bordering a worrisome two-mile gap in the U.S. front.)[1]

"I reported these strange noises to regiment," Bouck added. "We had heard similar sounds during the previous three nights, and we thought they came from heavy vehicles moving around, perhaps tanks."[2]

Bouck's platoon, a select group of thirty-two men, was hand-picked back at Camp Maxey by him and the regiment's intelligence officer, Maj. Robert L. Kriz. "We looked for bright, athletic, and enthusiastic individuals with a wide spread of ethnic backgrounds. We selected only those scoring 'expert' on the rifle range and those interested in patrol activity." On December 10, Bouck and his men had moved into prepared positions at the edge of a forest six hundred feet northwest of the Belgian border village of Lanzerath, sixteen air miles south of Höfen. His orders: "You are to occupy this position and be the eyes and ears of the regiment [394th], the division [99th], and the corps [V]. Maintain contact on an hourly basis with Task Force X, a tank destroyer [TD] unit just to your front in Lanzerath."

Dug in on a hill, Bouck and seventeen men from his platoon blocked German entrance to a strategic Belgian road junction. Supported by the nearby TD unit, they were manning a lonely, highly vulnerable outpost more than a mile from any other American unit. One of the roads, leading northwest from nearby Losheimergraben, provided one of the best routes from the Ardennes Front to the city of Liege, the Belgian heartland, and the Allied supply port of Antwerp.

Two of Bouck's men, twenty-year-old Pfc. Risto Milosevich and nineteen-year-old Pfc. William James (Sack) Tsakanikas, served in the same platoon with me in the ASTP program at Tarleton College. Tsakanikas also served with me in basic training at Camp Wolters.

At 5:30 A.M., life for the eighteen men changed dramatically. After a long, freezing night of peering into darkness and seeing only twenty to thirty feet of a partially visible, snow-covered slope, a stunned Tsakanikas saw the entire eastern skyline suddenly light up. The distant thunder of hundreds of guns followed a moment of eerie silence. Seconds later, heavy shells crashed on Lanzerath and then on top of the platoon's positions. On a ridge to the east, he saw self-propelled guns and tanks silhouetted by muzzle flashes.

The half-frozen men in the platoon's foxholes, most of whom had been awake all night, immediately forgot their fatigue and discomfort. "The portion of the barrage that concentrated on us lasted for fifteen minutes," Bouck estimated. "Then the shells fell sporadically on the platoon for two more hours. When the Germans finally stopped shelling us, I checked the damage and found no one killed or wounded, but the barrage knocked out telephone wire communications to regimental headquarters.

"Our confidence was shaken at about 9 A.M., approximately an hour after the barrage lifted, when our only U.S. Army neighbor, the nearby TDs, evacuated Lanzerath, leaving us alone in the area. Without a word," Bouck added, "they drove to the rear with their four three-inch guns." Also left alone in Lanzerath, four artillery observers (one lieutenant, one sergeant, and two corporals) pulled back to join Bouck.

After the German barrage lifted, Bouck, Tsakanikas, and another soldier went on a reconnoitering patrol into a wooded draw across the road. They saw nothing, but they heard scattered small arms fire to the south. Later in the morning, regimental headquarters assigned Bouck to lead another patrol into Lanzerath for the purpose of spotting German infantry. At this point, with small arms fire getting closer, Bouck decided to take over the OP in Lanzerath, formerly occupied by the departed TDs. He gathered Tsakanikas and two other men and took off on his second patrol of the morning. The tempo of events accelerated.

When the patrol reached the two-story OP, the men scrambled up the stairs and found the best lookout toward the German line. Much to their astonishment, a large man in civilian clothes was talking on a phone in German. Tsakanikas jabbed his bayonet at the man's abdomen and yelled, "Reach!" The civilian's hands shot up. Tsakanikas wanted to shoot him but decided it would be unwise to have a dead German around, in case of capture. Bouck took command. "Release him," he ordered. The German quickly disappeared down the stairs. Bouck could now look out the window. Shivers went up his spine. Through his binoculars, he saw German troops en masse about one-half mile to the east headed in the platoon's direction. They marched in close formation, oblivious to possible danger.

Bouck ordered two members of the patrol to remain at the window observing the troops. "When they are about to enter the village," he told them, "return quickly to the platoon." Bouck and Tsakanikas raced back to their positions.

Most of the men urged withdrawal from a hopeless situation, but Bouck rejected the idea. "Our orders," he said, "are to stay put and stop or delay the enemy. From our excellent positions we can do a lot of damage to them." To demonstrate his resolve, he shoved two reluctant men into their foxholes. He immediately called regimental headquarters on his radio to relate what he saw. He pleaded for maximum artillery on the advancing columns. But, because of "higher priority" targets, 99th Division artillery could not fulfill his request.

As soon as Bouck finished with regimental headquarters, one of the observers at the window called on the phone. "We've got some Germans downstairs in our house," he whispered. Bouck figured they were advance scouts for the approaching main body. When he tried to question the observer, there was silence. Bouck sent a three-man rescue team.

Before the rescuers arrived, however, Bouck's two observers sneaked down a stairway and escaped into a barn. Undetected by the Germans, they crawled under some cows and fled out the rear of the barn, crossed a road, and rejoined the platoon. The rescuers, meanwhile, got caught in a firefight with other German advance scouts. To escape, they fled north and became separated from the platoon. They were captured en route to Losheimergraben.

The tense platoon now settled down to await the approaching German columns. With plenty of backup ammunition, they aimed across a sloping snow-covered field at the still-empty road.

"I posted myself in the woods to observe," Tsakanikas said. He didn't have long to wait. "They're coming into view," he exclaimed. The Germans sang as they marched through Lanze-rath. (German sources described them as the leading battalion of the 9th Regiment, 3rd Parachute Division.) The Americans couldn't believe what they were seeing: two columns of singing German parachutists, walking close together on both shoulders of the road, looking straight ahead, weapons (mostly Machine Pistols 44) slung over their shoulders, with no flank protection. They wore the mottled uniforms of German paratroopers.

As the paratroopers passed in front of the Americans, one of Bouck's men aimed at a German leading one of the columns. "Hold your fire," Bouck snapped. He wanted to wait for the main body and its leaders. After about thirty paratroopers had passed by, three German officers appeared, separated from the other men. Tsakanikas figured one was the commander and the other two were staff officers.

Tsakanikas, in the most forward hole, aimed at the commander. He hesitated, however, when a blonde-headed girl of about thirteen darted from a house to speak to the German officers. He didn't want to kill her. She returned quickly to the house. Before Tsakanikas and the others could fire, the German commander yelled to his men. They dove into ditches as the Americans opened fire. Bouck had lost the opportunity for an ambush, and a firefight started.

Tsakanikas raced to a 50-caliber machine gun mounted on the platoon's Jeep. Standing on his knees to reduce his exposure, he aimed by observing where his hail of fire struck.

A force of 100 to 130 paratroopers rushed across three hundred feet of snow-covered field in front of the Americans. The Germans had no mortar or artillery support to keep Bouck's men pinned down. The Americans thought they were crazy.

The result was predictable. The Germans were mowed down. Many were so close that Bouck and his men could see their facial expressions as bullets struck them. Wave after wave, all were cut down. Many fell as they tried to climb over a fence that crossed the field, and their bodies hung in the barbed wire.

The Americans fired, reloaded, and fired again. Some of them felt a sickening sorrow as they slaughtered "the tall, good-looking German kids," as Tsakanikas described them. None of the Germans flinched or tried to retreat. Caught in an ultimate kill-or-be-killed drama, the Americans had no recourse but to continue the slaughter.

When not firing himself, Bouck briefed a highly concerned regimental headquarters on the attack, and he pleaded again for artillery support. The regimental contact again replied: "Unfortunately, artillery has too many high priority missions" (including Höfen and Losheimergraben sectors). When Bouck asked what his men were supposed to do without such support, he was told: "Hold on at all costs!" He interpreted this to mean "we stay on the hill, even if we all get killed."

By noon, most of the attacking Germans were lying in the snow, hanging lifeless on the barbed wire fence, or pulling back. A few Americans had minor wounds, none serious.

During the lull that followed, the Germans raised a white flag. They wanted time to rescue their wounded. Both sides stopped firing. German medics scurried around the field, picking up wounded. The dead and those who looked like they wouldn't survive were left in the snow. When the medics finished their job, the Germans launched a second attack. This time they had support from a mortar team.

Three Germans crawled close enough to threaten Risto Milosevich, who protected the platoon's left flank with a 30-caliber machine gun. Tsakanikas spotted the threesome. Using an M3 submachine grease gun, he cut them down, just in time. (Tsakanikas used three weapons, each with its own special purpose: the 50-caliber machine gun on the Jeep, the M1 rifle he carried, and the M3 grease gun hanging from his neck.)

Milosevich singlehandedly manned the 30-caliber machine gun, simultaneously feeding the ammunition belt and firing—a job that usually required two men. He directed heavy fire onto the Germans, who were concentrating their assault to the front and right of his foxhole. When Milosevich's machine gun jammed, he continued to suppress the attack with remarkably rapid and accurate fire from his M1 rifle.

Bouck's team started to suffer casualties. Cpl. Billy Queen, one of the four artillery observers who had joined Bouck's defensive position, was killed as he fired an I&R Platoon machine gun. (In February, his body was found where he fell.) One of Bouck's men, Pvt. Lou Kalil, suffered a severe wound when a German grenade hit him in the face. Fortunately, it failed to detonate. The force of the blow knocked Kalil unconscious, fractured his jaw, and drove four teeth into the roof of his mouth.

With bullets whizzing over his head, one of Bouck's sergeants wiped Kalil's wound with snow and forced two sulfa tablets down his throat. He then bandaged Kalil's face with gauze from two first aid kits. (No American medic was present at Lanzerath.) Kalil regained consciousness and started firing his M1 rifle again—despite his painful wound. He was so thoroughly wrapped up in bandages that Bouck did not recognize him.

Despite the mortar support, the Germans' second attack had results similar to the first. Another massacre began as the Germans rushed the platoon's positions. Most of the attackers ended up in the snow, wounded or dead. They met a hail of bullets, many from Tsakanikas's machine gun. Again, Bouck reported the attack to regimental headquarters and pleaded for artillery support. Just as he confirmed another order to "hold at all costs," a bullet struck the transmitter, which he held to his left ear. It hit with such force that it knocked him to the ground. Two men dragged the stunned lieutenant to safety in a foxhole. The bullet that destroyed the radio had miraculously missed him, and he recovered in minutes.

The last communication the 394th Infantry Regiment heard from Bouck's radio was the sound of the striking bullet. Lt. Edward (later Father) Buenger, with whom Bouck was talking, concluded that Bouck probably had been killed.

As the Germans charged up the hill, Milosevich helped William Slape, the platoon sergeant, fire a 30-caliber machine gun. Milosevich fed the ammunition belt until the gun burned out. Then, to continue the rain of bullets on the Germans, Milosevich fired his rifle, using ammunition from the now useless machine gun belts. "Milosevich's sustained weapons fire throughout the day contributed immensely to the platoon's ability to stop the enemy," Bouck said.

This third attempt to overrun the platoon's hilltop position failed miserably, but the Americans were exhausted and running out of ammunition. Tsakanikas had only one clip of 45-caliber bullets left for his M3 grease gun.

Daylight began to fade over the field of motionless German bodies. Tsakanikas felt like he'd been killing them all day. And he was right. The first German attack started in late morning. Now the day was almost over.

During the lull that followed the third German charge, Bouck told Tsakanikas to accompany any men who wanted to retreat to the regiment's CP before the route was cut off. Tsakanikas asked Bouck if he would come with them. Bouck replied that his orders would not permit his withdrawal. "We won't go, then!" Tsakanikas asserted.

Bouck told his men he would feel justified in pulling back when they ran out of ammunition. Looking at all of the dead Germans lying in front of them, he said the platoon had accomplished its mission. It had held up the leading element of an attacking enemy battalion for an entire day. In addition, it had held up the enemy parachute regiment that was waiting for its forward battalion to eliminate the Americans.

At this point, Bouck assigned two men to carry a message to regimental headquarters. In blunt language, it said: "Give us reinforcements or orders to pull back. We can't hold much longer." The two men reached the regiment's CP but found it abandoned. Two days later, Germans troops captured the pair hiding in a hayloft nearby.

Bouck made a last-minute check on all the platoon's foxholes. Then he and Tsakanikas took over a newly-dug BAR hole. Just as it was getting dark, the Germans started their fourth and strongest attack, this time with artillery support. The platoon received tree bursts, and all hell broke loose. One American jumped up on the 50-caliber machine gun on the Jeep and opened up. All platoon members were firing.

Realizing the futility of attacking across an open field, the Germans changed their strategy. They began infiltrating the American positions from a flank. In the growing darkness, the German paratroopers started to capture Americans at gunpoint.

"After a while, the battle started to die down," Tsakanikas said. "They must have knocked out some of our holes on the forward slope. Some crazy Jerry stood up and yelled for us to surrender. We ignored him. Grenades started exploding near our hole. I think ours was the only one still resisting."

Bouck leaned out the backside of their foxhole and emptied his carbine at two figures running toward a recently vacated bunker. In seconds, the barrel of a burp gun was pushed into the foxhole. A loud guttural voice asked, "How many you?" Bouck hollered "zwei" (two) and pushed Sack's shoulder away from the weapon.

A burst of fire, directed at Sack's face, roared from the burp gun. He slumped to the bottom of the foxhole and flopped against Bouck. A beam from a flashlight revealed that the right side of Sack's face was a mass of blood and tissue. The blast tore out most of his right jaw and right ear. His right eyeball was blown out, leaving it hanging loosely from its socket. He was conscious. (From this tragic moment on, Bouck regretted that he pushed Sack's shoulder away from the barrel of the burp gun. He thought the movement may have caused the German to pull the trigger.)

Two Germans helped Bouck get Tsakanikas out of the hole. One of them kept repeating, "Mein Gott!" Another kept asking, "Who is the commandant? Who is the commandant?"

German interrogation of Bouck was interrupted by a burst of automatic fire, which struck Bouck in the left leg. While one German medic bandaged him, another started wrapping Tsakanikas's face and head. The German interrogator stopped questioning Bouck. Instead, he directed the medic and another soldier to take the two wounded Americans down the hill.

Standing in the bloody snow and among the mangled German bodies, Bouck felt faint and started to dry heave. Tsakanikas, who was drifting in and out of consciousness, also remembered his reactions: "My feet dragged over one of the bodies, face up, a blonde kid, his eyes with a blank stare, his lips parted as though he were asking in disbelief, 'Why?' He didn't have a visible mark on him. No blood. But he was dead! My heart went out to the German who, after all of this killing, still helped carry me to safety. My thoughts went to the mothers of these boys . . . when suddenly I thought of my mother, just as obscurity obliterated consciousness."

One of the German soldiers started to question Bouck about St. Lo, Normandy. Bouck surmised that he had lost some friends there and wanted to know if Bouck and Tsakanikas had been there. He took his position behind the Americans and rousted them down the hill. They were taken to Cafe Scholzen, a tiny tavern in Lanzerath.

"Placed on a bench just inside the cafe door," Bouck said, "I sat with Sack, who leaned on my left shoulder, until after midnight. His blood saturated my field jacket. I would wear these marks," he added, "until I was liberated at Moosburg on April 29, 1945, by the 99th Division."

Others from Bouck's group on the hill filtered into the cafe. Most were wounded, but still able to walk. (The Germans had finally overrun all of the American foxholes.)

As the cuckoo clock on the cafe wall struck midnight (Bouck's twenty-first birthday), Col. Jochen Peiper, commander of the 1st SS Panzer Regiment, entered the room in a rage. He

demanded to know why his column had stalled all day in Lanzerath, only two or three miles from its original starting point in
the Siegfried Line. (At that time, Bouck didn't know it was
Peiper, the man Hitler had picked to lead the main German
thrust through the American lines.)

Bouck and Tsakanikas spent a sleepless night trying to encourage each other. "I was aware," Bouck said, "of a Bible he
carried and was hoping that it had not been taken from him.
Luckily, I found it still in his left shirt pocket under his field
jacket. I held the Bible against his chest and said a short prayer.

"Then, I told him the German doctors were going to take
good care of him and that we would get together after the war.
I told him how proud I was of him. I told him he would be all
right. I thanked him for his help and tremendous efforts. I felt
he understood me as he squeezed my hand. I told him the Germans were going to separate us—so goodbye and God speed."

Tsakanikas regained partial consciousness later in a German
Army hospital. "For a lone American infantryman, lying on a
stretcher in the cold, dark brown world of semiconsciousness,
everything seemed unreal," he said. "Am I dead and in another
world? Suddenly, a stretcher carried me from darkness into
blinding light, and I knew for sure I was alive. The room seemed
crowded with white tables and teams of ghostlike figures clus-
tered about each of them. The smell of ether permeated the air.
The white-clad figures, murmuring among themselves, congre-
gated at the foot of my table. Finally, I realized they spoke German—and I was their prisoner! Yet, they were about to inter-
vene surgically to save my life. New hope surged through me."

When a German surgeon asked him how old he was, he answered "nineteen." The German continued: "Und now you
die!" Tsakanikas thought "the monster" standing over him was
going to suffocate him with an ether mask. "My despair grew.
My head was swimming. Wait! What was that? He said 'in fifty
years.' My mind raced, and the German's voice trailed off in
echo—in fifty years, in fifty years, in fifty years—as the ether put

me to sleep. The German was trying to be helpful and friendly. 'In fifty years' was the rest of the sentence: 'Und now you die— [pause]—in fifty years.' He was joking in order to loosen me up for an operation to save my life!"

The day's fighting at Lanzerath had these results: Bouck's I&R Platoon suffered twelve wounded, and all eighteen became prisoners of war. The four-man artillery observation team (which joined the I&R Platoon when the tank destroyer unit pulled out of Lanzerath) suffered one killed and three prisoners of war. As to the German dead and wounded, Bouck said: "Conditions made it impossible to come up with an accurate number, but I can safely say it was a slaughter for the Germans."

For twenty-two Americans to hold up Kampfgruppe Peiper, Hitler's spearhead for his Ardennes Offensive, for nearly an entire day represented incredible skill and courage. The delay gave V Corps, U.S. First Army, time to reorganize and reinforce the north shoulder of the Battle of the Bulge by the nineteenth of December. Numerous other small American units, independent of higher commands, made exceptionally brave stands against overwhelming odds. Their combined efforts were a major cause of Hitler's failure to achieve the quick breakthroughs he needed for the success of his bold offensive.[3]

The war never ended for William James Tsakanikas. After suffering thirty-two years of constant pain, he died on June 27, 1977, at the age of fifty-two—after the thirty-seventh surg‑ ̣ reconstruction of his battered face (three done by German Army surgeons while he was a POW). Sack lies, finally at peace, in Arlington National Cemetery. To his wife, his four sons, and his many friends and admirers, he was a hero.

In 1981, the platoon received the Presidential Unit Citation (Army) for "extraordinary heroism." Tsakanikas, Bouck, William L. Slape, and Risto Milosevich received the Distinguished Service Cross (DSC). Platoon members awarded the Silver Star "for gallantry in action" were John B. Creger, Louis Kalil, Aubrey McGehee, Jordan Robinson, and James Silvola.[4]

9 • Battle of the Bulge: A Lost Platoon

I knew we were dead. Everyone just sat there, frozen.
—Pfc. John Thornburg, L Company, 394th
Infantry Regiment, 99th Division

DECEMBER 16–20, 1944

STANDING ON GUARD DUTY IN A FOREST OF TALL TREES, Pfc. John Thornburg, age twenty-two, felt the wrath of the German artillery barrage on the first day of the Battle of the Bulge. This was the beginning of a five-day drama for Thornburg, a second scout for the 2nd Platoon, L Company, 394th Infantry Regiment. Thornburg served in the 99th Division's only reserve battalion at the time of the battle. It was located near Buchholz (railroad) Station, Belgium, two miles to the northwest of Lanzerath, the location of Lt. Lyle Bouck's I & R Platoon.

"At dawn, the barrage ceased," Thornburg said. "We thought the danger was over at our behind-the-lines position, so our platoon headed for breakfast at the station." At the same time, however, a German patrol approached the station from the east.[1]

Before Thornburg and his comrades reached their breakfast, they heard nearby small arms fire and stopped in their tracks.

Thornburg's squad leader, Sgt. Chester Gregor, ordered the squad to disperse.

The Germans almost reached the station before L Company's first sergeant, stepping outside the station to urinate, spotted them. Unable to see clearly in the mist, the astonished sergeant yelled, "Halt." Then the shooting began.

"Our 1st Platoon chased some of the Germans into nearby woods," Thornburg said. "Other Germans ducked into a freight car parked on the tracks." This was a big mistake because Thornburg's battalion brought up a cannon and quickly demolished the freight car and the Germans hiding inside.

Thornburg saw three prisoners marched into a barnyard and then led away. A German corporal arrived next. "When ordered to stand against a stone wall," Thornburg said, "he screamed, 'Nicht schiessen, nicht schiessen'" (Don't shoot, don't shoot). Told he would not be shot, he, too, was taken away.

Forgetting breakfast, Thornburg's 2nd Platoon moved from a barn into a safer cellar. "My 1st Platoon buddy, Howard Suess, was there, still plucky and cheerful despite a serious wound from shrapnel that penetrated his ribs," Thornburg said. "Also there was Milton Crawford, a 1st Platoon sniper. But his helmet, along with the top of his head and brains, had been left on the road outside."

In the melee along the railroad tracks, all of the 1st Platoon's snipers had been killed, and two medics were wounded, one fatally. Thornburg and Dubby Wilson were ordered back to the barn to pack the squad's belongings. Due to renewed shelling, they hit a roadside ditch numerous times as they made their way, no farther than a city block.

En route, Thornburg spotted a unit's breakfast ready to eat, but no one was in the chow line. Very hungry, he disregarded the shelling and ate as much as he could. Dubby joined him. As soon as the shelling slowed, Thornburg dashed out and refilled his mess kit.

Later in the day, with only a few shells landing, Thornburg's platoon was ordered into a nearby woods to dig a defensive line of foxholes. Before platoon members finished this job, they were ordered to scout a forest believed to be in German hands. As they went farther into the woods, it grew darker and darker, but they didn't find any Germans. When they returned to the unfinished foxholes, two men were missing. Apparently they lost contact with the patrol in the now inky-black forest. One returned a few hours later, but the other man was never seen again.

Since everyone was exhausted after the long day, Lieutenant Green (name changed), Thornburg's platoon leader, told the men they could sleep in a cellar instead of in the new but unfinished foxholes. No one slept. Except for Thornburg and Dubby, no one had eaten since late afternoon the day before.

About midnight, the platoon received orders to move out in ten minutes to the platoon CP. The men dropped their packs at the CP and assembled under a shattered railroad bridge, ready to march. They had no idea where they were going or why.

Just after midnight of the second day (December 17), the 2nd Platoon moved out with L Company, minus thirty men from the still missing 1st Platoon. After following a long trail through woods, the company stopped. Lieutenant Green ordered the men to dig in for the second time that night. Before they finished, they were ordered to join in a dawn attack. "I was really scared," Thornburg said, "but we arrived too late [after dawn] to participate. We were exhausted. No one had slept during the entire night."

Confusion reigned. The men wondered if their leaders knew what they were doing. Thornburg had no idea what direction they were going (no sun, no compass, no maps). When they reached a group of abandoned log huts built by another rifle company in the 3rd Battalion, they halted. "John [Slim] Cunningham, a twenty-year-old Texan, and I stuck our heads into these windowless structures looking for Germans," Thornburg said. No Germans. But Sergeant Gregor found a lone candle burning on a table in a hut he checked. He suspected Germans were nearby. Now on high alert, most of Thornburg's 2nd Platoon were ordered to spread out across a road from the huts and prepare for action.

"It was very boring and cold waiting there," Thornburg said, "until a German machine pistol broke the silence. It was followed by a smattering of rifle fire. We couldn't see any movement. Suddenly, one by one, our men on that side of the road dashed to our side, Gregor being the last." A group of Germans had surprised Gregor and his men as they searched a dugout. Gregor grabbed a German machine pistol he found in a hut and shot the first two or three Germans. The others scattered into the woods.

L Company moved out of the area about noon, walking in the woods parallel to a road. Again the men had no sense of where they were going.

When the company reached an intersection, it spotted American trucks and Jeeps speeding down the road. Some of the Jeeps were making a great show, with their mounted machine guns at ready, spinning first up the road and then down. The drivers seemed unable to decide where they were going.

Thornburg's company stayed in the woods and turned left at a road crossing. About five hundred yards from the intersection, they finally caught up with the lost men from the 1st Platoon.

The company ran into trouble fifty yards farther down the road. A German burp gun started firing from behind. "I dove into a ditch, landing on my belly in three feet of snow," Thornburg said. "When the firing ceased, I raised up to look around. Several of our fellows had been hit."

As the men of L Company started walking forward again, they got another surprise. As far as they could see (perhaps two miles), American soldiers straggled along the road. It was a retreat. "So far, I had seen only a few Germans, and there were hundreds of us. We had prepared positions. It didn't make sense." Companies were intermingled, and packs and rifles were strewn along the road. "At least my squad still had rifles and ammunition," Thornburg said.

"The constant digging, marching, and no sleep or food for thirty-six hours had really worn me out. I got a charley horse in my left leg and wondered if I'd soon fall at the side of the road," Thornburg said. Gregor carried the BAR most of the time. To give him a little relief, several of the other men took it for short periods.

Hours later, Thornburg's company left the road, crossed a field, and passed a couple of occupied machine gun positions of the U.S. 2nd Infantry Division. "I could begin to see some sense in our retreat. We'd go back a little farther, where trucks would pick us up and take us to the rear. There we could rest and regroup. The 2nd Division would block the enemy from pursuit," Thornburg said.

The platoon came to another road junction at about 3:30 P.M., and someone indicated which direction to take. Thornburg thought they had finally reached their destination, and he flopped on the wet snow. In thirty minutes, the platoon was ordered to dig in for the night around two machine gun emplacements manned by the 2nd Division.

The men split K rations as a meager snack during breaks from digging. This was the first food for them in two days. They were so exhausted and cold that they decided to group three men per foxhole instead of one or two. Close together, they could warm each other. Someone asked Lieutenant Green about chow. He said he expected a hot breakfast to arrive in the morning. Was he joking? (It would be five months before any of them would eat breakfast.)

About dusk, rifle fire sounded from forward positions of the 2nd Division about a mile in front of Thornburg's new foxhole. The Germans were blasting them with everything in their arsenal. As Thornburg's company finished digging their foxholes, spasms of firing from rifles and machine guns were still audible. "We now thought the 2nd Division's forward positions were about wiped out," Thornburg said.

Green sent a runner to alert the platoon about a possible quick pull-out of the entire company in the middle of the night. Gregor, Hoppy (last name unknown), and Thornburg squeezed into their foxhole. "All we had to cover us was what we were wearing, which thankfully included overcoats. I thought I might freeze to death, and not even care," Thornburg said. Miserable as it was, the men had their first real sleep in forty-eight hours.

On the third morning of the German offensive, Gregor stuck his head out of the hole, only to pull it back three times as fast and reach for his rifle. Startled, Thornburg cautiously peeked over the foxhole's edge. At that moment, Germans opened fire. Slim Cunningham, the squad's first scout, stood up to urinate, only to have his helmet shot off his head. The impact sent it flying six feet from his foxhole with a bullet hole through the back. (He escaped injury.)

Looking out from their foxhole, Thornburg saw approximately thirty German soldiers moving into a gully about 150 feet down the slope in front of his position. Another group was out of sight on the right. From this direction, a burp gun opened up. About a half-mile down the road, several hundred Germans marched four abreast in the direction of the Americans.

Thornburg pulled in the ammunition bags from the ground beside the hole. Hoppy crouched down in a corner of the hole and volunteered to reload guns as needed. Gregor, a man of action, started picking off the Germans. He pointed and said, "Get him, Littlejohn [Thornburg]; I'll get his buddy!"

With the group of Germans still marching toward the platoon, Gregor called the command post by radio to find out why the 2nd Division machine guns nearby were not firing. No answer. The gunners had pulled out during the night.

The Germans were getting closer all the time. Less than

120 feet directly in front of the platoon, two Germans ran up and planted a machine gun in a fence row. The Americans fired round after round at them, but missed. The Germans flattened themselves on the ground and never attempted to return fire, for some inexplicable reason.

Gregor and Thornburg elevated the sights on their rifles to 350 yards and started firing on the marching Germans. "I don't know if we hit any of them, but they scattered off the road and hit the ground," Thornburg said. Gregor called over to the BAR gunner's hole and ordered him to start shooting. He gave an unintelligible reply, but he never fired a shot.

"I looked behind us at just the right moment," Thornburg said. "On the skyline, about a hundred feet behind our hole, I saw two Jerries running. Apparently they were from the hidden group on our right. I punched Gregor and told him to get number two. With one shot, he downed his man. I missed mine in my haste, but with my second shot, he collapsed. Then, looking down the road, we saw men marching with their hands up. Americans! Prisoners! We stopped firing in their direction. Soon they marched out of sight.

"I looked back at the two Germans we had shot. One of them, sitting in a gap in the fence row and supporting himself on one arm, was motioning to someone out of my sight to come forward. Again, in my rush to hit him, I missed my first shot. After my second shot, however, he slumped to the ground. No one else showed up," Thornburg declared.

"We had a good view of German soldiers in the large group lying near the road. We hollered again at our BAR gunner to open up, but he wouldn't pull the trigger. I didn't know why someone else in the hole didn't grab it and start shooting. Gregor and I cursed him, but to no avail."

The German to Thornburg's rear was moving again, trying to push himself along the ground. Thornburg hated to shoot him again. "But," he added, "I didn't want to worry about him encouraging others to hit us from the rear. Why didn't he just lie still? Anyway, I fired three more shots. He stopped moving."

After two and a half hours of the firefight, Gregor and Thornburg·realized they had not heard a word from the platoon sergeant, the platoon guide, or Lieutenant Green for some time. Then they both realized that L Company, including a few from their own platoon, had pulled out during the night, leaving most of the 2nd Platoon alone on the hill as a rear guard.

To provide the missing leadership, Gregor took charge of the 2nd Platoon. "He did not do it by declaring himself in charge, but by taking the initiative and directing our withdrawal from the hill," Thornburg said.

Gregor told Thornburg to go to their platoon's CP. After he had gone halfway safely, Gregor ordered the rest of the squad to follow. Thornburg reached the CP's first big hole, but it was empty.

The BAR gunner who would not fire and others arrived in the hole behind Thornburg, but the gunner failed to bring his desperately needed BAR. Gregor risked his life going back for it, only to discover the gunner had also forgotten the BAR ammunition belt. So they had the powerhouse weapon of a rifle squad with only one magazine of twenty bullets. Gregor yelled for the other squad leaders to send their men, one or two at a time, to join him at the CP. Apparently the Germans did not notice the pullback, because they didn't charge the just-emptied American foxholes.

Gregor sent Thornburg out to scout an escape route, and he headed for the nearest 2nd Division machine gun hole. As Thornburg approached the hole, he saw a figure sprawled face down in an American uniform. He slid into the hole to identify the man. It was Sergeant Fields, with a bullet hole centered in his forehead.

Thornburg then crawled to the second machine gun hole, also minus its machine gun. He saw a human figure lurking there. Scrambling into the hole headfirst, he was about to pull the trigger when he made out the outline of an American helmet. It was Lieutenant Green. The other platoon members crawled into the hole. They were now out of danger from flat trajectory fire because they were over the crest of the hill. They felt free to stand up.

Gregor commanded: "Scouts out!" Thus, the platoon moved out under very unusual conditions. Sergeant Gregor had taken command with the unspoken approval of Green, the official platoon leader. Green did nothing to reassert his command and became a follower. "It was the best decision Green ever made," Thornburg declared.

With the decisive Gregor now in charge, the platoon's first priority was to get back to the American line. After about two hours of walking, the group reached a cluster of log huts, abandoned by 99th Division engineers. Inside one of the huts were three lost men from the 99th's 393rd Regiment. They joined Gregor's group as it left the huts and headed toward small arms fire on a hill up ahead. They thought the shots came from an American outfit and hoped to link up with it.

They started single file across a field, keeping close to a fence. The last man had just exited the woods when six shells landed nearby. No one had time to flatten himself on the ground before the shells exploded. Two men didn't get up. One of the 393rd men was hit in the jaw, and he was patched up. The other man, the BAR gunner who wouldn't fire earlier, remained prone, a gaping hole in his back. There seemed to be no way to help him, so the platoon continued on, leaving him alone on the snowy field.

Meanwhile, seven men decided they would try to reach the American line on their own. (Presumably killed by the Germans, they were never heard from again.)

After encountering more artillery and eluding two groups of Germans, the remaining men of the 2nd Platoon decided to return to the engineers' huts and hide there until nightfall. It was now clear to them that a German advance had placed them in the uncomfortable position of being well behind the German front line.

"When we reached the engineers' compound," Thornburg said, "we moved into three huts and decided to wait until dark before trying again to reach the American line. Gregor, Lieutenant Green, and what was left of my squad moved into one hut; Sergeant Kinsley's squad moved into another nearby hut; and Sergeant Palmer's squad moved into a third hut."

Thornburg stationed himself at a rear window to watch for the Germans who had surprised the group in the clearing. What happened next verified his worst fears. He glanced through the dirty glass of the front door and saw someone trying to peer into the room while pushing open the door with his foot. Everyone was paralyzed. "I thought it was one of our men. But, as the door opened, I could see that it was a German carrying what looked like a machine pistol on a sling across his chest. Without thought, I pointed my rifle and fired."

The shot went off before Thornburg intended. He pulled the trigger for the second shot—but nothing happened. His rifle jammed. The German just stood there with a surprised look on his face. Thornburg worked frantically to fire again, but it was useless. "I knew we were dead," he said. "Everyone just sat there—frozen."

Then, to the amazement of everyone, the intruder fell backward with a soft "ugh." At first, Thornburg shut the door and left him lying on the steps. After five minutes of silence, he reopened the door and crawled out to examine the fallen German (he was dead) and to look around.

Two Germans appeared, apparently looking for someone. One started calling, "Ludwig, Ludwig!" Ludwig didn't answer. A third German appeared, also calling for Ludwig.

Thornburg slid back into the darkness of the hut and told the others what he had seen. They decided to pull the body into the room. Thornburg hurriedly examined the German again and found no wound, no blood. "Since my shot was high, I decided I must have hit the top of his skull. But I couldn't find a visible hole or blood on his forehead or his helmet. I don't know if my shot hit him, or if he died of fright." The men shoved him under the nearest bunk.

As dusk arrived, Thornburg saw German soldiers leading Sergeant Kinsley's squad out of its dugout at gunpoint.

Thornburg tried to relax in the broken-down bunk on top of the dead man. "Once he gave out a gurgle, and I feared he might be alive. I felt him, and he was as hard as a rock. I could not get any real rest lying on top of my victim. In addition, he had an odor about him that permeated my clothing."

Another day had passed with no food and no sleep.

Now in the fourth day of their incredible adventure, the 2nd Platoon decided to move out of the engineers' compound. Thornburg was told to search the surrounding dugouts for the remaining squad. It was a dangerous assignment in the black of night. "Jasper [name changed] was chosen to go with me," Thornburg said. "He was a good person, but was scared almost to the point of hopelessness."

The two men crept up to each hut to whisper, "Second Platoon, Second Platoon," and the names of some of the platoon members. Only one dugout remained, and they heard no answers. Then, slowly, the door started to open, and Pfc. Denzal Croft, one of Sergeant Palmer's men, stuck his head out. His squad joined Thornburg, Jasper, and the others. The 2nd Platoon was back together, minus the captured squad and the defectors.

The group moved out, traveling single file, with Sergeant Gregor leading the way. After crossing numerous fields, often under heavy artillery fire, the 2nd Platoon reached two fields where five of the enemy's sixty-three-ton Tiger tanks were parked. With the arrival of daylight, they hid in a large hole abandoned by an American antiaircraft crew and decided to stay there until dark.

"We were so hungry and thirsty. The last drink I had had was two days earlier at a dirty creek," Thornburg said. The last meal he had eaten was breakfast four days earlier. The rest of the platoon hadn't eaten anything but a few snacks for five days.

Gregor spied thirty to forty Germans walking down the road about seventy-five feet from the platoon's hiding place. The Americans remained hidden, waiting without sleep, until midnight. Then they headed toward a faint glow on the distant horizon, which they thought was an American-held town burning as a result of German bombardment.

On the fifth day, the lost 2nd Platoon continued its nighttime efforts to elude Germans and reach the American line.

Thornburg spotted a silhouette that made him gasp with fear. "A lone German was walking down the road toward us. He didn't seem to see us. I didn't intend to fire, except as a last resort. When he was fifteen feet from me, he detected us and asked in a frightened voice: 'Was ist das?'" (What is that?) "Das" was five shots from Lieutenant Green's German machine pistol. The surprised German collapsed on the road. "I expected all hell to break loose, but nothing happened. We all scrambled through the hedge row, and flattened ourselves on the ground, ready for trouble," Thornburg said.

Almost immediately, the platoon walked into another confrontation. Two Germans, mostly hidden in the darkness, were manning a tripod-mounted machine gun. "I could have reached out and touched the barrel," Thornburg said. "I couldn't say a thing to the others. I wanted to run, hit the ground, anything. But what I did was just walk on, keeping pace with the group, expecting to be cut down with bullets in my back. Nothing happened."

When Thornburg got within ten feet of a hedgerow, he dove

for the ground and clawed his way through. The Germans didn't fire. "Moments later," he continued, "some shadowy figures jumped at us." Gregor fired once or twice and smashed at something with his rifle. Green emptied the magazine of his machine pistol, and all was confusion for a few seconds. Five Germans lay silent on the ground, presumably dead, as the Americans moved past them. The shooting started fireworks in neighboring fields. Machine guns were burping, and flares shot up like skyrockets.

The 2nd Platoon raced through more hedges, and then encountered Germans again. "I had just emerged from the third hedge, crawling, when a German fired from a foxhole in the same hedge," Thornburg fired back at the flash of his gun. "Missed him. Then the Germans surrounded us."

Lieutenant Green suddenly became platoon leader again. He stood up, raised his hands over his head, and yelled: "Kamerad! Kamerad! Don't shoot! Don't shoot!" The Germans fired a dozen shots at him, but somehow missed him. A grenade exploded near him, but it didn't knock him down, either.

Another flare lit up the field, and almost everyone from the 2nd Platoon stood up. Thornburg did not. He was still near the hedge and thought he had a chance for escape. However, when one of the Germans started his way, he dropped his rifle and got up.

A German asked if that was all of the group. Green counted seventeen and said it was. "Incredible! We had gotten through the day without losing a single man," Thornburg thought to himself. "I was glad they captured us in a different field than the one in which Green and Gregor had left five Germans lying in the snow, apparently dead. Otherwise, our captors probably would have mowed us down."

In the first hour after capture, the Germans searched the Americans, removed some of their possessions, and moved them across the field. A German officer had them searched again. This time, those who had wristwatches lost them. Then, with hands still over their heads, the Americans started marching.

Once, when they crossed a small stream, they fell flat and lapped up as much water as they could before the guards got after them. After passing an endless number of German tanks stopped on the road, they wondered how the Americans could survive such massive power.

At a shell-shattered house with five armored cars parked outside, the Americans were stopped by a German officer who warned them that any attempt to escape would be punished by death for all. The men were then marched off into Germany as POWs. Thornburg was amazed he was still alive. The platoon had gone for five days without eating a regular meal and three nights without sleep.

When Lieutenant Green decided to take back his command and surrender, the 2nd Platoon of mid-November no longer existed. Ninety-nine percent of the platoon had become casualties, mostly prisoners of war. Almost all of the men became casualties between December 16 and December 20. Only one man out of the original forty managed to get back to the 99th Division at Elsenborn. He was Pfc. Charles Swann. When he reported to the L Company commanding officer and asked the whereabouts of the 2nd Platoon, the CO replied: "You're it."

By the end of March 1945, Thornburg's company had only twenty-eight men left of the 185 who had arrived on the front in early November.[2]

10 • Battle of the Bulge: Last German Parachute Jump

It sounded like an artillery shell in slow motion.

—THE AUTHOR

DECEMBER 17–22, 1944

☆ 3rd Battalion Morning Report to the 395th Regiment
December 17, 1944—

AIR ACTIVITY: HEAVY, STRAFING, AND NUMEROUS *dogfights through daylight hours of December 17. Few planes after dark. Several flares were dropped by planes during the hours of darkness. An extreme number of flares, mostly white, were also fired by enemy troops. [After the costly attacks of the day before, enemy infantry refrained from major attacks to break through our Höfen positions. Efforts they did make were beaten back by accurate artillery fire.]*

The 3rd Battalion is attached [temporary shift of command from the 99th Division] to the 47th Infantry Regiment, 9th Infantry Division.

A Company, 612th Tank Destroyer Battalion, and Reconnaissance Troop, 99th Infantry Division, attached to 3rd Battalion.

Miserable as usual, I kept stomping my feet to help blood circulation. In case of artillery fire, I could slip back into my foxhole in seconds. Because we were on high alert, I had climbed out of the hole to improve my hearing over the river's noise. The date and time: December 17, about 3:40 A.M. A mild wind was blowing. Considering the wind-chill factor, the temperature was about fifteen degrees.

Suddenly, the river's noise was interrupted by the strangest sound I had ever heard. A swishing, whooshing sound, first faint, then much louder, as something came right at me. It hit near the top of the twenty-five-foot fir tree I stood under, then flew on past me. It bounced with a thud, another thud, a final thud. Then silence. I figured it stopped between the trail in front of my foxhole and the river's edge. No one else seemed to hear it. Were they all asleep?

I got on my phone to the platoon CP. "I just heard the strangest noise," I told Lieutenant Goss breathlessly. It scared me because it sounded threatening. "It sounded like an artillery shell in slow motion," I explained. I told him it was a heavy object because of the thumps it made upon hitting the ground. "In fact, it came close to hitting me on the head." I'm sure Goss thought I had been drinking or had lost my mind. "Did you hear any other unusual noises?" "Not a thing," I answered.

Knowing I had a reputation for both sobriety and reliability, he took my call seriously. "Keep listening," he said. "I'll be over before dawn. Sergeant Mysliewiec is on his way right now." Before Mysliewiec reached me, I alerted the men in nearby foxholes and dugouts.

As dawn approached, Goss joined our vigil. We waited for enough light to see what, if anything, lay in front of my foxhole. The more I thought about the sound, the more I questioned my own hearing.

Finally, about 8:15 A.M., dawn arrived. In the foggy, dim light, we could see something out there—much to my relief.

More light solved the mystery. Shadows came into focus. In front of us lay an orange parachute attached to a large, tubular, bomblike object. The orange contrasted sharply with the snow.

Most of us suspected a delayed-action bomb, and we felt like getting to the bottom of our holes before it exploded. For a few moments, we just stared at it. Then I looked across the river at George Kelly's positions. Three more orange parachutes hung in the trees in plain view.

At this point, Goss "volunteered" George Prager to crawl out to the object to investigate. That he did—quite boldly, I thought. Prager looked it over carefully, then called back: "Relax, it's not a bomb; it's a container!" The methodical Germans printed instructions on its outside explaining how to open it. Prager, fluent in German, knew exactly what to do.

Goss and I joined him, and the second mystery was quickly solved. It contained factory-fresh Panzerfaust rockets with launchers. This was the German version of the American anti-tank bazooka. An effective, recoilless weapon, it fired deadly bulbous-nosed rockets for killing tanks, smashing holes in walls, and knocking out machine gun nests. Also neatly packed inside were printed instructions on use of the Panzerfaust, several new Schmeisser rapid-fire machine pistols, and plenty of ammunition.

Suddenly we realized that we were in great danger. These parachutes meant German paratroopers. Where were they? Obviously, they would be out looking for their weapons at daylight. "Let's move fast, men!" Goss ordered. "Get this container and parachute inside the tree line at once so the paratroopers can't see them. Bury everything as fast as you can."

He raced back to his CP to alert Kelly's team across the river of the danger caused by the parachutes near their foxholes. He told Kelly to bury all three immediately. He also alerted 3rd Battalion headquarters.

Goss placed me in charge of hiding the parachute near us, along with the container, Panzerfaust rockets, and launchers.

Since we were in a hurry, I decided to bury them in the bottom of our newly dug straddle trench. Even if the Germans found them, recovery would be extremely unpleasant. We filled in just enough dirt to cover them. Then I urged everyone to use the now-shallow trench to make it look really authentic—and uninviting! Since most of us had dysentery, it looked like any other well-used straddle trench in an hour.

We remained on tense alert, manning all foxholes. Everyone was now on the lookout for German paratroopers. Undoubtedly, they were in the forests around us in a state of panic, desperately searching for orange parachutes. Having dropped at night into deep ravines and thick forests, they could not know where they were. Or so we thought.

Throughout the gray, gloomy day, both sides fired artillery, but not as frantically as on the previous day. The Germans were licking their wounds. We also noted that our rooster was still missing in action.

About 2:30 P.M., I received a call from the platoon CP. The message was about the last thing I wanted to hear: "The battalion has a shortage of ammunition. Dig up the German equipment and ammunition you just buried. Let us know when you've got it by the road near your CP. We'll send a Jeep down to pick it up." I never dreamed that my efforts to hide the rockets would backfire, and that I would be the one reaching into human excrement to retrieve them. An irony to top all ironies. I used every cuss word I could think of. I went to work with the help of a couple of "volunteers." I will leave out the details.

When we had cleaned up the rockets, I slung my rifle over my shoulder, picked up four of the deadly weapons in my arms, and started walking carefully toward the platoon CP. The trail led over the blasted Siegfried Line concrete pillbox near the straddle trench. About halfway over the pillbox, I slipped on the ice-covered concrete and lost my balance. The rockets, which I'd been treating with tender, loving care, went up in the air and landed on pieces of concrete. This, I figured, was my last moment in this world. But they failed to explode. Were they duds? I got up and continued with only two tightly held rockets.

I learned later what can happen when someone drops the American equivalent of a Panzerfaust rocket on concrete. In early March 1945, many men in our I Company were in a barn in Kuckhof, Germany, when two bazooka teammates, loading their weapon, had an unusual accident. A rocket fell through the tube and hit the concrete floor. The impact caused the rocket to explode, instantly killing the two-man team. Many others suffered severe wounds, some fatal. In a few minutes, a German 88-mm gun, attracted by the blast, began shelling the barn. The company lost fourteen killed and forty injured, all within thirty minutes.[1]

We continued our lookout for German paratroopers. Goss spotted four on the road behind us after we retrieved their supply containers. He said they were "eliminated . . . rather quickly." Somehow, I missed that fracas.

ON THE OTHER SIDE. The parachutes dropped on us were just a minuscule piece of the last German airborne attack of World War II. Hitler named Col. Friedrich August Baron von der Heydte as commander of the attack.[2]

Colonel von der Heydte's adventure began on December 8 when he received a call from the Wehrmacht's Army Group West to report to headquarters immediately. On arrival an hour later, he learned that Hitler had ordered a large offensive against the Americans, including a parachute attack. Von der Heydte was to lead the parachutists. He was happy and a little bit scared of the new assignment. He feared he would get inexperienced men. Finally, after much persuasion, he received 150 men from his regiment and 850 more he deemed of good quality. Major Erdmann, known as a strong leader who had jumped with von der Heydte in a successful attack on Crete, became his second in command. The flight crews, however, were not properly trained for the job.

The jump was planned for the first day of the Ardennes Offensive (December 16), before the opening artillery barrage. That meant jumping before 5:30 A.M. in total darkness. There were other impediments. Von der Heydte did not know what was happening on the American side, what conditions were in the jump zone, or where American reserves were located and what their strength was. He asked for, but did not receive, aerial or ground reconnaissance, maps and photos of the area, and carrier pigeons as a backup for his radio.

At 5 P.M. on December 15, trucks arrived to transport the paratroopers to two airports for takeoff. There was one huge problem. The trucks arrived with almost empty gas tanks. After fruitless efforts to find more fuel, the jump was cancelled.

On the afternoon of December 16, the chief of staff of the Sixth Panzer Army informed von der Heydte that the Ardennes Offensive had not started as well as expected. Most German ground forces had failed to meet first day goals, and the Americans were moving reserves toward Elsenborn. To stop these reinforcements, the Sixth Panzer Army scheduled the jump for early the next morning.

Kampfgruppe von der Heydte, as the Germans called the new airborne unit, finally got under way at 3 A.M. on December 17. The colonel himself flew in the lead plane. One hundred twenty JU-52 three-motored air transports with one thousand German paratroopers took off from two Luftwaffe air bases east of the Rhine. They bucked strong head winds. Their destination: the Baraque Michel mountain area, located between Eupen and Malmedy, Belgium, ten air miles directly west of my foxhole. Their goal: to seize and block important multiple road junctions in the Baraque until the Sixth Panzer Army reached them.

Inside the aircraft, the nervous paratroopers were quiet. When they reached the front line, they could see artillery fire and burning houses. Von der Heydte knew that they had been in the air much longer than anticipated. He saw two of his planes crash after being hit by American antiaircraft fire. Then, they received orders to jump.

Von der Heydte hit hard and was dragged across the ground. Alone at first, he soon found some of his men at the assigned assembly point. They were far too few. Later he learned that part of the squadron got lost and that paratroopers were dropped near Bonn, along the Rhine, and in no man's land between the front lines. (And, as described earlier, some landed on the front line in the Höfen-Monschau area.) Everything seemed to be going wrong. When daylight arrived, von der Heydte counted only 120 of the thousand men who jumped. The men's only weapons and ammunition were what they carried with them. At first, the paratroopers couldn't find any of the containers. After a two-hour search, they found five or six. One contained a radio and a mortar with a few rounds of ammunition.

The German commander and his men waited until daylight for more of their force. No one showed up. But Americans did. They waved at the Germans as they passed by in trucks, and the Germans waved back. The Americans did not recognize them as the enemy because the steel helmets worn by the German paratroopers looked much like theirs.

After his close call with American truck convoys, von der Heydte moved his men into the woods to build a defensive position. He couldn't contact the Sixth Panzer Army because his only radio was broken. His reconnaissance troops obtained information about American artillery positions and reserve troop locations, and they captured American runners who were carrying corps orders. Von der Heydte sent volunteers to walk the information back to the German lines, but they never made it. An American armored car approached the Germans, but it fled when they shot at it with a Panzerfaust rocket—and missed.

Von der Heydte decided to move northeast, hiding in woods

along the way. At this point, he ran into 150 of his missing men, which more than doubled the total to 275. He still could not do much without the missing weapons and ammunition. He didn't dare harass U.S. truck convoys carrying 1st Division and 7th Armored Division troops. They were headed south to help stop the German Sixth Army's breakthrough south of Elsenborn and the Fifth Panzer's breakthrough east of St. Vith.

In the evening (December 17), one of von der Heydte's reconnaissance groups brought in twelve rear echelon American soldiers who had little important information and were more hindrance than help to the German commander. He freed them with the stipulation that they would take his wounded soldiers to American doctors for medical attention. As soon as they left, he changed his location. The next couple of days were similar to the first, with von der Heydte and his men moving every night to new locations. They captured thirty-six more Americans, but some were released because von der Heydte's men could not watch or feed them.

On December 19, when one of the German paratroopers was seriously wounded in a small arms fight, von der Heydte turned him over to some American prisoners to take to an American aid station. Then he moved his troops. He had other worries besides firefights with Americans. He and his men had nothing to eat. One JU-88 made an airdrop to them, but all they could recover was one canister containing water and wet cigarettes.

By the end of the next day, von der Heydte concluded that the Sixth Panzer Army was not going to break through the American defense at Elsenborn and that his assignment to block American reinforcements was impossible. Thus, he ordered his men to try to return to German-controlled territory by infiltrating through the American lines in groups of two or three.

Thinking the Sixth Panzer Army had captured Monschau, the exhausted colonel headed in its direction. Amazingly, he reached it on December 22 without being stopped by American soldiers en route. At the edge of the village, he knocked on the door of a house owned by a man named Herr Bouschery. Astonished to see a German airborne officer standing in front of him, Bouschery confirmed for the colonel that Monschau was still held by Americans.

The overfatigued, injured, and nearly frozen colonel had eaten nothing for nearly six days. In the morning, after a night's sleep, he wrote a letter in English offering his surrender to Captain Goetcheus, the American military government commander in Monschau. Bouschery's fourteen-year-old son delivered it to Goetcheus's headquarters at the Hotel Horchem.

Captain Goetcheus drove to the Bouschery home in his Jeep, accompanied by a group of American soldiers in another Jeep and an American doctor in an ambulance. Goetcheus accepted the colonel's surrender. After medical treatment, von der Heydte was transported to V Corps headquarters in Eupen. Thus, the war ended for the weary colonel about two miles from my foxhole. His fluency in English and the help of Herr Bouschery probably saved his life. A much less happy ending came to many of the men under his command.

A high percentage of von der Heydte's one thousand men had terrifying experiences in trying to return to the German front lines. Some tried to pass through the area around Höfen, often using empty houses and barns as hiding places. Of the 275 men who had joined von der Heydte on the ground after their jump, only about one-third made it safely to the German line. The fate of the other paratroopers is unknown.[3]

BACK ON OUR SIDE. One group of sixteen of von der Heydte's men passing through the Höfen area at dusk was spotted by a 3rd Battalion officer near our ravine and the bridge we protected. They were just out of earshot and sight of my foxhole. The officer hid behind some ground cover before the Germans saw him. When he threw two grenades at them, they ran.

The officer killed all sixteen of them with a blaze of bullets from his automatic weapon. The officer could not believe what he had just done. He immediately raced to battalion headquarters to report the incident to Colonel Butler.

Butler said the officer came to him out of breath and declared, "Colonel, I just killed sixteen German paratroopers." Butler found his story hard to believe. The officer responded, "Hell, colonel, if you want to go look at them, you can." He then gave the colonel their location.

Butler did not forget. His bodyguard drove to the site at daylight, where he found sixteen dead paratroopers. "An amazing feat for one man," Butler declared. "Since the officer had no witnesses," Butler explained, "the army would not even give him a Bronze Star."[4]

L Company sent out patrols with bayonets fixed for possible close encounters with the paratroopers. They had the unenviable job of checking empty houses and barns in Höfen. One of those assigned to this scary task was Olsen (name changed), a friend of mine from Nebraska. A strapping, blue-eyed blonde, he had attended the University of Nebraska before enlisting in the army.

After going through two houses with no problems, Olsen and his buddy opened the front door of the third house and quietly tiptoed inside. They checked the downstairs and then crept up the staircase to the second floor. Nothing. Relieved, they walked out the front door. They almost forgot the barn. Olsen volunteered to investigate. He checked out all potential hiding places downstairs. Nothing. He climbed a ladder leading to a hayloft and looked around. Nothing. As he turned to go down the ladder, however, he heard a rustling sound.

Instantaneously, he wheeled around and drove his bayonet into the hay. It struck something, and he heard an agonizing scream. Out of the hay thrashed a young German paratrooper—with Olsen's bayonet stuck in his face. The husky Nebraskan started to place his foot on his victim's bloody head for leverage to pull out the bayonet. But he hesitated for fear the German would grab his leg. Instead, he played it safe and pulled the trigger, just as they had told us in Texas training. The shot blew the German's head off the bayonet.[5]

Pfc. Bruce Waterman, an L Company runner, told me about another incident in which a lone paratrooper tried to reach the German line under the cover of darkness by going through the south end of Höfen. The paratrooper was less than two miles from German positions. He was walking by well-spaced homes he thought were empty. In the darkness, he didn't see an American guard standing next to the open garage of the house that was L Company's CP. The guard challenged the man with the password.[6]

The German responded by running. The guard fired, and the paratrooper fell in the snow. He lay silent and motionless. Thinking him dead, the guard let him lie where he fell. Since the men at the CP tried to avoid leaving the house after dark, they decided to check out the body at daybreak.

Shortly thereafter, the guard shift changed. The new guard was a New York City man noted for his great fears of darkness and cold. When the paratrooper regained consciousness and moaned "nicht schiessen, nicht schiessen" (don't shoot), the guard panicked, left his guard station, and ran into the house to get his sergeant. The sergeant was so upset he grabbed the New Yorker's arm and took him back to his post. The German continued to moan and call for his mother.

At this point, the sergeant contacted L Company's heavy weapons platoon and ordered it to shoot a flare over the CP so a sharpshooter could easily see his target. The sharpshooter, the same soldier who had shot the paratrooper initially, hit him several more times. Another of von der Heydte's men came to an agonizing end.

In a fourth incident, Paul Putty, an I Company rifleman,

heard crunching in the snow beneath a second-story window of a Höfen inn (Gasthaus Schmiden). Looking down, he saw one of the paratroopers crawling beside the wall right under him. The window was covered by a net to prevent enemy soldiers from throwing grenades into the room. Putty's rifle got entangled in the net, and he couldn't shoot straight down. Instead, he dropped a hand grenade. After the blast, the German raced off. But, unfortunately for him, he ran in front of two I Company riflemen manning a nearby foxhole. They both fired. The German fell dead in front of them.[7]

TD ACTION IN HÖFEN. Early on December 17, A Company's 612th Tank Destroyer Battalion was alerted for another enemy ground attack. Sgt. Sam Mestrezat of A Company recorded the attack. "Again, the Germans threw many shells into Höfen. But, our artillery sent ten for every one they threw."[8]

Mestrezat said an attempted attack was beaten back before it reached U.S. lines, thanks to the deadly accuracy of American artillery fire. "We suffered no casualties, but communications lines were severed. This kept the wire crews busy. We had little sleep during the night. Most of us were sleeping in cellars with no heat, and the temperature sank to below freezing. Perhaps the main reason we got so little sleep was that we were all fully aware of the grim situation confronting us."

Later that same day, the men of the 612th's A Company learned they were lucky compared to their "brothers" in B Company, who had just moved into two houses in Honsfeld, ten miles south of Höfen.

"In the early morning hours," reported Maj. James B. Kemp, 612th's executive officer, "Honsfeld was hit by a terrific concentration of artillery fire." As soon as the barrage lifted, German tanks and infantry fought their way into the village.[9]

"Our men fought desperately from their houses," Kemp said. "By firing two of their tank destroyer three-inch guns, they managed to knock out three half-tracks, two mobile guns, and three tanks. But, after a short siege, the Germans surrounded the village. The situation was completely hopeless, so they decided to surrender."

The Germans lined up a group of the company's men in a field. "Instead of being marched away as POWs," Kemp continued, "it became apparent that another disposition was to be made. They were to be murdered! The SS soldier assigned to the job started down the row of men, firing at each man as he walked by him. Men farthest from the assassin ran for a building and fields. Only two escaped through the German line to safety."

Later in the afternoon, Kemp added, a B Company roll call disclosed that the company lost 82 percent of its men in less than twenty-four hours: three of five officers and 110 of 128 men.

The worst atrocity against Americans on the western front occurred near Malmedy, twelve miles southwest of Höfen. A German SS panzer unit killed eighty-six American prisoners of war in a field by lining them up and mowing them down with machine gun fire.[10]

No 99th Division men were involved, but the ramifications affected attitudes along the entire American front line. As news of the incident spread, American feelings toward Germans hardened to vindictive hate. Chances of survival for newly-caught German POWs diminished greatly.

Meanwhile, German advances caused 99th Division headquarters to pull back four miles to the west, from Butgenbach to Camp Elsenborn, Belgium. General Lauer, division commander, gave the order. If we in Höfen had known about the pullback at this time, we would have been flabbergasted. However, no further significant withdrawals by division headquarters were necessary. Elements of the U.S. 1st Division bolstered the 99th's line near Butgenbach and helped the 99th stop the German advance in that sector. Even more important was the powerful role of the U.S. 2nd Division in helping to slow down the German advance on 99th Division positions at Krinkelt and to hold Elsenborn Ridge.

Third Battalion Headquarters also learned from documents captured on this day (December 17) that the German attack against Höfen was part of a massive attack against the entire American front line along the Ardennes. With this information, our leaders realized that it was not just a local episode, as they had originally thought.

11 • Battle of the Bulge: A Day Too Long

After you're in combat awhile, dying is a lot easier than living.

—BOB CONROY, 75TH INFANTRY DIVISION

DECEMBER 18–19, 1944

☆ **3rd Battalion Morning Report to the 395th Regiment**
December 18, 1944—

AT 4:35 A.M., AN ENEMY GROUP OF UNCERTAIN *number began infiltrating our positions in the vicinity of the battalion's key OP. Despite our concentrations of artillery and mortar fire, the enemy gained a few positions close to our front lines. All enemy positions could not be determined until daylight. Before and after daylight, our troops cleared enemy from positions, and by 8:18 A.M. enemy began to withdraw east.*

As enemy forces withdrew, we placed artillery on them. They reappeared and advanced toward our lines, placing heavy artillery and mortar fire on our positions. Our 81-mm mortars stopped them.

From approximately 8:30 to 9:30 A.M., a heavy barrage of artillery and rockets fell on our positions. The earth shuddered.

At 9 A.M., the enemy attacked us at three points with a

force that included two new regiments, the 752nd and 753rd, and what was left of the 751st [after its December 16 debacle] and 10–12 tanks. The attack was made with the main effort against our left front (I Company). The secondary effort was against our right front (K Company), with a minor attack being made at the center of our front (the boundary between I and K Companies).

At 9:30 A.M., K Company reported enemy tank and self-propelled guns withdrawing after most of enemy infantry was liquidated by artillery, mortar, and small arms fire. At the same time, I Company reported that the attack against the center of our battalion had withdrawn.

The attack continued in strength against our left front (I Company). At 10:10 A.M., the enemy moved up reinforcements at this location and succeeded in penetrating the 3rd Battalion's MLR [main line of resistance]. This penetration was approximately four hundred yards in width. The battalion's main OP was surrounded. The penetration was liquidated with artillery, mortar, and small arms fire by 11:30 A.M.

To restore our MLR and to repulse attacks, the Battalion commander was forced to call six five-minute artillery concentrations on his own men.

In addition, the battalion commander committed his reserve platoon [L Company's 1st Platoon] against the penetration of our left flank.

Heavy enemy concentrations of artillery and rockets fell on our positions throughout the day.

The results of today's fighting were as follows: 3rd Battalion captured 42 prisoners of war; 204 German dead were counted from 50 yards in front of our line to about 150 yards in rear of our line; at least 250 additional German dead in front of our lines could not be reached by our men; 3rd Battalion casualties included 5 killed and 7 wounded.

At approximately 8:30 P.M., an enemy patrol numbering

thirty to thirty-five attempted to infiltrate through the center of I Company. Fighting continued in this area until daylight, by which time the enemy patrol had been completely liquidated. We suffered one casualty.

At 10 P.M., an enemy patrol succeeded in infiltrating through L Company on the battalion's right front, an area weakened when the battalion's counterattacking reserve force was drawn from that area. Results: one killed, two wounded, and six men missing from A Company, 612th Tank Destroyer Battalion.

It was learned again from POWs that the mission of the enemy was to take Höfen at all costs. [Intelligence reports revealed that the attack on Höfen was one of Field Marshal von Rundstedt's main efforts for his Ardennes Offensive.]

At 2 A.M. on December 18, Pfc. George Northwang, I Company BAR gunner, was awakened with a frightened whisper. "Wake up, Northwang, we have big trouble. Lots of Germans right out in front of our foxhole." [1]

Without saying a word, Northwang followed his foxhole buddy from the cellar in which he slept to a nearby trench that led into their covered foxhole. Looking down the barrel of his BAR, he saw a group of Germans standing on a road he overlooked. They talked back and forth, as if they were having a conference. "They had no idea they were near any danger," Northwang said. What to do?

Northwang did not hesitate. He opened fire as his ammunition bearer threw two grenades from the trench outside the covered hole. His assistant gunner began firing an M1 rifle from another aperture. Several Germans fell on the road.

"Just as I finished my first clip of twenty rounds," Northwang said, "the Germans threw a concussion grenade at my firing aperture. Fortunately, it missed the opening and hit a board outside. It exploded and shoved some boards back on us and cracked one of the lenses of my glasses.

"I reloaded and kept firing. The Germans were so stunned they didn't fire back at us. I think we got most of them (about eight) in the initial clip. The survivors jumped into a ditch across the road and began firing back. Since we knew we were greatly outnumbered, we kept firing as fast as possible. Every time a German moved to fire we tried to fire back." The battle continued off and on until dawn, when the Germans withdrew, probably to an empty house.

The Northwang BAR team held its ground and, despite all the shooting, no one was hurt. The Germans left twelve dead in the ditch and on the road. I asked Northwang in an interview if he considered refraining from firing because the Germans clearly outnumbered his team. He replied, "Never thought of it." This deadly skirmish opened a long day of German attacks on the east side of Höfen—the fiercest encountered by the 3rd Battalion since its arrival in the village five weeks earlier.

Three hours after Northwang's firefight began, the Germans opened up on my platoon. I was on guard at 5:30 A.M. when they launched another violent artillery attack on our positions in the Perlenbach ravine. It continued for about thirty-five minutes. This time, because I was already in my foxhole, I felt more secure than I had during the December 16 barrage. I crouched in the bottom until it ended. Unlike two days earlier, we came through with no casualties. We were better prepared because we had placed more and thicker logs over both dugouts and foxholes. And we had dug even deeper. Leo Wresinski's former dugout was now much deeper into the slope and had a heavier log roof, but too late to do him any good.

Within thirty minutes, our artillery opened up. "Outgoing" shells whined over our heads toward Höfen, the same general target area as that of December 16. One of our artillery battalions said it fired thirty-six hundred shells supporting us on this day. (During the last three weeks of December, it fired twenty-six thousand shells. And this was just one of the many artillery battalions that supported us, including some in the Hürtgen

Forest. The Germans did not expect us to have this much artillery fire power.)

In addition to artillery, we added a terror weapon: 4.5-inch rockets fired by the 18th Field Artillery Battalion. Over the river noise, we heard its trucks forming a line on the Monschau-Kalterherberg-Elsenborn road eight hundred feet behind our holes. The battalion parked near our regiment's Cannon Company, the outfit with its guns aimed at our foxholes. In a few moments, the battalion launched two salvos of screaming rockets aimed at the village of Rohren. Totaling 1,025 rounds, they devastated the village. Before the Germans could return fire, the mobile rocket battery packed up and left. Scorch marks on the road gave evidence of its efforts.[2]

George Prager, our runner, called the barrage "the damnedest fireworks display any of us had ever seen." It was spectacular. The rockets were similar to the screaming meemies fired at us by the German nebelwerfer launchers two days earlier.

With the sound of exploding German shells in our midst, December 18 also got off to an exciting start for my 2nd Platoon. Artillery in the immediate Höfen area thundered back and forth for most of the day with varying degrees of intensity. After the Germans' initial blast, none of their shells fell on our 2nd Platoon positions during daylight. But the sounds told us that a vicious struggle raged nearby, probably in Höfen. My platoon remained on high alert all day, but there was no sign of Germans in our immediate area. Continuing a pattern that started on December 16, we had minimal sleep and food. Maj. Keith Fabianich, 3rd Battalion operations officer, said the Germans who entered Höfen during their 10 A.M. attack on this day moved into four large stone houses, where they fired from windows and doorways. At this point, Colonel Butler ordered his only reserve, L Company's 1st Platoon, to surround the houses and the Germans inside. Then he brought up two 57-mm anti-tank guns to fire armor-piercing shells into the buildings. With

L Company's 1st Platoon preventing the Germans from returning fire, the antitank guns methodically shattered the stone
walls.[3]

"The fire from the 57-mm guns proved effective," Fabianich
said, "but the Germans did not surrender until riflemen attacked
the buildings with white phosphorous grenades. That forced
twenty-five badly shaken enemy to come out with hands up.
Inside the buildings, we found approximately seventy-five dead
German soldiers."[4]

While the 3rd Battalion frantically tried to beat back German
thrusts into Höfen, misinformation became a destructive enemy.
Colonel Butler said U.S. V Corps artillery started firing eight-
inch shells into Höfen with its long-distance guns after its commanders heard, incorrectly, that the Germans had captured the
village.[5]

The shells arrived with "high whines," Butler said. Communications were mostly out, and Butler had no way for several
hours to inform the artillery team to move their guns onto German targets. To prove the shells were American, Butler walked
out on the main street in Höfen to check spots where they
landed. "You can tell the direction from which a shell is fired by
the scar it leaves after it hits and explodes," he said. "So I took
a compass reading on shell impacts while the firing was going
on. I sent a sketch of where several shells landed, together with
shell fragments, back through the lines of organization." After
V Corps received Butler's proof, its guns stopped shelling Americans and started firing at the enemy.

On I Company's front, with the arrival of daylight, Pfc. Don-
ald Stafford heard cries again from unseen wounded German
soldiers. Repeating the errors of two days earlier, these soldiers,
as they approached the Third Battalion's MLR, had walked into
withering fire from American artillery, mortars, machine guns,
BARs, and rifles. "As on December 16," Stafford said, "we did
not attempt to rescue any of them." With each new German at-

tack, more voices moaned in agony for water, help, and their mothers. The cries faded to silence by the time darkness descended on no man's land and the temperature slipped below freezing.

At about 10:30 P.M., the leaders of my 2nd Platoon surprised us with an order to "prepare to pull out" from our long-held positions along the Perlenbach River. A platoon of the 9th Infantry Division would relieve us so we could rejoin and thus strengthen the 3rd Battalion in Höfen, one of our sergeants declared. "We don't leave," he added, "until they arrive to take over our holes." They were walking to our area from Kalterherberg on the Monschau-Kalterherberg road. (The 9th Division was in familiar territory. It had captured Monschau on September 15 and Höfen on September 17.)

"Make up your full field packs," our assistant squad leader ordered. "We are not coming back here, so carry everything you want to keep. Carry two hand grenades where you can get them quickly. Also carry a couple of K-ration packages." We hated our miserable ravine, but we did not like the idea of leaving the holes and dugouts we had spent so much time preparing. We had finally settled in with our dugouts finished, and we did not know where we were going. We were leaving the known for the unknown, and we didn't want to go back to our pre-dugout days, sleeping in the snow or in a freezing pup tent.

I stuck a couple of candles—real luxury items—in my combat jacket, rolled up my sleeping bag, and put on my heavy, half-soaked wool army overcoat. (Wet and half-soaked, it weighed about fourteen pounds. Dry, it weighed six pounds.)[6]

We accomplished our packing in total darkness, proving possible the seemingly impossible. While we prepared to leave, two of our men, who had completed their packing earlier, manned two foxholes.

During our state of general disarray that night of December 18, a German shell exploded nearby. Everyone raced for foxholes. I slid to the bottom of my unmanned hole as more shells followed. This flurry of artillery was the third since the morning of December 16. The tempo of the barrage rapidly increased to a frenzy of explosions, the worst we had experienced. I pressed my body as deeply as possible into the slushy bottom of my foxhole while the Germans poured their firestorm on us. The noise was so loud I thought my eardrums would burst.

For the first time, I could clearly hear shell fragments falling like a hailstorm, slicing into the hard, frozen ground outside my foxhole. They were everywhere. Anyone outside of a log-covered, deep hole would be dead in seconds, bleeding from numerous bloody wounds. At this point, I felt too tired and numb to be afraid.

After fifteen minutes, the German gunners ceased as abruptly as they had started. We figured a German field artillery observer hidden nearby must have heard the men from the 9th Division approaching us and called for artillery fire on us. The Germans wanted to prevent our being relieved.

With the barrage over, the 9th Division men moved quickly into our wooded area. The man taking over my hole arrived, and I was ready to go. I couldn't see him, and he couldn't see me. Shadows in the dark.

With our leaders pushing us to move out, we barely had a chance to say hello and goodbye to our replacements. I tried to brief mine, but he asked no questions and sounded uninterested. I hoped our leaders told our replacements about the booby traps surrounding their new foxholes. We could not give them more precise information because of the darkness. We were all in a daze, however, after so much artillery.

We carried everything we thought we needed. We left any excess for the men of the 9th, or tossed it in the river. I carried at least seventy pounds, which included the BAR, a 240-round ammunition belt, and a 120-round bandoleer. I was a walking ammunition dump. Willie Cates, my assistant gunner and now also ammunition bearer, carried more ammunition than I did.[7]

It was now about 11:30 P.M. The next thing I knew, we were

out on the road leading up the awesomely steep hill to the north edge of Höfen with all of our possessions on our backs. (I didn't know who was leading us. I thought it was Sergeant Thompson, but I wasn't sure. Lieutenant Goss had just been appointed to replace our battalion's communications officer, who had been wounded the day before.)

Thick forests closely bordered both sides of the road. The sky was overcast. Thanks to snow everywhere, I could see the man fifteen feet ahead of me, but barely. I followed as much by sound as by sight. We moved in two columns, one squad on each side of the hard gravel road.

As BAR gunner, I came third in line. Out in front marched first scout Duane Shipman, followed by second scout Ensign Williamsen. Willie Cates and the remainder of the squad followed me. We moved at a fast pace, passing beyond the forests and into a wide, open area that extended to the top of the hill. All of us began breathing hard, gasping under our great weight.

We had no sooner passed into the open than a brilliant white flare lit up over our heads to the left toward Monschau. The enemy had us in the open, in full view. It was like daylight, and we were sitting ducks.

A sergeant yelled, "Freeze!" It was a reflex action resulting from night maneuvers in Louisiana, Mississippi, Texas, and Oklahoma. We immediately stopped, frozen in place. We remembered not to look up at the light as the flare's parachute floated slowly down, but we could see it out of the corners of our eyes. By standing still, faces down, German artillery observers would have more difficulty seeing us. Movement is much easier to spot.

As soon as the flare went out, we knew exactly what to do. In darkness again, we ran up the road as fast as we could—amazingly fast, in fact, considering the weight we carried and the steepness of the hill. The life or death incentive helped. We wanted to get away from where the Germans had last seen us because we knew what was coming next.

The shells came like bullets from a rifle. Almost simultaneously with the explosion of the first shell, we crashed full-force on the hard gravel—a painful experience, especially with a heavy BAR. We hugged the cold road to avoid the shrapnel.

At least five shells hit behind us. Apparently, the German gunner misjudged the distance we could move after the flare went out. No one was hit. The gun fired so fast that I thought it must be the highly respected German 88-mm, an artillery piece that can fire twenty rounds per minute under maximum conditions.

As soon as the artillery lifted, we rose quickly and literally ran for our lives. In two or three minutes, night turned into daylight as a second white flare floated high over our heads. Again, we froze. We just stood there waiting to see what the gunner would do. It was a cat-and-mouse game.

When the flare went out, we started moving at double time. Fright and our crippling loads were wearing us out. Within twenty seconds, the German gun fired another flurry of shells. We threw ourselves on the gravel as shells hit near the road, but again too far behind to hurt us.

By this time I was breathing harder than at any other time in my life. I welcomed the short rest on the road. When the shelling ceased, we somehow managed to get up off the road and start running again.

Within two minutes, a third flare lit up over our heads. We froze. By now, I thought, the German gunner would be on target. He should have caught onto our game plan. If nothing else, he was going to exhaust us to death. When the flare went out, we repeated our run and hit-the-ground procedure. It continued to work. The shells moved up the road, but still hit behind us.

I wondered where we got the energy to keep going. By now we were within three hundred feet of the plateau-like high ground upon which Höfen perched.

As soon as the shelling ceased, we ran again. A fourth flare failed to appear. The game was over—lucky for us. We quickly entered the north edge of the village and slowed to a regular infantry pace of 2.5 miles per hour. The light from burning houses revealed the severely damaged village. All of the damage had happened during this day and the previous two days, mostly as a result of German artillery, but some by long-range American guns.

When we reached the L Company CP (located at the south end of Höfen), the two BAR teams—mine and George Kelly's—formed a defensive position in the middle of the main street and waited while our leaders went into the CP to get our assignment for the night. (German soldiers were prowling through the village at the time, but only our leaders knew it.)

Lying on the road, Cates and I were aiming north while Kelly and his team aimed south. The glow from the fires provided murky visibility. Catching my breath, I was almost too tired to care about anything. However, one thought came to me: Why are we out in combat conditions carrying everything we have? I reasoned that we could not possibly function effectively while carrying so much weight. If we got into a firefight with a German patrol, I was so encumbered with straps and weights that I could not quickly meet a challenge from a direction other than the one I faced. This was a good way to lose men unnecessarily.

After about half an hour, our leaders returned. "Let's go," a sergeant said in a low voice. No one told us what we were supposed to be doing. The streets were empty. Snow lay on both sides of the road, but the road itself had only small patches. We headed south, one squad on each side of the road in single-file formation. We halted by one of the last houses on the edge of the village. Our leaders talked to some men at a dug-in position on the roadside. When they returned, we took off again.

We were now out in flat, mostly open country with few trees. The road was covered with snow, indicating that it wasn't well traveled. The snow covering the road improved our visibility. Our pace speeded up to a fast march of about 120 steps per minute.

After we left the village, I sensed increased tenseness and alertness among the men. (Colonel Butler told me forty-five years later that he had ordered the patrol to find out what, if anything, the Germans were up to on this lonely road. Butler was particularly interested in possible German preparations for a tank attack on Höfen the next morning. He was also interested in eliminating some Germans he thought were holed up in a house at the edge of the village. He assigned us to check both the road and the house.)

We had gone about a half-mile from our last stop. The bleak fields looked empty—no farmhouses beside the road. We could hear only occasional, distant grumbling of artillery. (I learned years later that we had entered no man's land, heading toward the German main line.)

Suddenly, with no warning, I fell on the road. With the helpless feeling of having no control, I went down with a noisy crash. My right foot had turned in a small shell hole partly covered with snow, and the tremendous load I was carrying threw me off balance. My weight came down on my left knee, tearing open my wool pants and my knee. It bled profusely. I tried to get up but fell back onto the road. My right foot couldn't hold me, and the pain was excruciating. The patrol slowed but kept moving. This was no place to be in trouble.

The patrol leader grabbed my BAR and gave it to a man near the end of the column. In exchange, he gave me the man's rifle as I sat helplessly—and ignominiously—on the snowy road. I turned over my BAR ammunition belt to the man who took the BAR; he gave me his ammunition belt for the rifle.

The patrol leader mumbled something to Warner Anthony, our platoon medic, as he raced back to the front of the column. (Anthony told me in 1992 that he was ordered to leave me in the snow and that the platoon would try to pick me up later when it returned to Höfen. Anthony thought the chances of that were slim. He knew German patrols were using the same road. Suddenly, I had become highly expendable.)

I told Anthony to stay with the patrol. "Leave me here. I'll be OK," I pleaded. "I'll get back to Höfen at dawn." (I wonder if I would have been so bold if I had known we were in that deadly empty space between the opposing front lines.) Anthony paid no attention to my pleas. He gave me a shot of morphine to relieve the pain. "We're going back to Höfen," he said as he pulled me up. He told me that he was convinced one of three things would happen to me if I were left alone: I'd freeze to death; the Germans would slit my throat or shoot me; or they'd scoop me up as a prisoner of war. (I learned later that a sharp bowie knife was a popular weapon for German patrols. They liked it because they could cut the throats of wounded enemy soldiers without making any noise.)

I put the rifle on my left shoulder and my right arm around Anthony's neck. With most of my weight on my left foot, I hobbled down the lonely road, hanging onto my unarmed medic. We kept going and stopping, going and stopping. We were easy prey for a German patrol. We could not see much because the flames of the burning houses had mostly died out as we approached the outskirts of Höfen. Suddenly, an American-sounding voice from the dark told us to stop. He gave the first word of a two-word password. We were stunned. It was not the password we knew. "Good God," I exclaimed, "the password has been changed, and no one told us." Anthony gave him the last password we knew. "Wrong," our impatient challenger said.

"We don't know the new password," I said frantically. We could not see the man, but we heard him pull back the bolt of a machine gun. I told him our names, ranks, and company and then listed as many L Company officers and noncoms as I could remember. I must have convinced him we were authentic because he let us come closer. We could vaguely see a form through the darkness. Anthony told him I was injured and could not walk alone. He pointed to the large red crosses on his chest and helmet, but the machine gunner couldn't see them. "Take another step forward," he ordered. Now he could see the red crosses. We didn't recognize him, but I think he recognized us. "We went through our lines with an L Company patrol about twenty minutes ago," Anthony explained, "and I need to rejoin it as quickly as possible." "OK," the machine gunner said. "There's a house behind me. Put him in the cellar for the night."

Neither Anthony nor I knew that 3rd Battalion men in Höfen had been alerted that morning to watch for German soldiers masquerading as Americans. They infiltrated our lines under direction of Lt. Col. Otto Skorzeny's Operation Greif. Wearing American uniforms, carrying American equipment, and speaking American slang, their job was to cause chaos inside our lines with acts such as cutting communications wires, changing road directions, and giving false orders on American phone frequencies. Thus, our inquisitor had good reason for his caution. Since we faltered on the password, he could have easily killed us.

Soon I was on the earth floor of a cellar with about ten other men. They were resting or sleeping. I removed my steel helmet, ammunition belt, grenades, backpack, galoshes, and the shoe from my injured foot. I lay there exhausted and numb. The cellar was cool, but definitely warmer than outside. It felt good to me.

Anthony cleaned and bandaged my bloody knee. He said the battalion aid station would fix my twisted foot in the morning. Then he left to catch up with our patrol by retracing our footsteps in the snow—a highly risky undertaking that night.

I had just started to doze when Anthony returned, greatly agitated. "You won't believe what just happened," he declared as he gasped for air. "In the short time since I left [about fifteen minutes], I was captured by a German and then released! I went back down the road retracing our steps in the snow. When I walked about a quarter-mile beyond where you fell, I realized there were no more footsteps. I spotted what looked like a clump of trees and bushes hugging the road, maybe a hundred feet ahead. I decided to walk that far and, if I didn't find the patrol by then, I would return and spend the rest of the night with you. I walked to within fifty feet of the trees when a German voice called 'halt.'

"I said I was an unarmed Amerikanser medic. The voice in the darkness replied in broken English: 'You are lost. Go back the way you came.' Amazed by my good luck," Anthony said, "I turned around, took about five normal steps, and then raced back here." Excited and in a state of disbelief, Anthony told his amazing story several times to different groups of GIs in the house. The more he talked about the incident, the more he realized his good fortune. For about a minute, he had been a German prisoner of war.

Exhaustion soon brought sleep to Anthony and me. We slept so soundly we didn't hear a German shell hit the east side of the house, destroying an outside wall and exposing the kitchen to the enemy.

Anthony's "good German" behaved very differently than the German SS troops who committed the mass murder of eighty-six captured Americans at nearby Baugnez, Belgium (near Malmedy), about one and a half days earlier (December 17). Anthony's short-time captor acted especially well. He obeyed international law, which says unarmed medics are noncombatants. (Two American medics were part of the Malmedy Massacre; one was unharmed, the other was shot four times but survived.) The German slaughter near Malmedy is considered "the most heinous crime inflicted on American troops during the course of the war in Europe." [8]

Colonel Butler told me that if the soldier waiting in the woods had been American and the medic had been German, the German would not have fared so well. Since it was the day after the Malmedy Massacre, he said, a German medic would probably have been shot or captured. "I don't think our guards would have let him turn around and return to his unit," Butler said. American troops, he explained, were in a vindictive mood toward all Germans—even medics.[9]

I awoke in the cellar about 9 A.M., after one of my best sleeps ever. The previous day's frantic sounds of battle had faded away. They had been replaced by occasional artillery. I heard no small arms fire.

Anthony, worried about his long absence from the platoon, was anxious to rejoin it. After looking at my swollen ankle and foot, he asked if I could hobble a quarter-mile to the battalion aid station. With his help, I tried a step or two. I winced from pain but decided to try, since I would not have to carry anything except a rifle. I also did not want to delay his return to the platoon. "Good luck," he said as he disappeared up the cellar steps.

Anthony soon found our platoon. It had returned safely to Höfen. After hearing the rest of the story of the patrol's adventure, he realized that he, too, was expendable.[10]

"After our patrol left us on the road," he said, "it soon spotted the makings of an enemy ambush ahead—trees and bushes close to the right side of the road." The patrol slowed down, pulled well off the road, and stopped to rest near the spot where the "good German" had stopped Anthony. The men hid in some low growth. "Our leader was waiting for someone else to walk by those trees ahead to find out if his suspicions were correct. I turned up just in time to serve as his stalking horse. When he heard me coming down the road looking for the patrol, he let me walk by and continue toward the trees. Then, as I approached them, he heard the German voice ordering me to halt.

"Our leader waited quietly for me to turn around, on the German's orders, and return toward Höfen. After I disappeared, several men from the patrol sneaked behind the German and killed him." The German obviously did not know the patrol was hidden nearby. Otherwise, he never would have revealed himself. Anthony was furious that he had been used as a ploy. The leader's rationale: "I did it for the platoon."

Our leader's split-second decisions concerning life and death for Anthony and me raise interesting ethical questions about difficult combat situations. Should a patrol leader abandon an injured man when his most likely fate is freezing to death or getting shot? And, should the leader allow one of his men to walk into a suspected enemy position? These tough questions must be answered in seconds by commanders in combat situations. They indicate the incredible difficulty of being a leader and of making fast decisions in stressful situations.

After the war, I asked some 3rd Battalion comrades for their opinions about the patrol leader's decisions. They did not give me a clear yes or no answer. But, they said, leaving me on the road is more understandable than using a medic as a stalking horse. How a leader decides on these questions, my comrades said, could seriously damage a platoon's morale. Platoon members could conclude that the leader would make similar decisions concerning them. One of those I questioned said the patrol leader should have delegated a rifleman to take me back to our lines, thus keeping the medic with the patrol. I feel this would have been the correct decision. Anthony's quick decision to disobey orders and get me to safety probably saved my life.

While Anthony and I slept in the cellar, our platoon returned to Höfen and surrounded a two-story house on the village's outskirts. Battalion headquarters suspected that German soldiers were hiding inside. To force the Germans outside, Captain Price, company commander, fired bazooka shells into the house, setting it on fire.

The riflemen waited for the Germans to come out, but none appeared. Apparently the house was empty. Meanwhile, the flames drew heavy German artillery on our men. Once the patrol was certain that no Germans lurked inside the house, it moved quickly to escape the barrage of German gunfire.

Another unit of 3rd Battalion riflemen surrounded a house near the center of the village with an undetermined number of

Germans inside. This time there was no doubt that Germans occupied the house because they returned fire from the windows. The exchange continued until daybreak, when the Germans offered to surrender.

A 3rd Battalion sergeant, accompanied by a group of his men, moved cautiously toward the cellar exit to meet the Germans. The surrender was a trick, however, and the Germans ducked back into the cellar after one of them threw a grenade at the Americans. It exploded, wounding the American sergeant.

Enraged, the Americans started firing at the house with every available weapon. This show of force convinced the Germans they were hopelessly trapped, and they offered again to surrender. Seven came out, all with their hands up. When asked if there were any more inside, they said "nein."

Suddenly, one of the Americans, a private, screamed, "You wounded my sergeant!" He started firing an automatic weapon and, before anyone could stop him, all seven Germans lay lifeless on the ground. There were no repercussions that I know of for the American private.

Because of their massive losses on December 16 and 18, the Germans gave up their efforts to overrun Höfen and Monschau. Our 3d Battalion in Höfen, along with A Company, 612th Tank Destroyer Battalion, also in Höfen, and the 38th Cavalry Squadron in Monschau were virtually the only American units on the entire Battle of the Bulge front that kept the Germans to a zero advance from the first to the last day of the six-week battle.

Years later, I asked Colonel Butler why we were so successful in Höfen. "The Germans made big mistakes when they committed their troops piecemeal," he said. "If they had used all three regiments of the 326th Volksgrenadier Division on that first day [December 16], they would have gone right through us."[11]

When I asked him to rate German infantry soldiers, he said

they were "excellent." In many cases, he added, they had better weapons than we had. He cited tanks, carbine rifles, and machine guns. "They were also better dressed for winter."

Maj. Keith P. Fabianich, 3rd Battalion operations officer, said the Germans would have succeeded at Höfen if they had concentrated on a narrow front. The way the German commanders employed their forces "aided us immeasurably because our 3rd Battalion line was not organized for in-depth defense." [12]

In my opinion, some additional reasons account for our success: (1) the high quality of the young American infantry; (2) the skilled artillery and mortar teams who supported us; (3) accurate fire from the twelve three-inch guns manned by A Company, 612th Tank Destroyer Battalion, which kept twenty German tanks at bay in front of Höfen; and (4) the cool, intelligent leadership of Colonel Butler.

By preventing the Germans from taking Höfen, we played, in my opinion, a decisive role in the successful defense of Elsenborn Ridge by the 2nd Division and the rest of the 99th Division six miles to our south. If the Germans had captured Höfen, they could have easily outflanked the Americans dug in on the ridge. With its failure to capture Elsenborn Ridge and Höfen, the German offensive was in trouble by the end of the fourth day of the attack. The north shoulder of the Bulge remained solidly in the hands of the U.S. First Army, and the best routes into the heart of Belgium were kept closed to the Germans. They never came close to reaching their goal.

Warner H. Anthony, medic who rescued author.

Lyle Bouck, accomplished the impossible.

Lt. Col. McClernand Butler, commander of author's battalion.

Jackson W. Goss, author's platoon leader.

Gene Oxford, killed in action.

William (Bill) Parmelee, killed in action.

William James (Sack) Tsakanikas, an incredible story.

John Thornburg, recounts five days of terror.

Ensign Williamsen, killed in action.

Grim riflemen from the 87th Infantry Division line up for a chilly dinner near the front line. Courtesy of the U.S. Army Military History Institute.

George Neill, the author, poses in the snow about ten feet from his foxhole near Höfen, Germany, December 10, 1944. The photo has a story that ended with the probable deaths of the three men in a German mortar team, as described in chapter 6.

Exhausted infantryman comes off front line after ten days of fighting in ice and snow. Courtesy of the National Archives.

Soldiers in Bullingen, Belgium, discover a German parachute container similar to one that nearly hit the author. Courtesy of the National Archives.

Two 99th Division riflemen in a foxhole watch for the enemy near Krinkelt, Belgium. Courtesy of the National Archives.

Lonely Hotel Perlenau where the author slept his only night inside a building in five weeks. This photo shows rough terrain near the author's foxhole.

Two dead American soldiers lie in a Honsfeld, Belgium, intersection on the 99th Division Front on the second day of the Battle of the Bulge (December 17, 1944). Note German soldier at left. German tanks later ran over the two Americans. The enemy then forced American prisoners of war to walk over the crushed bodies. Captured German photo. Courtesy of the National Archives.

Captured German Panzerfaust antitank rocket similar to ones the author dropped when he slipped on icy concrete. Courtesy of the National Archives.

Browning Automatic Rifle (BAR) gunner prepared for action. Courtesy of the National Archives.

Forward artillery observer reports by phone on enemy activity.
Courtesy of the National Archives.

Overview of Henri-Chapelle American Cemetery and Memorial—a special
place for men of the 99th Infantry Division—at Henri-Chapelle, Belgium.
Courtesy of the American Battle Monuments Commission, Arlington,
Virginia.

12 • Road to the Rear

My memories of that [hospital] train are strange
and rather terrible, for it carried a cargo of men in whose
minds the horrors they had escaped from were still vitalized
and violent. . . . Every bandaged man was accompanied
by his battle experience.
—Siegfried Sassoon,
Memoirs of an Infantry Officer

December 19–20, 1944

✰ 3rd Battalion Morning Report to the 395th Regiment
December 19, 1944 —

ENEMY AIRCRAFT ACTIVE OVER OUR POSITIONS *throughout the day. Little strafing. No damage done. Defensive positions being improved.*

On the morning after my rescue and night in the cellar, I prepared to go to the Höfen aid station. My swollen right foot would not fit into my shoe. I put my bandaged foot in my galoshes and started off down the road.

With only a loaded rifle to carry, I limped my way to the medics. The battered village looked empty. (I did not see any of the many dead Germans—the result of the previous day's fighting— lying nearby.)

Except for an occasional rifle shot or distant shell explosion, all was quiet in Höfen on this gloomy, overcast morning. Evidence everywhere attested to the ferocity of the artillery that blasted the village during the previous three days. All overhead telephone wires lay strewn in the slush at the roadside. Shrapnel had sliced off many of the telephone poles.

With each step, my foot grew more painful. I erred by trying to walk. The swelling in my foot increased considerably. When I dragged myself into the aid station, my friend Douglas Packard, L Company medic, greeted me. Packard was a former ASTP engineering student at Tarleton College who became a medic when ASTP closed down. He placed me on a table and took off my galoshes. As Packard flexed my foot, I yelled. The pain was excruciating. "Looks like a fracture," he concluded. "I'll have to evacuate you to a rear aid station. You can't walk. You can't remain in Höfen. Too precarious here."

That surprised me. I didn't expect evacuation. I thought I would return to my platoon after Packard's care and a day or two off my feet. He put a tight elastic bandage on my foot and covered it with a clean, dry sock. He took my rifle, rifle belt, and precious galoshes, which finally had kept my shoes dry after weeks of being wet. I had gotten them only a week earlier. "We'll need these here," Packard said. "Many of the men still don't have them."

We had a few minutes to talk before the medical Jeep arrived. Packard told me about trying to save the life of our mutual friend, Gene Oxford, on this very table just six days earlier. "There was nothing I could do but watch him die," Packard said. "The mine explosion shattered both of his legs." Packard already looked several years older than when we had arrived on the Continent, just six weeks earlier.

Another casualty arrived at the aid station. Packard assisted me as I hobbled to a chair to await evacuation, wished me good luck, and moved on to the next patient.[1]

When the medic evacuation Jeep arrived, I sat in front and turned around to say hello to two men in the back seats. They looked beaten. They showed no sign of recognition that I existed. They looked straight ahead with glazed, blank eyes. Their faces were covered with dirt and their beards four or five days old. Although physically uninjured, they resembled the living dead. I felt terribly sorry for them—a very different kind of war victim.

These two men apparently had experienced more than their nervous systems could stand. Perhaps a shell landed too close. Perhaps, like many of us, they had little food and sleep for weeks. But I don't think fatigue alone made them zombies. Something highly traumatic must have happened to them. I think the World War I term "shell shock" best described their state.

I thought of Gen. George Patton slapping the face of a soldier hospitalized for emotional reasons in Sicily in 1943. In the case of these two men, I thought such an act, by a general (or anyone else), would have been exceedingly out of line. If, after careful investigation in an army hospital, they were proven to be shirkers, military law would punish them.

Our medic Jeep drove out of Höfen, around "88 Corner" and down the steep Höfen-Kalterherberg road to our bridge. I looked into the ravine to locate the foxholes and dugouts we had worked so hard to build and left so abruptly only ten hours earlier. I couldn't see them, but I noticed that our 9th Division replacements were burning smoky fires in our stoves during daylight, something we would never do. Smoke drifted above the snow-covered trees where we suffered for five weeks. Apparently they did not care if the enemy knew they occupied the area, or maybe they thought the enemy could not see the smoke.

Much to my surprise, the Jeep stopped at a new medical aid station in the Hotel Perlenau, our Hansel-and-Gretel-like retreat, hidden alone in a dark woods. Sporting a big shell hole in its roof as a result of recent German shelling, it now also served as a morgue. Bodies of men of the 3rd Battalion and attached units were picked up and brought here (stacked in the hotel's garage and in an open-air shed) to await pickup to Henri-Chapelle American Cemetery for burial. (Later this same day, Warren Wilson of I Company picked up the bodies of Lt. Ernest Chiodi, Pfc. John R. O'Brien, Pvt. Oren Stott, and another man whose name I do not know—all I Company men killed in Höfen—and drove them to the Perlenau. It was the first time Wilson had driven a Jeep.)

The medics at the Hotel Perlenau were still nervous about the previous night's German artillery barrage. They checked us out but didn't treat my foot. (Perhaps they were double-checking to make sure that we really needed evacuation.) I expected to stay here for a few days until my foot got better, but the medics decided to send me farther to the rear. They gave me the impression that my injury might take some time to heal.

I couldn't believe what was happening. I was terribly torn. I worried about my platoon because I knew it needed every man. (The following day, December 20, Willie Cates, my assistant BAR gunner, was evacuated with trench foot and frostbite, thus making 100 percent casualties for my basic three-man BAR team after nearly six weeks on the front.) My guilt feelings disappeared when I realized I would be more hindrance than help to my buddies.

The medics worked in the hotel's two large rooms, the sitting room/lobby and the dining room. My mind drifted back to the memorable meal Carl Müller, the Perlenau's owner, served us in that dining room nearly a month earlier.

While we waited for the next leg of our journey, a medic showed me a slice in his pants. "Last night," he said, "I was sitting in this chair when a shell exploded outside. A large shell fragment slashed right though the thick wall over there and, like a razor, cut this piece out of my pants [at the crease], just missing my leg. One inch closer and it would have sliced a piece out of my shin. Four or five inches closer and my leg would be gone." He was impressed with his good luck. The fragment obviously came from a big shell because the hole it made in the thick wall was a foot long and two or three inches wide.

A medical Jeep arrived, and in minutes we joined a traffic jam of U.S. military vehicles, mostly trucks carrying troops, on the vital behind-the-lines Monschau-Kalterherberg-Elsenborn road. The tire chains clanked as we sloshed slowly along in half-melted snow. After leaving Kalterherberg, we moved into open snow-covered fields. The farther south we drove along the border between Germany and Belgium, the angrier the artillery sounded. In fifteen minutes we reached the 99th Division's aid station in the small, battered village of Elsenborn, Belgium.

The Elsenborn aid station was approximately two miles from a front that the German Sixth Panzer Army had pushed back six miles in the previous three days. The capture of Elsenborn had been one of Hitler's top priorities on December 18 and 19. Despite numerous German attacks during the next several days, our 394th Infantry Regiment, two battalions of the 395th, the 393rd, and the U.S. 2nd Infantry Division stopped the German advance at Elsenborn Ridge. Unsuccessful here, Hitler then moved his main Ardennes attack to the south to exploit a breakthrough that led to Bastogne and St. Vith and worthless objectives on narrow, winding roads far to the west.

Pandemonium reigned at the Elsenborn station. The place overflowed with groaning wounded on the floors, down the halls, and around the sides of rooms. Some lay outside on the snow. Most suffered from shell fragment and bullet wounds. I saw one, no more than nineteen years of age, who was dying. A chaplain knelt at his side, praying for him. Another man, farther down the hall, died. I saw a medic pull a blanket over his face. This most depressing scene made a big impression on me. "War is so stupid," I mumbled to myself.

As I looked at all this suffering, I again felt guilty because I didn't have a similarly terrible wound. The worse the wound, the higher one's badge of honor in this setting.

I started to wonder about people who start wars. If they could see this scene, I was sure they would try harder to settle disputes peacefully. But Hitler undoubtedly had seen similar scenes in World War I when he served as a corporal on Germany's Western Front. So much for that theory.

The medics scampered back and forth giving blood transfusions, cleaning and bandaging wounds, administering shots of morphine. All patients bore the same look: dirty, disheveled, unshaven, and the uniquely forlorn appearance of combat soldiers suffering from extreme fatigue.

The medics dispensed with us as effectively as possible under the circumstances. We were categorized depending on the answers to these questions:

1. Who needs immediate treatment?
2. Who should be evacuated, and who should stay near the front?
3. Who is ambulatory, and who should be placed on stretchers?

After looking at my foot, a doctor categorized me as nonambulatory. He had me placed on a stretcher and decided that I required evacuation farther to the rear. My ankle and foot were wrapped again in a larger bandage. The doctors based their decisions on estimated recovery time. The longer the time, the farther back a patient was sent. The most severe cases were sent to ZI (zone of interior) hospitals in the U.S. I learned that my stupid ankle injury would take longer to heal than most gunshot wounds.

The medics lined up the litters to await ambulances as artillery pounded away on both sides of the nearby front line. The American shells went over our heads, and most of the German shells landed along our line to the east. A few landed in the village, but not near the aid station. Every few minutes, an ambulance would pick up four litters and then move out quickly toward the west to safe territory.

My turn came within forty minutes. Stretcher bearers opened the back of the ambulance and placed me and three others inside, and we drove off. The three men with me hurt too much to talk. Each bump made them wince. I could hear the man above me groan when he tried to shift his weight on his stretcher. We drove in silence for about thirty-five minutes.

Our route took us through the exact Belle Croux intersection in the Baraque Michel Mountains where three hundred parachute troops of Kampfgruppe von der Heydte watched, hidden in nearby woods. Occasionally, they ambushed single vehicles, but they avoided U.S. military truck convoys loaded with combat troops. Apparently, they let us pass because we were in a well-marked medical ambulance. The original mission of the paratroopers, if the drop had gone according to plan, was to block passage of American reinforcements rushed to bolster the defenses of the Elsenborn sector and St. Vith to the south.

My ambulance stopped at a large tent field hospital about seven miles beyond the Belle Croux crossing. I noticed a Long Tom, one of the army's larger long-distance artillery pieces, placed in a snowy open field about a quarter of a mile from the tent. Just as I was carried into the tent, the Long Tom fired at a target on the German side of the line about ten air miles to the east. The tent's canvas billowed from the concussion.

"Where are we?" I asked my litter bearers. "Near Eupen, Belgium," one replied. In turn, they plied me with questions: "How close are the Germans?" "What's happening along the line?" "What did you see?"

"What's all the excitement about?" I asked myself. We had more to fear than I thought. I didn't know von der Heydte's para-

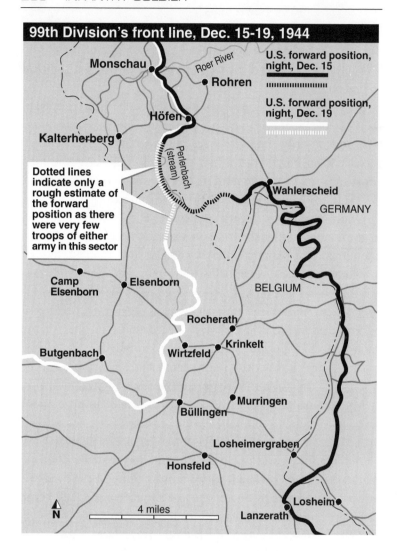

99th Division's front line, Dec. 15-19, 1944

Monschau
Roer River
Rohren

U.S. forward position,
night, Dec. 15

Höfen

U.S. forward position,
night, Dec. 19

Kalterherberg

Perlenbach
(stream)

Dotted lines
indicate only a
rough estimate of
the forward
position as there
were very few
troops of either
army in this sector

Wahlerscheid
GERMANY

Camp
Elsenborn

Elsenborn

BELGIUM

Rocherath

Krinkelt

Butgenbach

Wirtzfeld

Murringen

Büllingen

Losheimergraben

Honsfeld

N
4 miles

Losheim

Lanzerath

chutists were hidden in woods only seven miles southeast of Eupen. Nor did I know that the Germans had broken through the south end of the 99th's front and were threatening Elsenborn.

Actually, the litter bearers knew more than I did because the casualties from Elsenborn were pouring into their tents. They knew from questioning wounded men that Germans were attacking a big section of the U.S. line, something quite different from the localized attack I envisaged. They also knew the Germans were pouring through broken American lines in several sectors south of the 99th's line. An American rout, they called it. They knew the American line in front of Elsenborn had been retreating for three days. I didn't know that, even though most of my division (all except my 3rd Battalion) had to pull back a few miles.

"We're so concerned," one of the litter bearers revealed, "because our hospital administrators are planning a possible move to safer ground to the west. We don't want to become POWs in German prisons." I was surprised that I had to get ten miles behind the lines to find out what was really going on. Front-line soldiers know only what they can see from their foxholes, patrols, or marches. In some cases, that is less than three hundred feet.

I was placed in a waiting line for the orthopedic section. Patients did not say much to each other. The dying arrivals went to a special private area, near the morgue. Those needing emergency surgery went to an area near the operating room. And those in no mortal danger, like me, received nonemergency treatment.

After an hour's wait, I was lifted onto a table. A doctor turned my foot up and down and back and forth. He poked around the swollen area and then ordered a cast covering my right foot and leg up to my knee. A nurse gave me some pills and disappeared with the doctor.

With the cast completed, I was back on a litter, waiting in line for another ambulance. While waiting, I noticed something that infuriated me. Most of the medics at this rear echelon hospital had much better winter clothing than we had at the front. These people all lived in warm houses the army had expropriated from civilians in and around Eupen. I concluded that those who most needed the army's best winter equipment often did not get it. Those who needed it least usually had it.

The long supply pipeline that extended from the English Channel ports to the front line had many holes in it. Rear echelon army units took what they wanted. By the time shipments reached the front line, many of the best winter clothes and waterproof galoshes had disappeared. They were being worn by noncombat military personnel and even by French and Belgian civilians, who got them from Americans for big prices on the thriving black market (marché noire). The army did not count on the grand theft that took place. It sent only enough supplies for front-line troops. Thus, the infantry was literally left out in the cold.

Infantrymen in the rear for a rest or in hospitals increased their anger with the rear echelon and SHAEF. They asked bitter questions, such as "Why didn't SHAEF order all rear echelon units to turn in all new winter equipment their men acquired and ship it to the front?"

The only items General Eisenhower mentioned as short in supply on the front in the fall of 1944 were gasoline and cigarettes. A gasoline shortage was a real problem, but a shortage of cigarettes was hardly critical in comparison to our shortages of overshoes, waterproof boots, and good winter clothing. Eisenhower said he acted decisively on gasoline and cigarette shortages by putting a group of inspectors on the job and uncovering "all the sordid facts." Eisenhower learned that "practically an entire unit had organized itself into an efficient gang of racketeers and was selling articles [food and cigarettes] in truck and carload lots. Even so, the blackness of the crime consisted more in the robbery of the front lines than it did in the value of the thefts." To show his indignation, Eisenhower added: "I was thoroughly angry."[2]

The "value of the thefts," however, was not insignificant. On the French black market, one pack of American cigarettes sold for $1.50 to $2 ($15 to $20 per carton). American servicemen could purchase a single pack for only 5¢ (50¢ per carton) at a U.S. Army PX. For the enlisted men found guilty of theft, Eisenhower offered a pardon if they volunteered for the infantry. In other words, service in the infantry was considered a punishment. He did not offer this option to guilty officers.

Within an hour of my arrival at the tent hospital, the litter bearers placed me in an ambulance with three other men and off we went to another unknown destination. I fell asleep quickly.

I awoke to the sound of male voices speaking German. It was dark, with the exception of a dimmed outdoor light over an entrance to a large building. Litter bearers, wearing German Army caps and gray-green uniforms, including Wehrmacht caps, opened the back doors of the warm ambulance and reached in to take us out. They looked like kids sixteen to seventeen years of age. "My God," I thought, "we've been captured by the Germans!" Perhaps I'd been dreaming about it.

As the litter bearers carried me through the emergency entrance to a city hospital, I noticed the PW (prisoner of war) printed on their jackets. One fear down, but it was instantly replaced by another. I spotted ten to fifteen highly agitated civilian men and women, their faces and clothes splattered with blood. A GI who was directing the litter bearers told me the civilians were victims of a German V-1 buzz bomb explosion, and American medics were playing Good Samaritan. "Lots of V-1s are crashing into the city tonight," he added. "Where are we?" I asked. "Liege," the GI answered.

The bloody civilians went to an emergency center on the first floor where the halls were lined with occupied beds. We were lucky. The litter bearers took us upstairs into a ward where there were beds waiting for us. We undressed to our long johns with the help of our nurses and crawled into the luxury of beds with sheets.

I had barely settled down when the doomsday sound of air

raid sirens howled across the dark city. This was followed in three or four minutes by the familiar throbbing rumble of a V-1 overhead. A minute later, the sound abruptly stopped. As V-1 "experts," we knew what came next. An explosion followed moments later, a mile or two away. We felt sorry for the poor people it landed on. V-1s repeated this performance every twenty to thirty minutes for the rest of the night.

Since most of the men in my ward were front-line veterans, we tried to appear unconcerned. We were more worried than we admitted, but this was light years less scary than the artillery barrages we had experienced in Höfen. The nurses said the thick blackout curtains over the windows might prevent our getting cut by shattering glass if a V-1 landed too close. However, nothing could protect us from a direct hit. Although some landed within a few blocks, none damaged the hospital that night. My nurse said the attacks on Liege had become more intense beginning December 16 (the beginning of the Battle of the Bulge). She also told me Antwerp was receiving similar treatment.

The arrival of new patients triggered conversations with nearby ward mates. Most of the men, shocked by the strength and surprise of the German attack, were anxious to piece together what was really happening. Hospital personnel asked many questions, too. The medics were concerned about reports of Germans overrunning American positions to the immediate south and east of Elsenborn. They were relieved to learn that my battalion had beaten back several major German assaults on Höfen. "When I left this morning," I reassured them, "we still held the town." I added that the 99th Division held Elsenborn as of this morning, but the situation looked frantic.

As December 19 ended, I fell asleep quickly, despite the tensions caused by the V-1 blitz attack. My state of fatigue was overwhelming. I didn't know it at the time, but the outcome of the Battle of the Bulge had already been settled. According to General Bradley, the Germans had counted on a speedy breakthrough. They failed because of the many courageous small-unit stands made by rifle companies occupying the front-line foxholes and by powerful and accurate American artillery support. Sepp Dietrich (commander of the German Sixth Panzer Army), under Allied interrogation after the war, acknowledged that his offensive "had already slumped fatally behind schedule by December 19. Thus was the offensive doomed to failure, only three days after its start. . . ."[3]

I awoke the next morning (December 20) amazingly refreshed from a restful sleep, despite the buzz bombs. To sleep in a bed and have good food seemed like the ultimate luxury. The noise outside was a worry, but we had heard guns firing and shells falling day and night for weeks. Unfortunately, many of the men were hurting despite painkillers. I was lucky. The only impediment to my comfort was the large cast on my right leg.

I could not fully enjoy my good fortune because I missed my buddies, worried about what they were experiencing, and felt guilty about being away. Many of the others in the ward felt the same way.

After breakfast, I was told I was leaving by ambulance for the Liege railroad station where I and many others in the ward would be placed on a hospital train bound for Paris.

Paris? We couldn't believe what the nurse said. Since we had no personal belongings other than the mud-caked clothes we wore, we had nothing to pack, not even a toothbrush. German POW litter bearers arrived to carry us out of the hospital.

The streets of gloomy Liege were crowded with ambulances— clear evidence of the seriousness of the German attack only twenty-five miles to the east. Belgians stood along the sidewalks watching the ambulance parade crawling to the railroad station. They feared a return of the Germans. More German prisoners of war waited to carry us inside a long hospital train generously marked with red crosses on white backgrounds.

The medics divided us by those who could walk and those

who could not. The nonambulatory, like me, were carried to cars from which the seats had been stripped. Litters hung on each side of the cars.

The medics were jumpy because several hospital trains on this track had been strafed by German planes since December 16. Luftwaffe pilots were shooting at anything moving on the Liege-to-Paris line.

This train reminded me of the long hospital train we had seen from our truck convoy on the way to the front six weeks earlier. My litter hung close to a window, giving me a good view of the train's length. It picked up speed as it moved out into the open countryside. When we hit rough spots in the track, some of my companions groaned. Many were given sedation, and most fell into deep sleep. Many carried with them ghastly memories of battle.

I awoke about four hours later as the train approached Paris. I could not believe that I was lying on a litter, about to enter a city I had dreamed about. My high school French teachers had succeeded in promoting the wonders of Paris, and of France. So I was full of excitement and great anticipation. The backsides of worn, five-to-seven story apartment buildings lined the track for several miles before we eased into the Gare du Nord station. I saw no signs of war damage.

The train stopped amid a scene of great commotion. Scores of older French men in tattered overalls and dark berets were lined up waiting with litters. They smoked cigarettes so short they appeared burned into their lips. They came aboard, covered us with olive drab GI blankets, and started carrying us into the bedlam on the platform. They yelled back and forth with American nurses and medics, who spoke an Americanized version of French. Our brief medical records, created in the last two days, lay on our blankets.

While waiting to move us into ambulances, our litter bearers set us gently on the cold sidewalk. Our clothes still carried the caked mud of the front line. The scene was fit for a Hollywood movie. To the few passing Parisians, already aware of a scary German advance in Belgium, the sight of so many wounded American soldiers probably set off fears that the Americans were falling apart.

A line of U.S. Army ambulances, so long it disappeared out of sight, waited as the litter bearers placed four litters inside each vehicle. Our American ambulance driver tried to rouse our interest by becoming a tour guide en route to the hospital. I was thrilled by how much I could see out the back doors and through the front windshield.

Our friendly driver pointed to Galeries Lafayette and Au Printemps (two major department stores), the Opera de Paris, and the Madeleine Church. Then we drove out into the middle of the grand Place de la Concorde. At the Obelisk of Luxor, our driver told us that General de Gaulle had brought the pillar to Paris from Egypt. I winced, since my French teachers had told me (correctly) that it was a gift to King Louis Philippe in 1831.

Next, we headed west, up the broad, tree-lined Champs-Elysees. I made special note of the traffic. There was virtually none, except for ambulances. When we reached the high end of the wide avenue, our driver circled the Arc de Triomphe twice. From that moment, I could never forget the heroic figures adorning the four corners of the giant monument. We turned south, crossed the Seine, and entered the suburb of St. Cloud. In minutes, we approached the entrance to a modern hospital that looked much too good for the infantry. My road to the rear from Höfen came to an end—at least for now.

13 • Christmas Holidays, 1944

ONE AFTER ANOTHER, THE AMBULANCES DROVE UP TO the hospital unloading zone in St. Cloud. Inside, an attractive, sympathetic army nurse checked my medical records and asked basic questions. When she asked my age, I answered "twenty-two." (Actually, I was twenty-three. I had forgotten I had a birthday while on the front.)

She pulled the blanket off me, revealing what I wore to the front-line aid station the previous day. She looked appalled at my mud-caked field jacket and wool pants, cut back on my right leg to make room for the cast. "How long have you been wearing these clothes?" she asked. "I never took them off since we left England on November 1," I replied. "I haven't had a shower for seven weeks, either. My last shave was six days ago." She pulled back my shirt collar, revealing the top part of my long johns. She noted that the cloth appeared "glued" to my skin. "My God," she said, "you've been living a primitive life!"

I don't know why she seemed surprised. A high percentage of

the casualties coming into army hospitals in Europe were from front-line infantry rifle platoons. Most looked just as messy as I did. Some looked much worse.

At this point, the newly arrived wounded and injured went separate ways, depending on what was wrong with them. French civilian litter bearers carried me off to the orthopedics ward for enlisted men. (Officers were taken to special wards.)

In my new ward, at least one-third of the men lay trapped in various traction devices. Many had casts on their arms and legs. Those who were awake watched curiously as two nurses carefully moved me off the litter and onto a wonderfully clean bed with glorious white sheets. As in Liege, the unspoken and unofficial rank in this room was determined by the seriousness of the wound or injury and how it was obtained. Low man on the totem pole was the rear echelon guy who fell off a barstool in Paris and hurt his back.

The men here did not talk much. Most were fresh from the front and exhausted. In addition to their wounds and injuries, they were suffering from shock because of the drastic change in their lives. They lay in bed sedated, drifting in and out of sleep.

A well-decorated Christmas tree at the end of the ward surprised me. I did not realize Christmas was near. My Christmas present, I quickly decided, was making it to this hospital in one piece.

A nurse came by to introduce herself. She gave me a urinal and told me to make myself comfortable. "A doctor will check you shortly," she advised. Within a half-hour a doctor appeared. He cut off my leg cast to study my swollen black and blue ankle. After twisting it different ways, causing intense pain, he told the nurse he would check me out more carefully the next day. "Meanwhile," he added, "help him get out of those filthy clothes." He ordered the nurse to get X-rays of my injury. In lieu of the cast, he placed a tight bandage around my ankle and told me not to walk on it.

Taking off my field jacket, shirt, and pants was easy. I did that mostly by myself, but the long johns stuck to my skin. I was able to peel off most of it, except for hard-to-reach parts on my back. The nurse had to cut with scissors and peel those parts off of me. "Tomorrow," she exclaimed, "you get a bath." She tossed me a hospital gown and disappeared.

For others in my ward, who suffered from terrible wounds and injuries and the results of surgery, life was a greater ordeal than ever. Two beds were closed off with shields to give privacy to men in critical condition. One man had both legs amputated. We cried for him.

At least 90 percent of the men in this ward came from front-line combat activity. Most were from the Battle of the Bulge. Several were near death. I thought I had been through hell. But it was nothing compared with what many soldiers had endured. I make one big exception to this conclusion: Few on the American Western Front suffered more from the cold than my 2nd Platoon.

Our mood brightened with the arrival of a hot dinner in the hands of cheerful young French civilians, mostly girls. The stew and powdered potatoes with gravy tasted wonderful. Even more elegant was the dessert, a small dish of real ice cream, the first we had tasted since we left the States. That seemed like years ago.

Eager to test my French again, I got into a short conversation with two of the civilians. They declared great dislike for Germans. I think some French people felt they gained favor with Americans by saying this.

I kept repeating to myself my appreciation for a good roof over my head. (I still do, more than fifty years later, especially on rainy or cold nights.) After taking a sleeping pill and reading for an hour, I fell into another deep sleep.

The army operated a highly effective medical evacuation system that delivered me safely to Paris. It deserves high praise—from the actions of Warner Anthony, my platoon medic at the front, to the medical personnel and their facilities in Liege and Paris. I received first-class care.

General Eisenhower proudly called the army medical service "efficient." He pointed out that "the ratio of fatalities per one hundred wounded in the American Army of World War II was less than one-half the ratio of World War I." He cited several reasons: penicillin, sulfa drugs, blood plasma, and an efficient system of evacuation.[1]

ON OUR SIDE. On December 21, the Germans surrounded U.S. troops in Bastogne, Belgium, forty air miles southwest of Höfen-Monschau.[2]

Hospital wake-up came early. So did the doctor. "No fracture," he said, "but the ligaments holding your ankle together have been badly torn. It will take longer to heal than a fracture."

Following breakfast, an American male orderly removed the bandage from my foot and helped me hobble on crutches to a small room containing nothing but a deep bathtub filled with clear, hot water. I smelled like a pigpen. However, I was not infested with lice, as were many infantry comrades.

With the orderly's help, I slipped into the water for the first hot bath in more than five months (the previous time was on home leave in July). This was the most luxurious feeling I have ever had. I was left alone to soak and wash off the grime that encrusted my body. For at least ten minutes I just lay there, luxuriating. I raised my feet out of the water to compare the injured foot with the good one. My good foot stood straight up, but my injured right foot flopped over to the left at a sharp angle. The ligaments were not holding it in place.

After about forty-five minutes, the orderly returned with a wheelchair. The filth was now in the water and not on me. I could run a comb through my hair, which had been tangled and matted with gluelike muck.

My angelic-looking nurse said the doctor had ordered a new cast for my foot and lower leg. She brought me hot water, shaving cream, and a razor, but I was reluctant to shave. My beard was a souvenir of the front. I felt terribly proud of being a BAR gunner in an infantry rifle company.

The next day, I felt up to conversing with the soldiers near my bed. We talked most of the day, comparing notes on our battle-field experiences. We spoke with great admiration and pride of our squads and platoons, all except two replacements who were wounded a day or two after joining their outfits. They had not had time to become acquainted with anyone in their new units or to acquire unit pride.

Nearly everyone had wild tales to tell. Many had escaped death by fractions of an inch—bullets just missing their heart or arteries, bullets creasing their skull without smashing it, shell fragments stopping next to vital organs. Shell fragments and bullets had caused most of the injuries. The ghastliest wounds, loss of one or more limbs, resulted from encounters with various sorts of devilish mines. One unlucky soldier had lost both legs and one arm, but he was in intensive care.

I felt embarrassed to tell about my torn ligaments. I almost wished I had a bullet hole for these show-and-tell sessions. Yet many of the bullet- and shell-fragment victims could walk, and I could not. Although two men in my conversation group were in traction, they exhibited high morale.

We complained endlessly, and bitterly, about lack of decent winter shoes and clothing. Some in my ward had trench foot and its close cousin, frostbite-damaged feet and toes. I quickly learned that frostbite destroys body tissue as a result of freezing. Trench foot, a painful, inflamed condition, results from long pe-riods of exposure to cold and dampness.

In two cases of extreme frostbite in my ward, the toes looked like dried black prunes. The only answer for both men was am-putation of all their toes, thus making walking difficult for the rest of their lives. Some trench foot/frostbite victims lay in bed with their feet exposed at all times to prevent any pressure from blankets. Others had wire tentlike structures to lift blankets and sheets above their feet.

Despite the wide variety of discomforts, many of these wounded soldiers retained their sense of humor. In addition, the good nature of most of our army nurses, all second and first lieutenants, helped greatly. They kidded us, and we kidded them.

At night, when the lights went out, I lay on my back and enjoyed the quiet and warmth of my bed. I reviewed the previous days on the front, determined to remember details. I kept saying to myself: "Don't forget what happened, how bad it was, the suffering, the dead and wounded. Life on the front should never be forgotten!" An occasional groan or wince of pain interrupted the quiet. The few who had nightmares usually cried out in the early morning hours.

Meanwhile, six thousand miles away in California, this telegram arrived at my parents' front door in Pasadena: "Regret to inform you your son Private First Class George W. Neill was slightly wounded in action 19 December in Germany. You will be advised as reports of condition are received. Dunlop Acting Adjutant General."

I wrote to my parents on December 23. Although I told them that I was in a hospital somewhere in France, censorship would not permit me to explain why. The postmark on the envelope indicated that the army postal service held it in Paris until January 18. That meant my parents had no word from me for about six weeks. Previously, they had received at least two letters a week. During the same period at home, word of the German attack in the Ardennes dominated the news.

My letters were not the only ones held up. Letters from wounded and injured GIs in Belgian, French, and British hospitals were similarly delayed. The army apparently did not want to panic the home front at the time of the Battle of the Bulge with news of large numbers of wounded and injured men pouring into hospitals. That, the army thought, would damage civilian morale. Since the public thought the war was almost over, the army did not want the Germans to know the large numbers of casualties their offensive had caused.

On Christmas Eve, Parisian children's choirs strolled through the halls and wards of my hospital. They sang traditional carols—and some we had never heard before. Their young voices produced eerie echoes as they approached our ward and as they moved to other wards down the hall. I felt the true spirit of Christmas. I don't know whether these children knew they were singing to young men who had helped keep the war from returning to Paris this yuletide. They sang so earnestly, however, that I think they knew. By now, most of the approximately thirty men in my orthopedics ward were from the Battle of the Bulge. Several of us had misty eyes as the children departed. I doubted if I would ever experience another Christmas Eve with such poignant feelings.

In Höfen on Christmas Eve, Pfc. Warren Wilson wrote: "The fellows [in the freezing foxholes] are calling up and down the line wishing each other a Merry Christmas. It is a very pretty night with the ground covered with snow."[3]

In a German hospital, the Christmas spirit prevailed for Bernard Macay, B Company, 393rd Infantry Regiment, 99th Division. Wounded in the back, legs, and feet by shell fragments on December 18 and captured by the enemy two days later, he was in an American ward on the second floor of a German hospital at Attendorn (near Dusseldorf).[4]

"This day before Christmas brought back memories of home," he wrote. "We [American wounded prisoners of war] all reminisced about Christmas in the states. We felt pretty blue. All through the day, German officers brought their wives and girlfriends to look at us. I guess they presumed we were some kind of animals and should be observed only from a distance for safety reasons. One of our fellows had his right thumb and half his arm blown off. Part of the treatment was exposure to the air, so at times his unbandaged arm looked like a slab of raw meat. It really was a hideous sight."

In late afternoon, the American patients heard more German soldiers coming down the hall with their wives and girlfriends. The American with the battered arm dangled it out of the doorway. Upon seeing it, the women did an about-face and went screaming down the hall. That gave the Americans a good laugh.

As darkness descended, hospital staff hosted a Christmas Eve party downstairs in a ward full of wounded German soldiers. "We could hear the singing and laughter," Macay said. "That only made us more homesick." At 11 P.M., the Americans were surprised when a German nurse came upstairs and invited them to come downstairs and join the party. Amazed, the Americans hesitated but then, feeling they had nothing to lose, accepted. "It was quite a gala affair. The women wore long, elegant evening gowns," Macay said. "We first thought we were being put on display again, but we soon discarded that thought because of their genuine warmth."

Even more surprising, Macay said, "the Germans asked us to sing 'Silent Night' in English. They, in turn, responded by singing it in German. We stumbled through a few bars of 'O Tannenbaum,' sang other Christmas songs in German and English, enjoyed some dessert, and had a good time." Macay said he would never forget this Christmas Eve. For an hour or two, both Americans and Germans made a mockery of war by displaying friendship instead of hate.

Another bit of Christmas cheer occurred during the frenzy of the Battle of the Bulge in German-surrounded Bastogne, Belgium. During visits with his troops, Brig. Gen. Anthony McAuliffe, assistant commander of the 101st Airborne Division, heard male voices singing Christmas carols. He was near the city prison, and inside were four hundred German prisoners of war.

Lester David, a correspondent for *Stars and Stripes*, described what happened. "During a brief lull in the almost constant German bombardment, the general heard 'O Tannenbaum' and several other popular Christmas songs. Just as night enclosed the city, the loveliest of all carols: 'Stille nacht (silent night), heilige nacht, alles schlaft, einsam wacht.'"[5]

McAuliffe stopped. He went inside with a worried aide and circulated among the POWs. David said the German soldiers, "at first astounded, recovered and began ribbing the general. There was no arrogance, no nastiness. It was almost like a coach of a football team coming into an arch rival's dressing room and being told his boys won't win." One kid said to McAuliffe, "We'll be out of here soon, general, and you'll be in." Another said, "It's nice and cozy in here, general. You'll like it."

When the POWs quieted down, McAuliffe told them, "I just came in to wish you all a Merry Christmas." Amid silence, McAuliffe turned and left the enclosure. As he reached the gate, he heard shouts behind him. "Merry Christmas . . . Froehliche Weinachten."

In contrast to Christmas celebrations for some of us, one of the most tragic events involving Americans in the European war unfolded in the English Channel. It involved the sinking on Christmas Eve of the troopship *Leopoldville* and the deaths of 802 American soldiers from the 66th Infantry Division. The men followed behind us in the barracks at Dorchester and were being rushed to the front as reinforcements in the Battle of the Bulge. The *Leopoldville* was torpedoed by a German U-boat approximately five miles off the Cherbourg coast. The Americans drowned because of a combination of miscommunication and ineptitude. When I learned about it years later, I finally understood the dangers that lurked in the Channel when my 99th Division crossed it unprotected only six weeks earlier.[6]

ON THE OTHER SIDE. On December 24, the German Ardennes offensive reached just outside Dinant, Belgium, about seventy miles west of its December 16 starting point. (Located on the Meuse River, Dinant became the high tide for the German advance in the Battle of the Bulge.)

Christmas was a happy day for our ward of battered soldiers. The Red Cross left stockings on our beds; WACs (Women's Army Corps) sang carols and visited with us; and the hospital fed us lavishly. My thoughts returned, however, to the front and my buddies still there. In the early evening, my nurse told me that some survivors of a disaster off the French coast arrived at our hospital (probably survivors of the *Leopoldville*). She did not know any details.

The day after Christmas, the censor finally permitted us to write home about where we were and what had happened to us. The following letter ended much worry for my parents:

> Somewhere in France
> From a U.S. Army Hospital
> December 26, 1944

Dear Mother and Dad,

It is now possible to tell you that I have been in a hospital here in France since December 20.

My injury is nothing really serious—just my bad right ankle torn up a bit. I'm sure that the time I hurt my ankle in high-jumping left me with a vulnerable weak ankle. My doctor agrees.

It will take a little time to reach infantry standards again. My outfit is still "Somewhere in Germany."

> Love, George

On Christmas day I remembered the bad injury of my right ankle during high-jumping practice at Pasadena Junior College in 1941. I had no further trouble with the ankle, even in basic training and advanced infantry training at Camp Maxey. I had

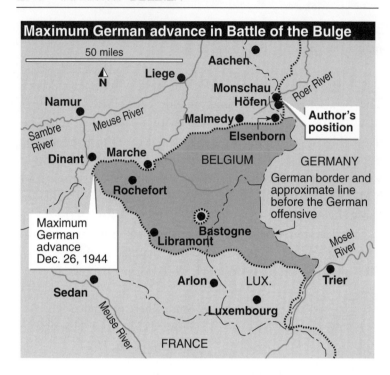

Maximum German advance in Battle of the Bulge

50 miles

N

Aachen

Liege

Monschau
Höfen

Roer River

Namur

Meuse River

Malmedy

Author's
position

Sambre
River

Elsenborn

Dinant

Marche

BELGIUM

GERMANY

German border and
approximate line
before the German
offensive

Rochefort

Maximum
German
advance
Dec. 26, 1944

Bastogne
Libramont

Mosel
River

Arlon

LUX.

Trier

Sedan

Luxembourg

Meuse River

FRANCE

forgotten all about it. As it turned out, my earlier injury and my
fall on the night of December 18–19 may have saved my life. I
know I would have been on the patrol a month later that took
the lives of two of my best friends. It amazes me how little things
that happen early in one's life can affect what happens years later.

On December 28, news services reported that prices of stocks
on the New York Stock Exchange reached their highest level
since 1937 as a result of the German Ardennes Offensive. Apparently, with the German timetable now badly behind schedule
and another big defeat facing them, investors thought the end
of the war had been speeded up. In reaction to this news, I
offered this comment in a letter to my parents: "I'm glad to
see someone profited from the attack." My sarcastic remark re-
flected the hostility I was feeling at the time about civilians'

complaints over gas and minor food rationing; what little food U.S. civilians were having to do without paled in comparison to what front-line soldiers and civilians in the war zone were doing without. My hostilities were shared by other soldiers overseas. At this time, I felt very uncomfortable living such a soft existence in a warm, dry hospital. News from the 99th usually triggered this reaction.

On New Year's Day, no one in my hospital ward was sorry to see 1944 fade away. I expected 1945 to treat me much better. However, for those still on the front and for those in hospitals who expected to return to the front, there was much trepidation. There was good reason for this, as we found out later. By the end of April 1945, my 2nd Platoon was almost a completely different outfit from the one I left in late December. Virtually everyone I knew was either in a hospital or buried at Henri-Chapelle.

On January 5, I got a big surprise. My wonderful nurse told me I was slated to go to England the following day in a hospital plane, along with several other men in the ward. The hospital needed space for the large increase in casualties coming from the front.

The weather did not look good for flying. Snow fell so heavily it blocked the view out of our hospital window. Shortly after breakfast on January 6, young French litter bearers arrived to take us to a line of ambulances waiting in front of the hospital. The snow had stopped falling, but a low, dark overcast blanketed the sky.

As we were carried out of the ward, our friends and nurses gave us a hearty goodbye—a goodbye like that of long-time friends, not of people who had been together for only a few days. We had shared a never-to-be-forgotten episode in our lives, including a special Christmas.

The ambulances retraced the route of my arrival in Paris. Traffic was heavier than on December 20 when I arrived. More civilian cars and buses sloshed up and down the streets, reflecting fading fears of a German return.

Near Place de la Concorde, my ambulance turned south toward Orly Field. The light gray buildings and gray streets lined with leafless trees contrasted beautifully with the white snow. Civilians walked hunched over, with their coat collars pulled up to protect them from the freezing wind. The famous outdoor cafes were empty.

Most of the chimneys in residential areas were smokeless. Behind those picturesque gray walls, hundreds of thousands of Parisians were cold and hungry. Their lives epitomized the plight of most civilians who lived in large European cities during the bitter winter of 1944 – 45.

When we reached the Orly runway, I saw a line of two-motored DC-3 hospital planes, clearly marked with red crosses. After my plane was loaded with litters, the pilot took off into low clouds. It was my second trip in an airplane. Upon reaching the English Channel, the plane started bucking fiercely. Several men got sick. Few talked. Rough flying continued until we landed near Blandford, Dorset. I breathed a sigh of relief. (In similar weather three weeks earlier, Maj. Glenn Miller, the conductor of the most popular swing band in the United States, flew across the Channel in the opposite direction, from England to Paris. But he didn't make it to the other side. Since no wreckage was found, investigators concluded that his plane crashed into the Channel.)

14 • A Time for Healing

JANUARY 6–APRIL 8, 1945

THE RAF AIRFIELD WHERE MY AMBULANCE PLANE touched down was only a short distance from my new home. No snow here, just cold and wet.

Located out in the country, U.S. Army Hospital 4117 looked like a recently built army hospital back home. And, much to my surprise, I was back in Dorset, only eighteen miles from Dorchester. The nearest town was Blandford. I was one of 125,000 American military personnel in U.S. Army hospitals in Britain at that time.[1] Many were Battle of the Bulge casualties or victims of trench foot, frostbite, pneumonia, and other cold weather ailments. U.S. Army figures revealed that twenty-three thousand American soldiers were evacuated with trench foot from the Western Front in November and December. Almost all of them came from infantry rifle platoons.[2]

Several men from my ward in Paris joined me in an orthopedic ward. As soon as I was placed in bed, the two men on both sides introduced themselves. Especially friendly, they wanted to know my division, my location on the front, what happened to me, and how we fared with the Germans.

One of my new friends came from a glider infantry company in the 82nd Airborne Division. He was shot through the shoulder, splintering bones, in the Ardennes. A cast covered his arm and shoulder. My other new friend was from the 80th Infantry Division in Patton's Third Army. He had several wounds—none critical—caused by shell fragments.

A third new neighbor was a soldier from the 99th Division's 394th Regiment. He had a fractured arm caused by small arms fire. He talked about the desperate plight of the men in his battalion's rifle companies. They were overwhelmed by Germans on December 16 and 17, and many were killed, wounded, or missing.

When a truck backfired just outside our ward, each of us discovered that he was not the only one oversensitive to loud noises that sounded like shells exploding. All the front-line veterans jumped. Thanks to the truck backfire, we got to know Manley, our ward's only representative from the gung-ho 101st Airborne Division.

Manley, a blue-eyed twenty-year-old sergeant, began yelling: "Look at that ack-ack, men! Look at that ack-ack!" (By "ack-ack" he meant bursting antiaircraft shells.) The backfire reminded him of the antiaircraft fire he had encountered in Normandy and in Operation Market Garden in the Netherlands.

Manley had been wounded just before German panzer units surrounded his division in the Belgian town of Bastogne. At first his yell startled us. We thought he had gone out of his mind. As we watched him, however, we noticed a subtle, in-command smile on his sober face. His was the yell of a macho paratrooper excited by the loud noise. A few days later, he bellowed a blood-curdling "Geronimo," introducing us to the scream his company used when it jumped from transport planes. The 101st Division called itself the "screaming eagles." If Manley was any indication, the division was well named.

Also in my new ward was a talkative buck sergeant from the 106th Infantry Division, located on the front immediately south of my 99th Division. I'll call him Sergeant X. He revealed that the 106th collapsed only four days after the Battle of the Bulge began, leaving the 99th in a dangerous situation on its south flank. I now listened to him with great interest. He had trench foot and a gunshot wound through his left foot. As with other trench foot victims, his sheet and blanket were held above his feet by a tentlike frame to prevent pressure on them. His face was pale and his beard so dark it left a shadow even after he shaved. He had a frantic look about him.

Located directly across the aisle from me, Sergeant X sat up in bed as he recounted what happened to him and his outfit. "We arrived on the front line from Camp Atterbury, Indiana, on December 11–12," he began. "We took over approximately twenty miles of the eerie Ardennes Front from the 2nd Division. We moved into its foxholes and dugouts, immediately south of the 99th Division. It was a world of ice, snow, and mud."

Sergeant X did not know that his division's three regiments, the 422nd, 423rd, and 424th, had been assigned to hold a vulnerable hole punched through the Siegfried Line when American infantry arrived at the German border in September. Defending the breakthrough, as ordered by Generals Eisenhower and Bradley, left the three regiments protruding up to eight miles into the enemy line. If the enemy turned aggressive, the 106th faced a serious danger of being cut off from the rest of the American line, a situation deplored by Maj. Gen. Alan W. Jones, commanding officer of the 106th.

Before the 106th knew the landscape, the Germans began their great attack. Almost immediately, the 106th was in trouble.

The Germans realized the 106th's vulnerability and launched a two-pronged pincer attack. Both succeeded. The north pincer left wide open the south flank of the 99th Division and the north flank of the 106th Division. The south pincer cut the 423rd Regiment off from the 424th.

Sergeant X continued: "Enemy patrols and artillery had cut most telephone lines. Radios had become almost useless because of enemy jamming of the 106th's radio frequencies. By the morning of December 17, we were nearly surrounded, and later in the day the German trap snapped shut. We tried to break out, but the enemy beat us back."

The next day, Sergeant X said, his squad lost contact with its platoon and company. "To save ourselves, we split into groups of two or three and headed west, hoping to find the new American line." Two riflemen joined Sergeant X. After surviving two nights outside in below-freezing weather without sleeping bags, they reached a quickly organized American infantry company composed of stragglers from the 106th. A first lieutenant immediately drafted them into one of the company's rifle platoons.

Sergeant X, now an assistant squad leader, soon found himself in action with advancing Germans. "During an exchange of rifle fire," he said, "I was hit in the foot." A medic heard his yells for help and evacuated him.[3]

I asked Sergeant X what happened to his regiment. "I think it surrendered. That's the rumor I heard." The grapevine was correct. Surrounded, two of the 106th's three regiments, the 423rd and Sergeant X's 422nd along with attached artillery units, surrendered to the Germans on December 19. As a result, at least seven thousand officers and men were taken prisoners. The figure was probably closer to eight or nine thousand, an official Army report said. This was the most serious reverse suffered by American arms during 1944–45 in the European theater.[4]

By December 30, the 106th reported that it had only 5,005 men on its roster, compared to 14,024 on December 15. In addition to those who surrendered, the division reported 415 killed in action, 1,254 wounded, and 529 lost to trench foot. Few American divisions had ever lost so many men so quickly.

When we woke up the next morning, Sergeant X's bed was empty. I asked my nurse what happened to him. "He's gone." He was given sodium pentothal, known in the army as "truth serum," to find out if the bullet wound through his foot was self-inflicted. He confessed that he had shot himself, and he was moved to a prison ward. We never saw Sergeant X again.[5]

On January 11, the army admitted for the first time that the 99th Division was on the front line. It lifted a news blackout in effect since September. *Stars and Stripes* published its first pictures and information about some of the 99th's combat successes.

Our hospital life was enriched every day by the best radio had to offer, including big-name American programs hosted by celebrities such as Jack Benny, Fred Allen, and Bob Hope. Thanks to the BBC, we enjoyed a mixture of music, comedy, and news. One of the songs it played often, "We'll Meet Again," sung by popular British singer Vera Lynn, haunted me then, and it haunts me now. Reflecting wartime feelings, it goes like this:

> *We'll meet again,*
> *don't know where,*
> *don't know when,*
> *but I know we'll meet again some sunny day.*
> *Keep smiling through,*
> *just like you always do,*
> *till the blue skies drive the dark clouds far away.*

These words may sound corny today to many people, but combined with the music, the times, and Vera Lynn's voice, they brought tears to many sentimental GIs—including me.

While we basked in the warmth of a hospital ward, our buddies along the front continued to suffer from extreme cold. Lt. (formerly Sgt.) Richard Byers, 99th Division artillery, wrote to his wife about the weather on January 21 at Elsenborn Ridge, ten miles south of Höfen:

> A fairly warm day here is 20 degrees F. Lately the snow and wind have been enough to make a stove-warmer out of me for the rest of my life. Recently it was my unhappy duty to arise at 5:30 in the god-awful morning . . . and struggle 300 yards to our observation post through three feet of snow against a hurricane wind blowing stinging sleet. I sat there for four hours in a snow-filled hole while the wind covered me quickly and completely with a three-inch layer of snow.
>
> Miller, my radio operator, and I started out at 6 A.M. in the worst storm I have ever seen. We became lost three times and had to start over again, gaining no more than 50 yards each time.
>
> Finally, we called for a guide to come down from our OP and lead us up. By sheer luck we met him and he led us back up to the vicinity of the dugout, where he became lost. We wandered around in the blizzard within 25 yards of the hole for a half-hour before his partner inside the OP happened to see us and yelled us in.[6]

On January 28, the Battle of the Bulge was officially over—forty-four days after it began. It was the "greatest battle ever fought by the United States Army."[7]

The American front in the Ardennes had returned to its approximate position of December 15, the day before the Germans launched their offensive.

Surprisingly, statistics on American casualties resulting from the Battle of the Bulge vary greatly from four of the best sources over the course of fifty years, from 1948 to 1998:

1. In 1948, General Eisenhower put total American casualties at 77,000, which includes 8,000 deaths, 48,000 wounded, and 21,000 captured or missing in action.[8]

2. In 1951, General Bradley put total American casualties at 59,000, which includes 6,700 deaths, 33,400 wounded, and 18,900 captured or missing in action. (In addition, Bradley stated that 15,000 soldiers were disabled by frost-bitten feet or trench foot during the forty-four days of the battle.)[9]

3. In 1984, Charles MacDonald put the total American casualties from the Battle of the Bulge at 81,000, which includes 19,000 deaths and 15,000 captured or missing in action. No specific figures are provided for wounded.[10]

4. In 1998, the U.S. Army Center of Military History cited casualties from the Bulge *and* Operation Northwind, a concurrent limited German diversionary attack on January 1 in Alsace, France. The center does not have separate figures specifically for the Ardennes and Alsace battles. The casualties in Alsace represent perhaps 12 percent of the total. American casualties for both actions totaled 105,289, which includes 19,246 deaths, 62,489 wounded, and 23,554 captured or missing in action.[11]

One conclusion is commonly accepted: the Germans lost significantly more than the Americans. Eisenhower used his field commanders' estimate of 120,000. (The Germans admitted to a loss of 90,000.)[12] U.S. Army historian Charles MacDonald concluded that the killed, wounded, and captured on the German side totaled "at least" 100,000. No official German figures are available.[13]

When American and German casualties are combined, the total reaches nearly 200,000—a huge figure for forty-four days of combat. Grave diggers worked overtime on both sides of the front. Hospitals and prisoner-of-war camps were bulging. A flood of telegrams went out to next of kin.

In the 99th Division alone, 465 men lost their lives in the Battle of the Bulge. Of these, a majority—268—fell in just four days, December 16–19. The division evacuated 2,524 men for medical reasons between December 1 and December 31, which includes the first fifteen days of the battle. The largest categories break down as follows: wounded/injured, 850; trench foot, 681; combat exhaustion, 261.[14]

After seven weeks of no mail, I received an avalanche of forty letters on February 3, all written after my injury. It felt good to know so many cared. The mail also brought some bad news about a friend, Bob McNeill. He was listed as missing in action during the first days of the Battle of the Bulge. He had been in my section at Tarleton College and sat next to me in American history. My mother got this bad news from Bob's mother, one of four mothers of 99ers in the Los Angeles area with whom she kept in contact. (McNeill was later declared killed in action.) Two letters were from former teachers at McKinley Junior High School in Pasadena. (Altogether, over a period of nineteen months, I received two long letters from my English teacher and six from my home room teacher. I appreciated their thoughtfulness.)

February 4 was a day of happy anticipation for Pfc. Harry S. Arnold and his comrades in E Company, 393rd Regiment, 99th Division. Their leaders scheduled the first showers for the company since the 99th left England on October 31.

Arnold's battalion moved off the front for the first time in three months to regroup, receive replacements and fresh clothing, and wash off an accumulation of filth. The men loaded aboard trucks to go to Verviers for their showers. "This was perhaps our fondest desire, for the collection of months of grime and sweat was in untold layers on skin and clothes," Arnold said. "God! To be clean again. The prospect was delicious!"[15]

Belgians along the way waved happily and threw whatever

they had to give to Arnold and the men with him. The trip was not all happiness because many of the men had urgent and frequent attacks of diarrhea. Supplications to the drivers to stop the trucks for relief periods were ignored, and the convoy charged along roads and through towns with dozens of bare behinds hanging over side rails and tailgates. "So much for the dignity of war," Arnold declared.

When the trucks reached Verviers, these heroes of the front—with their frayed uniforms, unkempt hair, bullet-ridden helmets, and hollow eyes—offered a stark contrast to the garrison (rear echelon) soldiers who walked the streets with a certain stride in their freshly cleaned and pressed uniforms. "They scarcely noticed our passing," Arnold asserted. "Some regarded us stonily and damn near shook with revulsion. This reception sans compassion or cheer began to sink into the marrow of our souls." As a further indignity, the combat veterans were told they could not use the shower facilities because this was shower-day for the garrison troops who lived in Verviers. "Never mind that they had showered three days earlier, and we had last showered more than three months ago. This rebuke shall always remain in my memory as one of the most callous and unpalatable of my life."

Arnold and his comrades could not believe that their officers apparently gave no thought to arguing the point. "Had I been the officer in charge of our group, we would have been in the showers in an hour by employing whatever means necessary (at gun point) and at whatever cost to my personal career. Moreover, the Verviers garrison would have been left fully cognizant that they existed for one reason only—to support the front-line troops 100 percent."

Two weeks later, Arnold and his buddies finally got their coveted showers, just before they joined a massive attack to the Rhine. The rest period they had been promised never materialized. Instead, Arnold and his fellow riflemen were used as labor in repairing local roads. They cut, hauled, and placed logs to form corduroy road sections in places impassable with mud. They also were assigned to washing and cleaning the motor pool vehicles. From these incidents, Arnold concluded that the infantryman is "a breed apart" who may have "more in common with enemy infantry across the way than with his own army in the rear."

I received a letter on February 6 that told me something awful had happened to my front-line comrades in the 2nd Platoon on the Höfen front. It came from platoon medic Warner Anthony. Writing with a censor in mind, he told me in carefully constructed language that the platoon was still in the Höfen area, but that the following men had been killed, wounded, or injured: S.Sgt. Bill Jenkins, Sgt. Bill Parmelee, Pfc. Bill Harmon, and Pfc. Ensign ("Willie") Williamsen. Shipman, first scout in my squad, was still okay.[16]

It took me two months to learn some of the highlights of what happened, but more of the story dribbled in during the next fifty years. My suspicions of heartbreaking disaster were eventually totally confirmed. All the men mentioned in Warner's letter went out on a combat patrol on January 25. Their experience illustrates what often happened to those who volunteered or were assigned to such ventures. Although higher commands would classify such an experience as a "minor skirmish," it terrified the men involved.

Those selected for the patrol were ordered to gather in predaylight darkness at a house in Höfen with elements from other L Company units. They were assigned to a combat patrol composed of approximately two squads. Its purpose: to gain information and to eliminate possible German strong points in a hilly, wooded area on L Company's right flank preliminary to the First Army's offensive to the Rhine.

Two of my good friends were assigned to the patrol's first squad: Sgt. Bill Parmelee (from North Hollywood, California, and a friend from Camp Wolters, ASTP, and the 99th) and Pfc.

Ensign Williamsen (from Ogden, Utah, and my squad's second scout). Williamsen's foxhole and dugout had been next to mine in the ravine. Pfc. Duane Shipman (from Eagle Grove, Iowa, and first scout of my squad) and Bill Harmon (from Missouri, and a member of my extended BAR team along the Perlenbach River in November and December) were assigned as scouts for the patrol's second squad.

The men moved out before daybreak (approximately 7:30 A.M.) in single file. Shipman's squad followed the fast-moving lead squad but lost track of it in the darkness. "We were now split into two patrols, a terrible outcome," Shipman said. "Now on our own, we followed the directions given at our briefing. The air temperature was below freezing. No signs of footsteps in the snow to guide us to our lost buddies." [17]

Spread out about thirteen feet apart, Shipman's squad cautiously passed through a strong point in the 3rd Battalion's front line. "No one had seen the squad we were supposed to be following. We moved into no man's land, crossed an icy bridge over the Fuhrtsbach stream, an upstream tributary of the Perlenbach, and began climbing a steep, slippery hill." The snow was three feet deep, making progress difficult.

As first scout, Shipman watched intently for possible danger ahead and for the other part of the patrol. He wondered what eyes were watching them. The only noise to disturb the stillness of the morning was the trudging sound of the men moving through the deep snow. No one spoke. Tension mounted as the men approached possible enemy positions. Shipman noticed the clear sky and the beauty of the forest and hills. "What an awful way to spend such a beautiful morning. I felt just plain scared." He had been around Höfen too long not to recognize the sinister potential of the area.

Shipman's fear escalated when he spotted German anti-personnel mines bound to trees with trip wires strung between them. That probably meant enemy positions nearby. Fortunately, the snow did not completely cover the wires, so the squad skirted the mines without incident. (The tricky Germans often placed trip wires at higher and lower levels, so troops could see some above the snow and not see others hidden under the snow.)

About two hundred feet up the hill, Shipman spotted German log bunkers that the mines were supposed to protect. Were they occupied, or empty? Shipman and Harmon didn't know. But they knew that if German soldiers manned the bunkers they were much too strong for this portion of the patrol to attack. The Germans had the high ground with clear fields of fire. Shipman and Harmon hit the snow and motioned for those following them to do likewise.

Neither side fired a shot. The silent standoff exuded a feeling of eeriness. Shipman knew that many eyes were probably peering at them through the sights of rifles and machine guns, all with tense fingers on triggers.

The wary Americans looked at the fortified area again and again, searching for any signs of the enemy. Like prairie dogs, Shipman and Harmon raised their heads above the snow level and turned to see if the other men were still behind them. They were, but almost invisible in the deep snow. "Do we advance or pull back?" Shipman asked himself. "We were there in view of the Germans for only a short time when we received a signal to withdraw. Harmon and I were now alone. The men behind us had withdrawn without incident."

As the two men started to pull back, Harmon tripped on a wire attached to an antipersonnel mine. The explosion fractured his leg and nearly blew his foot off, making walking impossible. Shipman tried to figure out what to do. He knew he could leave Harmon and notify medics, who could return and carry him back on a stretcher—if the Germans didn't mow them down. Or he could help Harmon through the mine field and out of sight of enemy positions.

"The only solution was to get both of us out of there as quickly as possible," Shipman decided. "I couldn't move too fast, however, because we were lying in the middle of a mine field. Getting out alive required delicate, super-cautious steps."

To make matters worse, Shipman spotted a German officer standing next to a bunker watching him pick up Harmon and carry him back through the mines. The deep snow and the weight of the rifle made the task extremely difficult. "I expected a bullet in my back at any moment," Shipman said. "Incredibly, miraculously, the kindly German elected not to fire. For all the years since, I have wondered who he was, and hoped he survived the war."

Shipman carried Harmon out of enemy view and placed him partially hidden among some small pines. He made Harmon as comfortable as possible and then retraced the patrol's steps until he reached the bridge. In a few minutes more, he was heartily welcomed by the part of the patrol that had withdrawn earlier.

Two riflemen moved out with a stretcher to pick up a lonesome and badly wounded Harmon. Shipman's rescue of Harmon and prompt medical treatment undoubtedly saved his life.[18]

Meanwhile, the lead part of the patrol was in deep trouble. It had crossed another small bridge over the Fuhrtsbach and soon found itself also facing a series of German log bunkers located on high ground with excellent lines of fire.[19]

No one on either side fired a shot. The leader of the patrol's first squad decided to withdraw because the German positions looked too strong for his split patrol. Just as he gave the pullback signal to his men, all half-buried in the deep snow, he heard the explosion triggered by the out-of-sight Harmon. A German officer jumped out of his hole near the bunkers to see what happened.

The patrol leader couldn't resist such an easy target. He and a sergeant with him fired six 30-caliber bullets into the startled German before he hit the ground. The Germans responded with a blaze of rifle and machine gun fire. The Americans returned fire, but the high-ground location of the bunkers gave the Germans a big advantage. The Americans were pinned down. To make matters worse, German mortars began lobbing shells on them.

The situation looked hopeless to some in the patrol. They knew they could not lie in the snow all day, waiting for darkness. They would be frozen or wiped out. Minutes passed. At this point, Ensign Williamsen courageously jumped out of the snow with a hand grenade held between his teeth. He charged the machine gun bunker, firing his rifle from his hip as he tried to run in the deep snow. The German gunner cut him down before he could toss the grenade into the bunker's embrasure.

The patrol leader started to send a message to an L Company observation post calling for artillery and mortar support. Before he could reveal the enemy's location, a German machine gun silenced his radio with a direct hit. Now, he reasoned, the only way to get that vital information to the 3rd Battalion was to go on foot to the OP. He crawled slowly backwards to the rear of his men, and then tried to run toward the OP. But the enemy pinned him down again, just after he crossed the bridge. He was five hundred yards from the OP. The patrol looked doomed.

Fortunately, twenty-year-old Lt. Jackson W. Goss, our former platoon leader and now battalion communications officer, was working at the OP trying to maintain communications with the patrol. He was particularly concerned because he knew and had formerly led most of the men involved. Goss asked the battalion executive officer for permission to go out and help them. At first, he was told "no." But Goss's persistent begging finally resulted in the permission he sought. For his role that followed, Goss was awarded the prestigious Silver Star medal by General Lauer on March 13, 1945.[20]

Taking along with him a radio operator who carried a forty-pound Signal Corps Radio #300, Goss moved as fast as he could in the direction the patrol had taken. Just before getting to the bridge, heavy enemy small-arms fire pinned them down. At this point, Goss decided to go on alone. He strapped the radio on his back and headed for the bridge. Enemy fire whistled all around him.

After crossing the bridge, Goss worked his way toward the sounds of a firefight. On a slightly elevated point, he spotted both the American patrol and the enemy positions. Calling the OP, he gave exact locations of the patrol and the German targets. Before supporting fire arrived, however, two enemy soldiers worked their way to Goss's right flank and fired on him with automatic weapons. One round pierced his radio, making it impossible for him to receive. But he could still transmit.

With the two Germans now firing at him, Goss wheeled around quickly and blazed away with his 45-caliber M3 grease gun, killing both of them. By this time, the barrage he called for, including smoke shells, began exploding near the targets. Despite the danger of his location, Goss remained at this position and continued to direct the barrage, enabling most of the patrol to withdraw safely.

As the men crawled backwards, they noticed that Sgt. Bill Parmelee, Pfc. Ensign Williamsen, and Sgt. Bill Jenkins did not move. When the men reached the American lines at 11:30 A.M., they called for a rescue attempt.

Sgt. Bruce Mather, a member of the retrieving group, told me that he came under intense fire in trying to reach the lifeless Parmelee. He was also unable to approach Williamsen, whose motionless body was lying too near a firing German machine gun. (Parmelee, I learned years later, was killed by a snow-covered German booby trap.)

Warner Anthony (who rescued me on December 19) found Jenkins lying in the snow with a shattered leg. He fixed him up the best he could, then "walked" him to safety. Jenkins put one arm around Anthony's neck to lessen the weight on his bad leg, but he still suffered excruciating pain with every step. Left behind, both Williamsen and Parmelee were reported to their parents as "missing in action."

On the plus side, Colonel Butler and his company commanders learned that the Germans had formidable positions at accurately identified points south of Höfen. Presumably, this information was helpful to planners of the forthcoming offensive to the Rhine.

After the incident, L Company discovered that both bridges the two parts of the patrol had used had been heavily booby-trapped by the Germans. The deadly devices had failed to explode because of water frozen on the triggers.

Goss's Silver Star citation praised "the coolness of this officer as well as his complete disregard for his own personal safety." Goss was not injured in this encounter, but he was slightly wounded twice by enemy fire in later engagements.[21]

After the snow had melted in March, the bodies of Ensign Williamsen, age twenty, and Bill Parmelee, age twenty-one, were found where they had fallen. My mother learned the bad news about Parmelee from her Mothers Network in the Los Angeles area. Mrs. Parmelee, who lived in North Hollywood, was a member of the group. Of the five mothers in the network, two of their sons were killed and the three other sons were hospitalized with wounds or injuries—for a casualty rate of 100 percent.

Williamsen and Parmelee, both ASTPers, were two of our best soldiers. A German soldier, captured a few days after the encounter, told interrogators that he and his comrades praised "that young American [Williamsen] for his fantastic courage" in his effort to knock out their bunker.

The tragedy of this patrol hit me hard. Many times over the years, I have fondly remembered Williamsen and Parmelee and mourned their loss. If I had not had my accident, I would have been with them.

When some war correspondents talked about "quiet" fronts

along the Ardennes and soldiers frolicking in towns and cities behind the lines in November and December 1944, they created the false impression that front-line rifle platoons were on vacation. To the contrary, these men kept going out on scary patrols to probe enemy positions. The enemy's riflemen did the same. Those not on patrol manned freezing front-line foxholes twenty-four hours a day, seven days a week. Their "vacation" came when they were wounded or killed. Few got passes to rear areas. Most war correspondents did not get close enough to the front to know what it was really like. They were seeing and talking to press officers and rear echelon soldiers in the damage-free towns eight to fifteen miles behind the front lines.

ON OUR SIDE. On February 11, after a series of thwarted and excessively costly American attacks that began in October, the U.S. First Army finally gained control of the Roer River dams, thanks to the efforts of the 9th Infantry Division. The attack succeeded because of smarter strategy and an enemy fatally weakened from heavy losses in the Bulge.[22]

With the successful U.S. drive to the Rhine River under way, conditions changed radically in the villages of Höfen and Rohren. Their ordeal of four and a half months in a front-line zone, reminiscent of the stagnant front lines of World War I, finally ended. Overnight, they were no longer on the front line, taking a constant pounding by guns from both sides. This was one of the few areas on the Western Front of World War II that became a war zone for such a long time. Residents returning in late spring found their homes in ruins and their fields and forests full of hidden live mines and booby traps. Nearby Monschau, however, was lucky. It escaped serious damage. All three villages were located inside the Siegfried Line.

Captain Goetcheus, the U.S. military government representative for the Monschau area, took Monschau burgermeister

Walter Scheibler to Höfen to see its condition. Scheibler was the first German civilian to visit Höfen since the Americans had captured it in September. Everywhere, the two men saw U.S. Army engineers filling up craters and moving trees placed across roads. Many West Wall bunkers had been blown up, and many dead cows lay in the fields. The bullet-spattered church and its steeple still stood. Many homes had been burned to the ground, and many others had their roofs blown off. Most of the furniture from the homes sat outside in the snow. Many more dead cows lay within the village.[23]

In the village of Kalterherberg, the damage was much lighter than in Höfen. A mountain of furniture stood in front of the village, placed there by American soldiers. The people from both villages wanted to return home, but the U.S. military would not issue passes.

Meanwhile, in London, the spirit of Christianity received a boost. On February 12, I made another visit to the city on a pass from the hospital. I attended a Sunday service at St. Paul's Cathedral. I described my experience in a letter to my parents. Most of the letter follows:

> Somewhere in England
> U.S. Army Hospital 4117

Dear Mother and Dad,

I returned to the hospital from London this afternoon after an enjoyable 48-hour pass. . . . I attended services at St. Paul's, a beautiful concert at Royal Albert Hall, and had a lively time at the Stage Door Canteen.

After seeing so many V-1 bombs on the front line, their presence in London didn't disturb me. They reminded me of the last time I was in London in October.

I was much impressed by the sermon at St. Paul's. The theme centered on the power of love and justice in dealing with people, no matter how much one despises them for ravages they have done to you. This theme was elaborated in reference to Germany.

Imagine the scene at St. Paul's, bordered on four sides by ruins caused by the German blitz, and itself damaged. Deep in the heart of this destruction, stood a clergyman of the Church of England advocating to his audience, his church and, above all, his country, to stand as a bulwark against the hate campaign now reaching a frenzy against the German people. Justice, not retribution and revenge, should be the theme of our eventual armistice, he declared. Imagine such magnanimity!

My admiration for the ideals of the British people and the Church of England certainly improved. For even a small segment of a war-ravaged people to feel in such a manner indicated greatness to me.

May their voices be heard at the peace table.

Love, George

There is no question in my mind (and in the minds of many historians) that if the vicar's magnanimity had prevailed when the Versailles Treaty was drawn up, Hitler and World War II in Europe never would have happened. Imagine the human misery avoided. Historians have long said that one war often creates another. World War I and its peace treaty certainly sowed the seeds for World War II. And World War II sowed the seeds for the Cold War.

ON OUR SIDE. On February 13 and 14, British and U.S. bombers conducted a devastating raid on Dresden, Germany, causing an estimated thirty-five thousand deaths (reliable figures for injured unavailable).[24] A total of 796 RAF Lancaster bombers and 311 U.S. Flying Fortresses (B-17s) participated.[25]

On February 25, U.S. troops gained a bridgehead across the Roer River with the capture of Duren, the major objective of the U.S. First Army since October. A little over a week later, the U.S. First Army entered Cologne, approximately fifty miles east of Höfen-Monschau. It was the first major German city captured by the Allies. On March 8, when my friend Don Stafford rode through the city with the 395th Regiment guard, bodies of German soldiers were "everywhere," Stafford said.

On March 7, the First Army's 9th Armored Division captured the Ludendorff Railroad Bridge (also known as the Remagen Bridge) over the Rhine before the Germans could blow it up. This remarkable feat of daring and initiative gave the Allies their first crossing of the Rhine barrier. (The 99th Division was the first complete infantry division to make the crossing.)

ON THE OTHER SIDE. To fill its depleted ranks, the German Army began on March 5 to draft boys fifteen and sixteen years of age. By the end of April, units of the 99th Division discovered they were fighting German boys as young as ten. Most Americans in front-line foxholes in the European Theater of Operations were nineteen or older. In my platoon, we had no eighteen-year-olds when we moved into the front line. But, as replacements arrived after the Battle of the Bulge, more eighteen-year-olds appeared in 99th Division front-line outfits. The United States never drafted seventeen-year-olds.

On March 7, my 3rd Battalion, 395th Regiment, was one of two battalions (out of nine) in the 99th Division to receive Presidential Citations for its defense of Höfen at the beginning of the Battle of the Bulge. The citation was presented to the Battalion at Gohr, Germany, by the War Department. General Lauer read it to the assembled battalion at a wet outdoor ceremony:

The 3rd Battalion, 395th Infantry Regiment, is cited for outstanding performance of duty in action against the enemy during 16–19 December 1944 near Höfen, Germany. During the German offensive in the Ardennes, the 3rd Battalion . . . was assigned the mission of holding the Monschau-Eupen-Liege Road. For four successive days, the battalion held this sector against combined German tank and infantry attacks, launched with fanatical determination and supported by heavy artillery.

No reserves were available to the battalion, and the situation was desperate. Disregarding personal safety and without rest, the men fought vigorously to hold their positions. . . . On at least six occasions, the battalion was forced to place artillery concentrations dangerously close to its own positions in order to repulse penetrations and restore its lines.

On other occasions, men came out of their fixed defenses and engaged in desperate hand-to-hand fighting in order to repel enemy assault teams. Enemy artillery was so intense that communications were generally out. The men carried out missions without orders when their positions were penetrated or infiltrated. They killed Germans coming at them from the front, flanks, and rear.

Outnumbered five to one, they inflicted casualties in the ratio of eighteen to one. With ammunition supplies dwindling rapidly, the men obtained German weapons and utilized ammunition obtained from casualties to drive off the persistent foe.

Despite fatigue, constant enemy shelling, and ever increasing enemy pressure, the 3rd Battalion . . . prevented the German breakthrough from extending to the Monschau area, guarded a six thousand-yard front, and destroyed 75 percent of three German infantry regiments.

[It also prevented the enemy from outflanking the Second Division and most of the 99th Division during their successful stand at Elsenborn Ridge. In the view of historian John Eisenhower, the action of the two divisions "could well be considered the most decisive of the Ardennes campaign."][26]

The Germans also were impressed by the fighting ability of my 3rd Battalion during the Battle of the Bulge. A German captain who participated in the unsuccessful attempt to capture Höfen revealed that almost every man in his company was killed or wounded by the 3rd Battalion during the attack. His revelation came during his interrogation by Roger Moore, in the town of Glefdorf in central Germany. Moore was a 3rd Battalion radio operator and interpreter.[27]

In another interrogation, this time of an enemy lieutenant in Hausen, Germany, the 3rd Battalion won more praise. The German said his company was almost wiped out by the Americans in Höfen during the Battle of the Bulge. At the conclusion of the interrogation, he commented to the American interrogator about the unit that had held Höfen: "They must have been one of your best formations." The interrogator asked the German the reason for his opinion. The German answered: "Two reasons: coldbloodedness and efficiency."[28]

On March 9, I received some good news. My doctor gave me a final check and pronounced me ready to return to duty. "Lie down, raise both legs, and let both ankles hang loose," he said. My injured right foot tipped sharply left while my left foot had no tilt at all. "Your right foot will probably cause you some trouble for years to come. I recommend that you wear an Ace bandage to provide more support. You can work in an army office, but the infantry is out."

The doctor proceeded to give me a minimal physical exam. When he told me to hold both hands in front of him with fingers stiffly extended, I noticed for the first time that my fingers trembled slightly. The doctor said the sudden shock of going from the tenseness of the front to the calmness of a hospital ward often caused this symptom. He called it "post-combat letdown."

The slight trembling of my fingers continued, even into civilian life. To keep people from noticing, I used one hand to steady the other. This mild leftover of the war lasted for ten years. My weak ankle flipped me to the ground numerous times over the next fifty-five years, sometimes requiring me to use crutches for several days at a time.

ON OUR SIDE. The battered Remagen Bridge finally collapsed into the Rhine River on March 17, but U.S. combat engineers had already built pontoon bridges nearby. Thus, American soldiers continued to cross the last major barrier between U.S. forces and Berlin.

I was released from the hospital on March 21, after a three-month recuperation period. Many of my ward mates with serious wounds had already returned to their combat units and were once again living the front-line life. My orders required me to report to the Tenth Reinforcement (replacement) Depot at Lichfield, about twenty miles north of Birmingham. I had seven days to get there—a nice holiday, I thought.

My friend Louis Pedrotti, a trench-foot victim from L Company in Höfen, was also released on March 21 from another hospital in England. Since we both had seven-day passes before reporting to the same replacement depot, we decided to visit London. We spent six days sightseeing, attending concerts, and dodging the last of the V-1 jet-powered flying bombs and V-2 rockets to land on London.

Louis and I were walking a block or two north of Piccadilly Circus when a V-1 hit a couple of blocks north of us. The sidewalks were full of people. Pedestrians, including Louis and me, hesitated a moment when the bomb crashed and exploded. Glass windows next to us shattered. The English civilians continued on their way as if nothing had happened. Not to be outdone, Louis and I struck the same nonchalant attitude. A few minutes later we heard ambulances arriving at the explosion scene to pick up the dead and injured. A tough lot, Londoners of 1945. A day or two later, we were walking between Trafalgar Square and Parliament when a German V-2 rocket exploded thousands of feet over our heads. Only minutes earlier it had left its launching site on the Continent. The V-2 represented a historic achievement because it opened the long-range rocket age. Fifty feet long and weighing thirteen tons, it carried a one-ton warhead.

My furlough over, I arrived at Lichfield on March 28. The army called this dismal, impersonal place a "reinforcement" depot, not a "replacement" depot. GIs called it a "repo depot." The original name, "replacement," sounded too much like its real purpose—replacing men killed and wounded with fresh cannon fodder. Bradley admitted that the replacement depots developed a reputation among the troops for callousness and inefficiency.[29]

Theoretically, the center placed men in jobs for which they were most suited. But, with the frantic need for infantry replacements, this refinement was mostly ignored—unless, of course, one had influential friends.

I did not know it at the time, but I lived in a camp where guardhouse beatings and other gross injustices reportedly occurred. Although Lichfield probably was a brutal place for some, it was just another cold, grim army camp for most of us.

I received orders on April 8 to report to Hounslow Barracks, only forty-five minutes from central London. There, I was assigned to all kinds of jobs—from kitchen police (washing pots, pans, and dishes) to typing.

One day I joined three other "volunteers." We were marched to a great mound of coal dumped near headquarters. An army truck drove up, and a sergeant gave each of us a shovel. "Fill it up." The sergeant explained: "The colonel says this here coal don't meet his standards." As we started shoveling, he sat down in the truck's cab to read a comic book. One of our group, who apparently knew something about coal, said it looked all right to him. I could not tell one way or the other. I just knew that civilians in the United Kingdom had a hard time getting coal. When we loaded the last piece, the sergeant told us to climb aboard with our shovels. "We're going to the London dump."

A half-hour later, we drove into a large open area. Small groups of older men and a few women searched through debris for useful material. Our truck stopped in a clear area. "Shovel it out here," the sergeant commanded. Within five minutes after we started unloading, three sickly-looking men in rags came over to see what we were doing. They couldn't believe their eyes. "The Americans are dumping good coal," they yelled in glee as they started picking it up. For containers, they used sacks and buckets in rickety wagons. Word spread quickly. Soon scavengers from all parts of the dump were busy picking up the coal as fast as we unloaded it. As we finished unloading, about twenty bedraggled men and women fought over the coal remaining on the ground. Thus, we had given further proof to the English that Americans were too rich for their own good.

15 • London, Again

IMAGINE MY SURPRISE, AFTER SPENDING SO MUCH TIME in foxholes, to receive orders to report for duty in central London. I didn't have far to go from Hounslow, about 11 miles. I was driven with my few belongings to Montague Square, a fashionable London address in the West End.

My new outfit, part of the 3113 Signal Service Battalion, operated most functions of the U.S. Signal Center in London and housed the center's men in several five- and six-level townhouses that looked out on a narrow rectangular park. Famous Marble Arch and Oxford Street, part of one of the busiest shopping areas in London, were four blocks to the south. This was my chance to learn how the rear echelon lived. Infantrymen, I thought, did not live in cushy places like Montague Square.

I arrived in time for lunch. The kitchen was below street level, and the mess hall for enlisted men was next to the kitchen. In normal times, this was where the servants ate. The BBC played background music. Much to my surprise, the enlisted men had no KP duty. The army hired English civilians for this job. The battalion's officers had their meals at the U.S. Officers' Mess at Grosvenor House, a luxury hotel near Hyde Park.

I joined several fellows who had just sat down to lunch. They told me we worked in shifts forty-five feet below ground level in the sub-basement of the Annex of Selfridges Department Store on Oxford Street. The London Signal Center operated twenty-four hours a day, seven days a week. My lunch companions explained that it ran one of the two most vital U.S. communications centers in Europe. The other one operated in a five-story former German blockhouse in central Paris near the Arc de Triomphe and SHAEF headquarters. Before the invasion of France and for two months after, the London center served as SHAEF's single communications hub in Europe. Even though the Paris center picked up part of its load, the London center remained as the vital link among President Roosevelt, Prime Minister Winston Churchill and his Cabinet, the British War Office and Admiralty, the Pentagon, and SHAEF's Paris headquarters. As my lunch companions described the center, I thought they exaggerated its importance. It did not take long for me to learn differently.

I immediately disliked the men of my new outfit because I still carried the contempt held by rifle platoon men toward the rear echelon. My hostility, at least in this case, was unwarranted. These highly skilled men were trying to be friendly and helpful. After lunch, one of them took me to my new home, a five-story townhouse at Number 2 Montague Square. The walls of each house joined the walls of its neighboring house; frontage was narrow. Several houses on the square stood gutted, victims of German air raids.

On the second floor of Number 2 was a large room full of double-decker bunks. Sleeping men who had worked the night shift occupied several of them. I was assigned to the top of a double-decker in the middle of the room. Formerly the large so-cial or "drawing room," it had a pleasant view of trees and lawns in the park. The great house had been stripped by its owners of all furniture and rugs.[1]

"There's an air raid shelter under the park," my guide said, "but I doubt that we'll have any need for it." After showing me around the rest of the house, he added, "You're on your own for the afternoon and evening to get acquainted with the area. Report to the orderly room at 9 A.M. tomorrow."

It didn't sound like the infantry. Work schedules resembled those of civilians. No one had any weapons—no pistols, rifles, or BARs. No steel helmets. Well-functioning coal furnaces kept sleeping quarters warm and, unlike the infantry, there was no mud to be seen.

Anxious to revisit central London, I took off to see Selfridges Department Store and the Annex where I would soon be working. I discovered that it was larger than Bullock's or Robinson's, two of the largest department stores in Los Angeles in 1945. Founded in 1909 by Minnesotan Gordon Selfridge, the store contained eleven acres of floor space. To reduce possible bomb damage, Selfridges had its windows on Oxford Street bricked to the second floor.

The bomb-scarred Selfridges Annex was located behind the main building. Its display windows were sealed off by a thick, eighteen-foot-high concrete blast-protection wall. An armed U.S. military policeman stood guard near the entrance to the Signal Center. More MPs stood guard just inside and out of sight from the street. The second floor of the three-story building exhibited damage from bomb blasts. Passers-by on Duke Street knew Americans worked in the Annex, but their jobs were supposed to be secret. I quickly concluded that this was no routine assignment.

When I started to do research for this book, I learned more about the role the Signal Center played in the war. My first clue of its significance came in an interview I had with Fred Redding, archivist for Selfridges.[2]

Redding briefed me on U.S. Army activities in Selfridges Annex during the war. As soon as the war began in 1939, the British government took over the Annex and made it into a military telecommunications center. When the Americans came to London in 1942, the British leased the site to the U.S. Army Signal Corps. The Americans wanted it because of its underground location and its nearness to U.S. military headquarters at Grosvenor Square.

The Signal Corps expanded the site, making it SHAEF's Signal Center—one of the most sophisticated communications operations in the world outside the Pentagon. Among other refinements, the U.S. installed new code-protected radio-teletype machines and a new central switchboard. When completed, it handled high-level communications for the entire European Theater of Operations during the months before and for many weeks after D-Day. To protect this vital facility, the Americans surrounded its sides and ceiling with reinforced concrete and brick walls. The result was a "virtually impregnable" bunker forty-five feet below Duke Street. The army considered it safe from anything but a direct bomb hit.

During my visit with Redding, I learned that a new secret invention by Bell Laboratories had been operating in the Signal Center at the time I was stationed there. It provided total secrecy for top-level worldwide telephone conversations, and it helped prevent any leaks about D-Day invasion plans. Redding suggested I contact Stephen Geis, an expert on the project, for more information. Geis, a Signal Corps lieutenant and later captain, worked at the Signal Center on the secret invention in 1944–45. He told me its story.[3]

With the improbable name of SIGSALY, it remained top secret until 1976. Geis told me it was an unbreakable voice scrambler and played a crucial role during the war. It made its first successful contact with the SIGSALY station at the Pentagon on June 29, 1943, from the sub-basement rooms of our London Signal Center, next to the room where I worked. The operators, all with top-secret clearances, reported directly to the U.S. Army's chief signal officer in the Pentagon. To help maintain the secrecy of their job, they kept to themselves, maintaining as little contact as possible with other soldiers. Their attempts to maintain secrecy worked with me even though I worked next to them.

SIGSALY served as the world's first radio-telephone "hot line." Prime Minister Churchill and President Roosevelt and later President Truman used it regularly to discuss major policy issues, and they placed high value on it. After they got used to it, they could recognize each other's voices, and it gave them the personal touch they desired. Expert stenographers at each end of the line produced backup transcripts of their conversations.

When a Churchill-Roosevelt or a Churchill-Truman call was scheduled, a SIGSALY expert traveled the short distance from the Signal Center to the Cabinet War Rooms to make sure everything went smoothly for Churchill. The phone was tucked away in a small booth that looked like a lavatory. Its door had a lock that signaled "engaged" or "vacant." Inside was a small desk with a black telephone.[4]

SIGSALY came just in time. This top-secret, sixty-ton voice-coding terminal, which had its own diesel-powered generator, allowed the Allies' top political and military leaders to confer between continents in perfect security. Its arrival was especially important because, unbeknownst to the Allied high command until after the war, a German communications unit had broken the code for SIGSALY's predecessor, a much less sophisticated voice scrambler called A-3. Without SIGSALY, D-Day could have been a disaster. Alerted Germans would have been much tougher.

SIGSALY pioneered the age of digital transmission, making it, in the opinion of some historians conversant with communications technology, one of the greatest technological advancements to come out of World War II.

SIGSALY was threatened only once during German attacks on London. A V-2 rocket hit within three hundred feet of Selfridges Annex at 11:07 P.M. on December 6, 1944. My fellow workers, trying to impress me with their rough wartime life in London, told me about the explosion. They said it gave the men on the night shift in the Signal Center a "severe shock," but no one was hurt.

The rocket slashed straight down to the basement of a multistoried building across Duke Street from the Annex and exploded. The building, including the pub on the first floor and the people in it, disappeared. A U.S. Army military police guard also evaporated from his station outside the thick wall protecting the Signal Center and its entrance.

The men at the Signal Center didn't know it at the time, but Germany had an efficient spy system in London that reported to the directors of the V-2 program where V-2 rockets landed. Such was the case with the V-2 that landed near the Signal Center. A German spy in London reported a direct hit on the Signal Center to Dr. Walter Riedel, director of development and design at the wartime Peenemunde Proving Grounds in Germany. Riedel revealed the spy operation to me in an exclusive interview in the early 1950s. He and his staff were particularly pleased about this hit because destruction of the Signal Center would have disrupted U.S. military communications throughout Europe. Riedel and his staff were celebrating with champagne when they heard again from the spy. This time he told them the V-2 had hit the pub across the street. "That was the end of our party," Riedel said.[5]

Riedel's disclosure that the spy knew the location of the Signal Center made a joke of our efforts to treat its existence and location as secret. It was obviously not a secret to the German high command.

I broke the news to my Mother and Dad about my new assignment:

> 3113 SIGNAL Service Battalion
> Central London
> April 11, 1945

Dear Mother and Dad,

Notice the change of address. I don't know the exact deal. Since I'm no longer considered fit for combat infantry, I'll probably remain in this or a similar organization. My infantry communications training at Camp Wolters apparently qualified me for a Signal Corps assignment. In all probability, my job will concern message center work.

I shall, however, always consider myself an infantryman. The best fellows I have ever known were the boys of L Co. and the 99th Division. . . .

This morning I had the first fresh eggs since leaving the States last September. We had steak for lunch. . . .

> Love, George

Gradually, I learned more about the secrecy that surrounded the operation of the Signal Center. On April 14, I was assigned to a three-man task force that had one final daily chore at the end of our eight-hour shift. Led by an officer in charge of the message center, we collected all paper not filed during the last eight hours from desk tops, wastepaper baskets, and on the floor. We could leave nothing, including any notes made by the staff during the previous eight hours.

Under close direction of the first lieutenant, we dumped all this litter into large containers and carried them up four flights of stairs to the Selfridges Annex roof, two floors above ground.

While the lieutenant watched, we tossed the paper into a special army incinerator and set it ablaze. The area was protected so gusts of wind could not blow any of the papers away. When every last scrap of paper was burned, we returned the empty containers to the Signal Center. Only then could we leave. The officer made certain we performed the task properly.

On April 19, the battalion decided that it needed more good teletype operators. Five of the new men who knew how to type, including me, "volunteered" for training. Our little group, with a sergeant in charge, met at a bus stop on Oxford Street. We got off at the Goodge Street Underground (subway) Station on Tottenham Court Road and entered an army-protected area. Our sergeant used appropriate passwords and keys to get us into an elevator, which took us one hundred feet below the station.[6]

Underground, the sergeant gave us a tour and explained the purpose of the facility. We were in a maze of fully furnished but spartan offices. A highly secret place devoid of people, it was set up as a military command post with telephones, a battery of teletype machines, office supplies, extra parts, neatly-made beds in barrack-like rooms, water, and food rations. This was the ultimate foxhole. The officer in charge of London's SIGSALY terminal called it "the alternate underground headquarters." If our Signal Center and/or Churchill's Cabinet War Rooms had been knocked out by enemy action, the Goodge Street facility would provide an excellent, totally bombproof alternative.

Although not used in the spring of 1945, this fallback command post actively supplemented our SHAEF Signal Center in the period prior to and immediately following D-Day. Its conference telephone system served the meteorological staffs of the British Admiralty, the Air Ministry, the Allied Naval Expeditionary Force, Allied Expeditionary Air Force, and SHAEF. It provided the latest weather reports, using findings from weather ships far out in the Atlantic. The Goodge Street Station War Rooms remained a secret for years.

So far underground that London's subway trains passed overhead, the facility was truly bombproof. In fact, some American officers with access privileges came down to sleep during the height of London's buzz bomb and V-2 rocket attacks. It was the safest place in town.

Our sergeant explained that the Allied high command never had to use these facilities as a "last stand" headquarters because the situation never got that desperate. It gave me an eerie feeling to see these offices intended to house the leaders of the final battle to save Britain from German occupation. I reminded myself that Germany, not Britain, was approaching a complete collapse. Germany's top military and civilian leaders were probably using a similar command post deep under Berlin at that very moment. (This was Britain's version of Hitler's underground bunker headquarters where he made his last stand and then killed himself.)

After our tour, we began training exercises on the unused teletype machines. My course continued for two weeks. By that time, the battalion gave up on making me a teletype operator because I had few talents for the job. I returned to the message center and work I much preferred.

In mid-April, an attractive young woman, about nineteen years old, came to the front door of our Montague Square townhouse pleading for a place to sleep. It was about 4 P.M. Whoever let her in said she could stay overnight if she would have sex with those who wanted to use her.

I was asleep in the large second-floor dorm room. I awoke when I heard a girl's subdued voice intermingled with male whispering, heavy breathing, and squeaky bedsprings. The girl slipped into different welcoming beds while the rest of the night shift tried to sleep. When she finished in a bed across the aisle from mine, she called over: "Can I join you?" I said something like "no thanks."

By this time the dark shadows of early evening had descended on the room. The girl was escorted downstairs, supposedly to visit a waiting member of the battalion. Instead, she was put out onto the now dark street. She protested as the door was locked behind her. Alone again with no shelter, she had only Hershey bars, nylons, and American cigarettes. Tossing the girl into the street seemed cruel to many of us who were involuntarily involved in the sordid episode.

ON OUR SIDE. Communicating through the Red Cross, the Germans offered to surrender on April 22 to the Western Allies, but not to the Soviets. Meanwhile, Allied strength in Europe reached overwhelming proportions. It peaked in April with 28,000 aircraft (14,854 were American), including 5,559 heavy bombers and 6,003 fighters. In contrast, the Luftwaffe had only 1,500 operational planes of all types on all fronts. Between D-Day and V-E Day, a total of 5,400,000 Allied troops had entered western Europe along with 970,000 vehicles. In addition, General Eisenhower now had ninety-one divisions under his command, sixty-one of which were American.[7]

On April 23, General Eisenhower required all Allied military personnel in Europe to view an explicit film that showed the ghastly situation our soldiers discovered when they liberated Nazi death camps in Germany. Within two hours of seeing the film, I wrote home: "It must be a subtle pleasure to the survivors of the Battle of the Bulge as they advance to the east to see the ruin of Germany and the awful plight of its people."

What happened to the idealism and magnanimity I felt upon hearing the forgiving vicar's message at St. Paul's Cathedral in February? Fortunately, my negative attitude toward the German people did not last long. That, of course, excluded members of the SS. In retrospect, I still believe the vicar at St. Paul's was right. A vindictive peace creates the climate for another war. I realized that *all* Germans could not be held accountable for acts of their government, just as *all* Americans cannot be held responsible for some of the dumb things our government does.

As the end of the war neared, American soldiers were in a hateful mood toward Germany and the German people. Hard feelings eased as Americans in Germany got to know the people better. Many GIs in Germany quickly found an affinity for German girls, and many of them reciprocated. This social interaction happened despite frantic efforts by the U.S. military to prevent Americans from "fraternizing" with Germans.

Also on April 23, the blackout ended in London. This was a big, big event for a city that had lived in the dark every night since September 3, 1939—almost six years.

I walked down Oxford Street to experience the great event. As darkness enveloped the city, the street lights came on—full instead of dimmed—as did auto and bus lights, lights for store displays in windows, and marquees. They all came on! People poured into the streets by the hundreds of thousands to witness and celebrate the return of wonderful light. I thrilled at the sight and the great joy shown by war-weary Londoners. No more fears of bombs and rockets. Theater lines were blocks long. While people waited to get in, all forms of beggars sang, played instruments, and even danced for a sixpence tossed to them by the more fortunate.

In late April, as the war wound down, the Soviets completed their encirclement of Berlin, and Americans troops met Soviet troops at the Elbe River. Italian dictator Mussolini was captured and executed in Italy. President Truman rejected a German offer to surrender only to the Americans and the British; he said that Germany must also surrender to the Russians. And on May 1, German radio announced that Adolph Hitler was dead. A day later, the Soviets completed their capture of Berlin.

On May 5, in a clue of things to come, the British and the Americans broke off talks with the Soviets about the composition of Poland's government until the Soviets explained their arrest of Polish democratic leaders. (In my opinion, this was the beginning of the Cold War.) Rarely had so many big stories occurred in such a short space of time.

On May 6, after almost six months on the front line, 3rd Battalion Headquarters, 395th Regiment, 99th Division (my old outfit), now located at Landshut, Germany, received word from higher headquarters that the war was over for the 99th Division.

16 • V-E Day—At Last

May 6–9, 1945

WITH THE GERMANS IN A STATE OF COLLAPSE, THE atmosphere at the Signal Center's Sunday night shift (May 6–7) was more anxious than usual. London waited to explode in celebration. When and how was the war going to end? Was the killing going to stop in the next few days? Or was fighting going to continue for a few more weeks in the German and Austrian Alps? Those were the big questions on everyone's mind.

I was one of a small night crew running the Signal Center's Message Center. As usual, we were routing messages, mostly routine, from top levels of command in Washington, the United Kingdom, and various military headquarters on the Continent. Also, as usual, we initiated messages from the United Kingdom to commands in France, Germany, and the United States. Teletype machines, operating with secret codes, provided our principal means of communication.

At around 2:55 A.M. on May 7, activity slowed a bit. I was getting drowsy, fighting sleep. "This is it!" one of my comrades declared in a low, but excited, voice. "It's over! The war's over!" He read the copy, marked "Urgent Top Secret," as it came off the teletype machine from General Eisenhower's forward headquarters in Reims, France.

Instructions said to relay the message immediately to the War Department at the Pentagon (for President Truman and General Marshall) and to Churchill's underground Cabinet War Rooms.

The message announced that the German High Command had signed the following "Act of Military Surrender" at 2:41 A.M., just fourteen minutes earlier:

1. We, the undersigned, acting by authority of the German High Command, hereby surrender unconditionally to the Supreme Commander, Allied Expeditionary Force, and simultaneously to the Soviet High Command, all forces on land, sea, and in the air who are at this time under German control.

2. The German High Command will at once issue orders to all German military, naval, and air authorities and to all forces under German control to cease active operations at 2301 hours (11:01 P.M.) Central European Time on Eight May and to remain in the positions occupied at the time. No ship or aircraft is to be scuttled, or any damage done to their machinery or equipment.

3. The German High Command will at once issue to the appropriate commanders, and ensure the carrying out of any further orders issued by the Supreme Commander, Allied Expeditionary Force, and by the Soviet High Command. . . .

Signed at Reims, France, at 0241 hours on the seventh day of May 1945.

On behalf of the German High Command—Jodl.

On behalf of the Supreme Commander, Allied Expeditionary Force—W. B. Smith

On behalf of the Soviet High Command—Ivan Susloparof

On behalf of the French—F. Sevez.

For some strange reason, no one signed "on behalf" of the British.

After we relayed the message to the British War Office in London and to Washington, a sergeant for whom I worked came up with a very bad idea. "I'll run off copies for our war scrapbooks," he said. "They may be worth lots of money someday." He ran four or five copies for those of us who knew its contents. I hid mine in the bottom of my left shoe.

Since the Germans had actually surrendered and they already had a copy of the agreement, the sergeant thought it would not hurt if we had copies, too. Most important, we understood and agreed not to divulge the contents. (But that did not begin to excuse what we did.)

When our shift ended at about 8 A.M. I walked out onto the London streets. I thought the good news was probably no longer secret. But the streets looked normal for a Monday morning. I looked for the surrender story in the morning edition of *The Times*. Not there! Not a word about the official German signing of a total surrender agreement five hours earlier. Our news appeared still hot, and very secret.

I felt very strange. In fact, I was scared. I carried the official message the whole world awaited with greater anticipation than almost any message in history. I could have set off the biggest celebration of all time. I could have upstaged President Truman, Winston Churchill, and Joseph Stalin. None of us, however, intended to do anything but keep the document totally secret until long after the official announcements.

I hurriedly read the newspaper as I walked back to Montague

Square. I ate breakfast with my comrades from the night shift and with others who had just gotten up, the latter of whom speculated on the ending of the war; we of the night shift kept quiet. There was not a word of the signing on the BBC.

When I retired for sleep, I was almost afraid to take off my left shoe. After seven hours of fitful sleep, I awoke, confirmed that the message was still in my shoe, dressed, and went down to the mess hall for an early dinner.

Conversation centered on the crowds gathering in the streets for a celebration. Someone said that the Associated Press (AP) had sent a story to the United States reporting Germany's unconditional surrender. The AP story, he added, pointed out that SHAEF refused to confirm the report. Our night shift crew remained silent. The mood in the city had changed since 8 A.M.

Since I was free until midnight, I joined three other fellows who wanted to see the celebration, if one evolved. Many more people than usual strolled the sidewalks. They sensed something was about to happen. As we approached Piccadilly Circus, there was barely room for one lane of vehicles. Although the crowds knew there would be no official announcement on this night (May 7), they appeared determined to celebrate anyway.

Cheering civilians and uniformed military personnel from Allied armies, including large numbers of Americans, thronged the sidewalks and filled the roads. They climbed on the tops of buses slowly working their way through the crowds. Cars entering the swarm of celebrators emerged with men and women clinging to their sides and backs and others on top trying to wave flags and hang on at the same time. Young women, arm-in-arm with servicemen, marched through the mass, singing at the top of their voices.

We quickly found ourselves swept into a mile-long procession. Servicemen from virtually all Allied nations decided to join in. We marched up and down the Strand several times and then through the Admiralty and the Mall to the front of Buckingham

Palace. Numerous voices yelled, "We want the King!" No one appeared on the balcony. Then the crowd sang "God Save the King," thinking that would bring out the royal family.

I thought the royal family would not appear until the Allied governments announced a definite German surrender. I felt nervous again when I thought of the message in my shoe. I wished the governments would hurry up and make the announcement. Then I could relax.

In all this hilarity, I found myself both happy and sad. I thought of my buddies from the 99th who did not make it. This was nothing to celebrate. Because of my conflicting emotions, I could not get into the full spirit of the evening.

If the high commands lived up to their surrender agreement, all fighting should officially stop within another day. Since both Churchill and President Truman were scheduled to speak simultaneously the next day to their nations, I figured they would disclose the news then.

As rumors of the unconfirmed surrender spread, three RAF Lancaster heavy bombers flew over, dropping red and green flares. (They would not be needed anymore for marking bomb-drop zones over German cities.) Great bonfires ringed the horizon and created a glow around London. Many of the fires blazed in gaping cellars of bombed-out buildings. American soldiers got a big boost when a huge sign in the Rainbow Corner Red Cross Club informed them that all passes and furloughs were to be extended forty-eight hours upon official notice of V-E Day.

The crowds peaked about 9 P.M., then gradually subsided when SHAEF appeared firm in its statement that there would be no official announcement on this night.

I arrived back at the Signal Center just before midnight. Almost as soon as I sat down at my desk, I was told to report to our lieutenant's office. A group was forming, and it appeared to be composed of the men on the previous night's shift. When all had arrived, our lieutenant strode in. He had a grim, angry look on his face. "I understand some of you have copies of last night's big message," he declared. "We will search you and all of your personal effects, and if we find a copy, I promise we'll throw the book at you." He continued in this vein for five minutes. After this tirade, I was really scared. I didn't want to spoil my good army record now.

When the lieutenant dismissed us, I walked swiftly to the latrine, locked myself in a toilet booth, took off my left shoe, pulled out the message, tore it into little pieces, and flushed it into the London sewer. I felt fantastically better. I do not know what the others did; some may have kept their copies. I do know that no effort was made to search me or my belongings. Ironically, this message that scared me so much probably disclosed the best news of the twentieth century.

At 8 A.M., I finished my shift. Since everyone now knew this was V-E Day, I was anxious to get up to street level to watch the show. Today was the real celebration. On Oxford Street, Selfridges was decked with British and American flags. The crowds were starting to build, but it was still early. The day was clear and sunny.

I picked up copies of *The Times* and *The Daily Mail*. The front page headlines announced: V-E DAY DECLARED TODAY; KING AND MR. CHURCHILL TO BROADCAST; GERMANS ANNOUNCE UNCONDITIONAL SURRENDER. One article said Churchill would officially announce the ending of hostilities in Europe in his 3 P.M. broadcast. It said simultaneous announcements would be made in Washington and Moscow, but there was still no official confirmation by SHAEF of a German surrender. At the top of another page, I discovered a bitter irony. Two columns listed casualties. Some of the casualties came from the ending European fronts and others came from the still active war with Japan in the Far East. Getting killed in the last few days of a war had to be the ultimate in bad luck, I muttered to myself.

A short article summed up one reason Britain was so thankful the war was over. It said the British government had released wartime figures showing Britain's civilian death toll from air raids and V-1s and V-2s to be 60,595 dead and 86,182 injured.[1] German civilian casualties, mostly caused by British and American air raids on cities, totaled approximately 2.1 million— 500,000 killed and 1,600,000 injured. The German casualty figures included all German citizens plus citizens of other countries working in Germany.[2]

At Montague Square, I went directly to our mess hall for breakfast. The men were regaling each other with their wild experiences of the previous night. Everyone seemed especially happy. All had an abundance of funny stories to share. Exhausted from a long night "on the town" and a full shift at the Signal Center, I ate quickly and went to bed. Tonight, I wanted to experience the "real" V-E Day celebration.

I awoke in time to hear Churchill's broadcast at 3 P.M. When he said, "From midnight tonight, hostilities would cease," we yelled approval. Cheers got even louder when he added, "The German war is therefore at an end."

After an early dinner, I left Montague Square on foot to become part of the great citywide party. Unlike the unorganized spontaneity of yesterday's unofficial hilarity, this day's celebrations showed signs of organization. Buildings and lamp posts were decked with Union Jacks. Many people wore red, white, and blue hats and carried flags and party whistles. British military bands marched through the streets serenading the crowds. People came to London on trains from all over the United Kingdom to join the celebration and to see the king and queen.

I headed toward Piccadilly again. The crowds were much larger than on the previous day. Many danced to "Lambeth Walk" as they sang the familiar tune. I joined a mass of young civilian women and uniformed service personnel in an irresistible tide, arm-in-arm—all instant friends. As we left Piccadilly Circus and headed for Leicester Square, we began singing a famous World War I song, "It's a Long Way to Tipperary." When we approached nearby Leicester Square, we sang the part that goes like this: "Goodbye Piccadilly, farewell Leicester Square." That thrilled me—to sing those lines as we walked from one to the other.

Our surging tide squeezed into Trafalgar Square, where an estimated sixty thousand people waited to hear the king's address on loudspeakers. The great crowd absorbed us, and we joined in singing stirring tunes played by an inspired military band.

As in the previous night's celebration, I could not get fully into the wild, unbridled spirit of the evening. I was more observer than participant. As I watched the crowds, however, I thought: "Why not celebrate? These people have been sad for too long. This historic night can be both a celebration and a solemn occasion."

I hurried over to Buckingham Palace and squirmed my way up near the front of the vast crowd (estimated at a quarter million people) waiting for the king and queen to appear. We didn't have long to wait. The curtains in a window near the balcony moved two or three times. It was 5:25 P.M. Then, one of the balcony doors opened and out stepped King George VI and Queen Elizabeth, along with their daughters, nineteen-year-old Princess Elizabeth (now Queen Elizabeth) and fourteen-year-old Princess Margaret Rose. They waved, and the vast crowd waved back. Princess Elizabeth, in a British Army female officer's uniform, stood ramrod straight, with sharp military bearing.

A few minutes later, the king called Prime Minister Winston Churchill, age seventy, to join the royal family on the balcony. The roar was deafening! Churchill did not wave or give a "V" for victory sign, nor did he sport his usual cigar. He just stood there bareheaded looking out at the crowd. He wore a satisfied-looking smile. The drama was incredible! As the cheers subsided, Churchill made one deep bow. The crowd erupted with a roar even louder than when he first appeared. Some people near me had tears in their eyes. The royal family waved, then stepped inside with the prime minister.

At 6 P.M., from a broadcast room in the palace, the king delivered a brief speech: "Today," he said, "we give thanks to Almighty God for a great deliverance." He thanked his countrymen for their tireless war effort. To many in Britain, this speech was the highlight of the day. When he finished, the crowd cheered and began singing the national anthem, then began calling again: "We want the king. We want the king."

In a few minutes, a face appeared in a window behind the balcony. With a rustle of curtains, the king and his family stepped out again on the balcony. The royal family waved. A pause, and then the prime minister joined them. Another thunderous roar! This was Churchill's finest hour. It was probably Britain's as well. The king and queen made their seventh and last appearance on the balcony at 12:15 A.M.

Tired of standing in one place, I left Buckingham Palace for the rowdier celebrations in Piccadilly Circus, Leicester Square, and Trafalgar Square. I joined a group of American and British servicemen and women who, like the earlier crowd, were also caught up with "It's a Long Way to Tipperary."

As dusk settled over central London, powerful floodlights lit up the fronts of most public buildings, monuments, and major commercial buildings. Antiaircraft searchlights formed great "V" (for victory) signs far into the sky as part of a planned light show. The lights proved that peace had really arrived. Only six weeks earlier, V-1 and V-2 bombs had still crashed into the city.

Virtually every able-bodied Londoner was in the streets; the total was in the millions. They displayed infectious, but disciplined, high spirits. Few were inebriated. It was a scene of fantastic camaraderie and goodwill.

With the approach of midnight, many people began drifting toward Parliament Square. I went with them. They wanted to count to twelve in unison as the hands of the brightly-lit Big Ben crept toward midnight. When it began to strike, we waited in silence. At the twelfth strike, the crowd responded with a thunderous cheer. One minute later—at 12:01 A.M., May 9—the long-awaited cease-fire on all fronts became official. A cluster of tugboats floating in the nearby Thames noisily blared out "V" in Morse code.

World War II, by far the greatest event of the century, had ended in Europe.

As I walked back to Montague Square, I again slipped into a mood of sadness and fond remembrance of the men of the 99th Division who had sailed across the Atlantic with me eight months earlier. I thought of 99th Division friends who now lay in Henri-Chapelle American Cemetery: Gene Oxford, Ensign Williamsen, Bill Parmelee, John Corrigan, Robert McNeill, and Leo Wresinski. Their faces, one by one, crossed my mind.

Then I had a happy thought. As of this night, all of the thousands of foxholes were empty. Overnight, they became ghosts of a tragic, stupid past.

17 • Reflections

L OOKING BACK AT THE WAR, I AM STILL AMAZED THAT the world's greatest industrial power (even in the 1940s) sent its army overseas to fight a war with inferior tanks, inferior footwear, and inferior winter clothing. We did not have a flat-trajectory gun equal to the German 88 until the last days of the war. The simple compass was nonexistent in my squad. Our platoon leaders and platoon sergeants had compasses, but, in some cases, they were defective World War I models. Our M1 Garand rifle, however, was an excellent weapon.

Front-line infantry cannot forgive their high command for the scandalous lack of adequate winter footwear and clothing during November, December, and January. The responsible generals could not help but notice that many American rear echelon servicemen walked the safe streets of Paris and other liberated cities wearing new U.S. Army winter clothing supposedly designated for the men at the front. Civilians wore it, too, thanks to a massive black market. But our leaders took no effective action to change this situation.

Lt. Col. McClernand Butler, commander of our 3rd Battalion, identified part of the problem after the war. "There is too big a cushion between the top brass and where the fighting is going on. The brass tend to be all theory, and know little about the life of their men on the front." In the five weeks I was on the front, I never saw a single officer other than Lieutenant Goss, my platoon leader.[1]

Other questions still plague many of us in the 99th Division. We still wonder, for example, why the Germans achieved total surprise when they launched the Battle of the Bulge. The American front line began reporting greatly increased German activity all along the sixty-mile Ardennes Front more than a week before the attack began. At night, front-line soldiers heard the sounds of many trucks and tanks just behind the German line. Why would SHAEF and General Bradley's Twelfth Army headquarters so completely disregard these reports? And how did they miss the fifteen hundred troop trains and five hundred supply trains crossing the Rhine during the first half of December carrying tanks, guns, and troops to the borders of Belgium and Luxembourg?[2]

Even the U.S. Army's official historian of the battle, Hugh M. Cole, called the surprise attack a "gross failure by Allied ground and air intelligence."[3]

With the war over, the army started adding up its human cost. It learned, for example, that from the time my 99th Infantry Division arrived on the front line until the war ended six months later, we suffered 11,987 casualties. That's 84 percent of our original compliment of 14,253 men. Army historians said that is about average for World War II infantry divisions on the Western Front for a similar period. The 99th's battle casualties totaled 6,103, including 1,130 killed, 3,954 wounded, 421 missing, and 598 captured. Nonbattle casualties—including trench foot, frostbite, psychological breakdowns, and injuries not resulting from combat—totaled 5,884.[4]

These casualty figures take on new meaning when one considers their implications for rifle platoons. To illustrate rifle platoon losses, General Bradley cited 30th Infantry Division casualties in Normandy. He pointed out that the 3,240 men in its rifle platoons took 75 percent of the division's casualties.[5] If the percentages of casualties in the 99th Division were similar to those of the 30th, the average rifle platoon of the 99th would have incurred approximately 277 percent casualties in its six months on the front.

Replacements replaced the original rifle platoon members, and they, in turn, were replaced by other replacements. These are fearsome, demoralizing figures, but the survivors kept plodding along until they, too, became casualties. Almost everyone in rifle platoons along the Western Front in late 1944 became a casualty by the time the war ended.

Many of the friends who rode with me in the truck across France and Belgium on November 4 to the front line lost their lives. Gene Oxford, age twenty, was dead thirty-nine days later, killed by a mine on December 13 near Höfen, Germany; Leo Wresinski, age twenty-one, was dead forty-two days later, killed right next to me on December 16 in the first German artillery barrage opening the Battle of the Bulge; Bill Parmelee, age twenty, was dead eighty-two days later, killed on a patrol on January 25, 1945, near Höfen. Ensign Williamsen, age twenty-one, was also dead eighty-two days later, killed by a German machine gun. Two or three others in the truck—including John Corrigan, age twenty, a rifleman in my squad—were killed later in Germany. All of us were members of the 2nd Platoon.

So what happened to those of us who survived?

Most of the men mentioned in this book said their wartime experience changed their lives. "We grew up in a few weeks in the foxholes of the Ardennes," one former soldier declared. He was nineteen, just out of high school, when he arrived in Belgium. Almost all of his comrades were similarly young, ranging in age from eighteen to twenty-two. Few boys become mature men overnight, but we on the front did. Many said the war made them a better person. But, they added quickly, they would not want to repeat the experience.

As for me, I decided after several weeks on the front line that war was humankind's most insane endeavor. The grim death of friend Gene Oxford, a fellow BAR gunner, hit me hard. At the time, I was alone in my foxhole where I swore that I would dedicate my life to helping prevent another catastrophic war. That night of grief became a watershed in my life. After the war, I changed my career goal from professor of history to journalist. My goal was to promote international understanding through the mass media. Having luckily survived the ongoing slaughter of the rifle platoons—while so many good men I knew died—made me feel subconsciously guilty. I had to make my life count to feel worthy of survival.

I came home a more serious person. Upon returning to the University of California at Berkeley in 1946 (using the GI Bill), I added journalism as a second major to my original one in American history. I worked harder at everything, with a new sense of purpose. I was far from alone. Professors at the university said they had never had such good students as the GIs who filled their classrooms between 1946 and 1950. I graduated in 1947.

For the next thirteen years, I initiated a series of journalistic projects to further my goal, all in addition to my full-time job as a newspaper columnist, news editor, and city editor. One of my projects, called "Nations Speak," featured a panel of political leaders representing the six major political parties in Britain and France. Every month I sent a question involving an international issue to the six parties, and they selected an official spokesman on the issue. The resulting series was distributed nationwide from 1947 to 1949 to large- and middle-sized dailies by the North American Newspaper Alliance. In 1954 and 1955, I wrote a monthly column called "Action on the Peace Front" for *The Christian Science Monitor.*

Another project featured leading journalists in the United States, Britain, France, Germany, the Soviet Union, Japan, and India. Under my guidance, they answered questions about political developments in their respective countries. Each participating journalist received the articles written by the other panel members for use in their newspapers.

When I look back on these quixotic efforts, I can't believe that I really thought one journalist could make a difference. I gave up my "labors of love" when I realized that not enough newspapers were interested in the articles. I then turned to reporting education issues to national audiences for the next twenty-five years.

The war experience opened an exciting new world to me. My one and a half years with the army in Europe aroused my interest in Europe and in the development of the European Union. I supported the Marshall Plan in my newspaper efforts and rejoiced with the Europeans when the Iron Curtain lifted and European unity neared reality. The war made me a better person and vastly broadened my horizons.

After living through so much hell, I learned a big lesson: to know what's important and what isn't. I became less tolerant of things I considered fluff. "Life is too short for such nonsense" became a favorite comment of mine.

Having experienced extreme living conditions in the Ardennes, I knew the difference between real and pseudo hardship. Life on the front gave me great appreciation on wet, cold nights of having a roof over my head and a warm, dry bed with a mattress. We survivors had so much to be thankful for. On the negative side, the army taught me to fear authority, even though in many cases I did not respect it.

In the 1970s, I served as assistant superintendent of public instruction for the State of California.

I asked several of the former infantrymen featured in this book to tell me how the war influenced their lives. They agreed with me about growing up—fast, dramatically, traumatically—on the front line.

During a 1998 interview, Ivan Bull, a rifleman in my platoon and later a squad leader, told me his war experiences made him a better person. "There is no question in my mind about that. But, I would not want my children to have similar experiences. The price and the risk were much too great. I learned a lot. I learned to take responsibility. And, because some of our leaders were clearly incompetent, many of us also learned *not* to respect authority. After having so many awful experiences, I learned how to deal with fear, a very valuable lesson for civilian life." Bull became a professor of accountancy and finance at the University of Illinois at Champaign. In 1975–76, he served as chairman of the board of the American Institute of Certified Public Accountants.

George Prager, our platoon's runner and translator, declared that the war experience made a man of him. "I went into the service as a high school senior, and I came out as a man who could act and think for myself, without having to ask questions of my folks or anyone else. I made my own decisions as much as six years earlier than if I had not had those war experiences. The most important thing I learned in those tumultuous years was how to deal with people. Before entering the army, I had never dealt with people on my own. I always had my parents, teachers, or others to back me up." Prager was thirteen when he came to the United States from Germany in 1938. He ran his own successful business after the war.

John Thornburg, who experienced hair-raising days with his lost platoon, said he felt that any years of his life after the war were an undeserved bonus. He described his attitude as one "of treating many problems as trivia—problems that would be major to others." He said the title of a 1997 book by Richard Carlson summed up his new outlook: *Don't Sweat the Small Stuff.* This attitude saved him much grief. "I doubt that I am a better person because of my war experience. I'm much more cynical. I wonder how people like us could be motivated to lay our lives on the line, especially under the inept leadership that seemed to predominate in the military."

Thornburg became a dentist in Kansas after the war.

Lyle Bouck, leader of the intelligence and reconnaissance platoon of the 99th Division's 394th Regiment, said his stressful experiences during the war made him a better person. "They influenced me to lead a no-nonsense life. I had a more serious perspective and attempted to achieve and win and perform things that would be meaningful and productive. The silliness that goes on in life did not fit in my life. I learned that attitude, attitude, attitude was the big thing. When I didn't have a positive attitude, things didn't go well. I also learned the importance of being prompt and considerate," said Bouck, one of the youngest officers in the army. "These lessons and the GI Bill of Rights, which allowed me to go to college, helped me greatly in leading a productive life." Bouck was awarded the Distinguished Service Cross for heroism at Lanzerath during the Battle of the Bulge.

After the war, Bouck became a chiropractor in the St. Louis area.

Jack Dowell, who entered the army with me at Berkeley, said the war really determined his choice of profession. "I was thinking of going to law school before the war. But, after my war experience, I kept asking myself how such a thing could happen. That's why I began to study politics and history. That led to my going into teaching." After the war, he became a professor of political science at Washington State University.

John (Jack) Mellin, a fellow BAR gunner and ASTP student at Tarleton College, said the war had both positive and negative influences on his postwar life. "One adverse effect was my automatic dislike of anyone who was an officer. I know this phobia affected my actions dealing with subordinates. I've been a supervisor, group leader, and veterans' group leader, and I've bent over backwards to never treat anyone like an army officer would." Mellin became a mechanical engineer after the war.

Jackson W. Goss, the unusually young leader of my rifle platoon, said surviving his war experiences gave him the mental conditioning to believe that he could do anything in business situations and not fear problems that might develop. When he left the army in 1946 as a twenty-two-year-old captain, he joined the *Kansas City Star*. In the early 1950s, Goss started writing about mutual funds and was hired in 1955 by Putnam Funds of Boston, one of the largest mutual fund companies in the nation. Two years later, he became president of Putnam Funds Distributors and a partner of Putnam Management Company. In 1970, Goss helped organize Investors Mortgage Insurance Company, which eventually had $6 billion of insurance in force. When this company was sold, he formed an investment management group that managed $1.6 billion for corporate pension funds and college endowment funds.

The men I write about in this book are rapidly fading away. We are part of the 16.5 million Americans who served in World War II. As of July 1999, only 36 percent (5.9 million) are still living, the Department of Veteran Affairs (DVA) reported. As of

1999, none of us is younger than seventy-two. The DVA estimates our death rate is 1,038 per day, 31,600 per month, and 379,000 per year. The rate accelerates monthly. We entered the military en masse during 1941–45, and now we are departing en masse. Our influence in business, labor, politics, the military, and government, still significant in the 1980s, is now barely felt. Unique in American history, we experienced two of the nation's greatest challenges in one lifetime—the Great Depression of the 1930s and World War II. As a result, we leave with memories of extraordinary times that our children and grandchildren know virtually nothing about.

I know one thing for sure. Never had so many suffered so much. No other event in history matches the disaster that was World War II. I fear that few appreciate the vastly disproportionate share of suffering and dying that fell on the men on the front line. People need to know—and never forget—the appalling cost and those who paid it.

May the last words of the last survivor be a vigorous "Don't forget. Don't forget the lessons of World War II. Don't forget the grit and suffering of the men. Vow you'll never forget."

NOTES

Preface

1. "Henri-Chapelle American Cemetery and Memorial" (information sheet), American Battle Monuments Commission, no date.
2. *United States Temporary Military Cemeteries, European Theater Area, World War II,* American Graves Registration Command, Paris, September 1946.
3. Omar Bradley, *A Soldier's Story,* 445.
4. Percentage of personnel based on figures given to author on July 8, 1999, by Vincent Demma, U.S. Army Center of Military History, Washington, D.C. U.S. Army personnel in the ETO totaled 2,588,983 as of November 30, 1944. Approximately 152,280 of these men were in rifle platoons in forty-seven infantry divisions, forty-two on the Continent and five in England.
5. Omar Bradley, *A Soldier's Story,* 445.

Chapter 1

1. The ERC was created as a recruiting device in April 1942 to encourage college men earning good grades to enlist in the army. Those who joined the program were placed on inactive duty and could continue their college education until graduation, or until "unforeseen circumstances" required that they go on active duty. Those circumstances occurred in less than a year, and the army closed down most of the ERC program.
2. *Digest of Education Statistics, 1997,* U.S. Department of Education, Washington, D.C.
3. Lee Kennett, *GI: The American Soldier in World War II,* 34.
4. Dwight Eisenhower, *Crusade in Europe,* 314.
5. Smithmark Publishers, *D-Day: Operation Overlord,* 190.
6. Charles B. MacDonald, *A Time for Trumpets,* 80. (MacDonald was also an official U.S. Army historian for World War II.)

Chapter 2

1. Louis E. Keefer, *Scholars in Foxholes,* 164.
2. Ibid., 169.
3. Ibid., 171.
4. *Logistics in World War II: Final Report of the Army Service Forces,* 1948.

Chapter 3

1. James Hare, telephone interview by author, 1993.
2. After the war, Anthony earned a Ph.D. in chemistry at the University of Wisconsin.
3. Walter E. Lauer, *Battle Babies,* 102.
4. John Eisenhower, *The Bitter Woods,* 111.
5. Ibid., 112.
6. Harry C. Butcher, *My Three Years with Eisenhower,* 685.

Chapter 4

1. Richard Byers, interview by author, 1996.
2. Robert J. Mitsch, "Lucking Out: A Recall of World War II Survival and Observations," and interviews by author, 1991, 1993.
3. U.S. Navy statistics disclosed that German U-boats sank only one seven thousand-ton Allied ship in the European Theater of Operations during the month of October, the lowest monthly figure for 1944. The sharp decline took place when the Germans were busy establishing new submarine bases in Norway to replace those lost when the Allies invaded France. Once reestablished in Norway, German U-boats became much more active in late October, November, and December in coastal waters around England and along the French coast. Between September 1939 and May 1945, Germany lost twenty-eight thousand of the forty thousand sailors who manned its submarine navy. Vice Admiral Friedrich Ruge, *The German Navy's Story—1939–1945,* U.S. Naval Institute.
4. John Eisenhower, *The Bitter Woods,* 119, 122.
5. Vincent Demma, U.S. Army Center of Military History, phone interview by author, 1999.
6. Information about death notices given to author by Vincent Demma, U.S. Army Center of Military History. General Eisenhower does not mention the Slapton Sands disaster in his book, *Crusade in Europe.* General Bradley provides a brief description in *A Soldier's Story,* 246–49. See also Paul Fussell, *Wartime,* 25–26.
7. John Eisenhower, *The Bitter Woods,* 122.

8. After the war, Marshal of the Royal Air Force Sir Arthur Harris, boss of RAF's Bomber Command, revealed the difference between bomb damage in Britain and in Germany: 600 acres of London were leveled, compared to 6,427 acres of Berlin. Harris said Bomber Command attacked 70 German cities, causing 60 percent destruction in 23 cities and 50 percent damage in another 46. More than 500 acres were leveled in each of 31 German cities, including 6,200 acres in Hamburg, 2,003 in Dusseldorf, and 1,994 in Cologne. In the following cities, 1,000 to 2,000 acres were destroyed: Bremen, Dresden, Essen, Frankfurt-am-Main, Hanover, Mannheim-Ludwigshafen, Munich, Nuremberg, and Stuttgart. The much-publicized bomb damage to Coventry, England, totaled 100 acres. Source: *Bomber Offensive*, 261.

9. Harry T. Butcher, *My Three Years with Eisenhower*, 14.

10. John Murphy, *Dorset at War, 1939–1945*, 5–8.

11. Ibid., 8.

12. Charles A. Olsen, "History of the U.S. Navy in Le Havre," 1–2.

13. Ibid., 12.

14. Ibid., 3–8.

15. Arthur Harris, *Bomber Offensive*, 214.

16. The wartime story of Le Havre is recorded in *Le Havre 1940–1944: 40e Anniversaire de la Libération*, Jean Legoy, ed., published by the City of Le Havre, 1984. It is also told in numerous French newspaper reports.

17. Arthur Harris, *Bomber Offensive*, 214.

18. Harry Arnold, "'Easy' Memories," 12.

19. Charles B. MacDonald, *The Siegfried Line Campaign*, 621.

20. John Eisenhower, *The Bitter Woods*, 136.

21. McClernand Butler, audiotape for his family, 1985, and interviews by author, 1990–98.

22. Siegfried Sassoon, *Memoirs of an Infantry Officer*, 148.

23. Charles B. MacDonald, *A Time for Trumpets*, 28.

Chapter 5

1. Charles B. MacDonald, *The Siegfried Line Campaign*, 30–31.

2. Höfen is located sixteen miles southeast of Aachen and forty miles west of Bonn on the Rhine River.

3. Unknown to us, the enemy had fortified positions and an artillery observation post hidden in trees at the top of the steep slope about eight hundred feet to the southeast. Rudolph Jansen, the only German soldier I could find after the war who served in the German Army opposite us, gave me this information in 1997. Jansen told me that he could easily see Höfener Mühle and American

soldiers walking around in Höfen. "Your location was inside the German line. You crossed into what we considered our territory when you walked over the bridge on your approach to Höfener Mühle. The Perlenbach River was our dividing line." Jansen served the Wehrmacht as communications specialist. In 1998, he lived in his family home in Monschau.

4. Omar Bradley, *A Soldier's Story*, 445.

5. Percentage based on figures given to author on July 8, 1999, by Vincent Demma, U.S. Army Center of Military History, Washington, D.C. U.S. Army personnel in the ETO totaled 2,588,983 as of November 30, 1944. Approximately 152,280 of these men were in rifle platoons in forty-seven infantry divisions, forty-two on the Continent and five in England.

6. General Bradley said, "Previous combat had taught us that casualties are lumped primarily in the rifle platoons." *A Soldier's Story*, 445–46.

7. Bernard Law Montgomery, *The Memoirs of Field Marshal Montgomery*, 34.

8. Harry Arnold, "'Easy' Memories," 15.

9. Ibid., 17.

10. Ibid., 18.

11. Hugh Cole, *The Ardennes: Battle of the Bulge*, 63.

12. Ernie Pyle, *Brave Men*, 103, 141.

13. Percy J. Pace, interview by author, Kansas City, 1998, and telephone interviews, 1999.

14. Roger J. Moore, letters to author, January 1996.

15. McClernand Butler, audiotape for his family, 1985, and interviews by author, 1990–98.

16. Keith Fabianich, "Defense of Höfen, Germany," *Infantry School Quarterly*, July 1948, 48–50.

17. Charles B. MacDonald, *The Siegfried Line Campaign*, 36.

18. Walter E. Lauer, *Battle Babies*, 123.

19. William Cavanagh, interview by author in Höfen, 1993.

20. McClernand Butler, audiotape for his family, 1985, and interviews by author, 1990–98.

21. Brown (name changed) was evacuated as "lightly wounded in action" in December 1944. He returned home safely after the war. In civilian life, he became a prominent attorney and served for several years as chairman of the board for one of the nation's most prestigious nonprofit organizations.

22. Bill Huffman, "Hold the North Shoulder," and interview by author, 1995.

23. Gibney's body was sent in a truck approximately fifteen miles to the Henri-Chapelle American Cemetery. He was buried there the next day, along with others killed on November 15 in other parts of the Ardennes Front, in the

Aachen area, and in the Hürtgen Forest. The fifty-seven-acre cemetery had opened only six weeks earlier, on September 28, 1944.

24. McClernand Butler, audiotape for his family, 1985, and interviews by author, 1990–98.

25. Ibid.

26. Omar Bradley, *A Soldier's Story*, 440–41.

27. Walter Scheibler, *Zwischen Zwei Fronten*.

28. Karin Uhl, interview by author, July 1993, Höfen, Germany.

29. Louis Pedrotti, letter to author, 1994.

30. Paul Fussell, *Doing Battle*, 141.

31. Robert J. Mitsch, "Lucking Out," and interviews by author, 1991 and 1993.

32. A few days later, the survivors of the patrol were awarded the Combat Infantry Badge. Pfc. Slaybaugh, the BAR gunner, received the Bronze Star. Bob Mitsch saw nearly four more months of combat with L Company, 394th Infantry. After crossing the Rhine River on the Remagen Bridge, he was evacuated to a hospital in March with a shell fragment in his elbow.

33. McClernand Butler, audiotape for his family, 1985, and interviews by author, 1990–98.

34. Walter Niedermayer, *Into the Deep Misty Woods of the Ardennes: The Battle of the Bulge in All of Its Fury and SS-Terror*, 124–25.

35. Quentin Reynolds, *Dress Rehearsal: The Story of the Raid on Dieppe*, 194–96.

36. McClernand Butler, audiotape for his family, 1985, and interviews by author, 1990–98.

Chapter 6

1. McClernand Butler, audiotape for his family, 1985, and interviews by author, 1990–98.

2. Edward Anderson, notes in personal journal, no date.

3. Paul Putty, interview by author, 1991.

4. *The Checkerboard* (99th Division Association newspaper), "First Combat Patrol—First Casualties," April 1993; Seymour Saffer letter to author, 1994, and interview by author, 1994.

5. Saffer's company of 193 men sustained more than 35 casualties (18 percent) on December 13 during an aborted attack aimed at the Roer River dams near Höfen. At least two men became prisoners of war. Saffer was wounded by small arms fire and evacuated to a hospital in England.

6. John Eisenhower, *The Bitter Woods*, 139.

7. Dwight Eisenhower, *Crusade in Europe*, 332–33.

8. Omar Bradley, *A Soldier's Story*, 445.

9. Dwight Eisenhower, *Crusade in Europe,* 316.

10. McClernand Butler, audiotape for his family, 1985, and interviews by author, 1990–98.

11. Harry Arnold, "'Easy' Memories," 25.

12. Willie Shipp and I both attended the University of California at Berkeley before entering the army. In 1946, when we were back at Berkeley, his parents invited me to dinner at their home, a mansion in San Francisco. His father was a captain in the navy, but Willie never used his father's influence to keep him out of combat infantry.

13. Richard Byers, "An Artilleryman's Recollections of the Bulge," 1983.

14. John Eisenhower, *The Bitter Woods,* 150–51.

15. Charles B. MacDonald, *A Time for Trumpets,* 44, 45.

16. Walter Scheibler, *Zwischen Zwei Fronten,* 93.

17. Will Cavanagh, author of *Dauntless: A History of the 99th Infantry Division,* documented the incident. He told the author about it in an interview in July 1993.

18. John Eisenhower, *The Bitter Woods,* 179–80.

19. Ibid., 180.

20. Ibid., 146.

Chapter 7

1. Charles B. MacDonald, *A Time for Trumpets,* 29.

2. Hugh Cole, *The Ardennes: Battle of the Bulge,* 71.

3. Charles B. MacDonald, *A Time for Trumpets,* 44.

4. Hugh Cole, *The Ardennes: Battle of the Bulge,* 56.

5. Charles B. MacDonald, *A Time for Trumpets,* 45.

6. Omar Bradley, *A Soldier's Story,* 450.

7. Charles B. MacDonald, *A Time for Trumpets,* 11.

8. Ibid., 161–63.

9. McClernand Butler, audiotape for his family, 1985, and interviews by author, 1990–98.

10. Keith Fabianich, "Defense of Höfen, Germany," *Infantry School Quarterly,* July 1948, 52–53.

11. Don Stafford, interviews by author, 1991, 1993.

12. Paul Putty, interview by author, 1993.

13. Bruce Waterman, letters to author, 1990–94.

14. Warren Wilson, notes in personal journal, no date.

15. Sam Mestrezat, diary, December 1944.

16. Don Stafford, interview by author, 1993.

17. Ibid., 1993.

18. Walter Scheibler, *Zwischen Zwei Fronten,* 101–103.

19. John Mellin, "Memories, November–December 1944," and interviews by author, 1991, 1993, and 1998.

20. Description based on information in the citation for the Congressional Medal of Honor awarded to Vernon McGarity, January 11, 1946.

21. C. Eugene Kingsley, notes in personal journal, written about 1946.

22. These statistics (from the official records of Kingsley's B Company, 1st Battalion, 393rd Infantry) drive home the horrendous losses suffered by infantry rifle companies, and especially their rifle platoons. They are available, thanks to careful record keeping by Ben Nawrocki, B Company's first sergeant.

Chapter 8

1. Bouck, born on December 17, 1923, enlisted in the National Guard at the astonishingly young age of fourteen. He joined Headquarters Company, 138th Infantry Regiment, on August 3, 1938. At eighteen, he successfully completed Infantry Officer Candidate School at Fort Benning and became a second lieutenant. This made him one of the youngest infantry officers in the U.S. Army. Only two men in his I&R platoon of 1944 were younger.

2. This account is based on interviews and extensive correspondence between Bouck and the author (1993, 1994, 1998) and notes by Bouck and William James Tsakanikas.

3. Additional sources about the ordeal of Lyle Bouck and William James Tsakanikas: John Eisenhower, *The Bitter Woods,* 183–92; J. C. Doherty, *The Shock of War, Volume I,* 242–56; Charles B. MacDonald, *A Time for Trumpets,* 174–79.

4. Tsakanikas's admiring friend, Lieutenant (later Captain) Bouck said his big regret is that Sack died before he and the platoon were finally recognized at an honors ceremony at Ft. Myer, Virginia, in 1981. Tsakanikas was nominated for the Congressional Medal of Honor (the nation's highest military award) for his courage, leadership, and determination to hold his defensive positions and keep his team together in the face of overwhelming odds. Bouck said he regretted that Tsakanikas was not awarded the Medal of Honor. "If anyone deserves this award, he did." After two years of study and consideration, the army and navy approved the award to Tsakanikas in 1988, but the Marine Corps turned it down. Since approval from the three services must be unanimous, the secretary of defense said the award could not be granted. Tsakanikas dropped his last name after the war and became just plain William James. He graduated from the University of Pennsylvania and attended Cornell University Law School.

Chapter 9

1. This account is based on John Thornburg, "One Fly, All Die," August 1945, and interviews by author, 1994.
2. The Russians "liberated" Thornburg and his comrades in April 1945 from Stalag IVB near Muhlberg, about fifty miles south of Berlin. He and a friend escaped from Russian detention in May when he learned the war had ended. He had lost fifty pounds in five months. After the war, he graduated from the University of Kansas City's dental school and practiced dentistry in Ottawa, Kansas. Before joining the 99th Division, he was an ASTP student at Baylor University in Waco, Texas.

Chapter 10

1. Thor Ronningen, *Butler's Battlin' Blue Bastards*, 104–105. (Ronningen was a member of I Company.)
2. This account is based on a report by Friedrich August Baron von der Heydte which is included in *Zwischen Zwei Fronten*, 252–61. It was translated for the author by George Prager, Douglasville, Georgia.
3. Charles B. MacDonald, *A Time for Trumpets*, 371.
4. McClernand Butler, audiotape for his family, 1985, and interviews by author, 1990–98.
5. This horror story did not end with the dead German. Olsen became a victim, too. Almost immediately after the incident he started having disabling head-aches. Evacuated a few days after the incident, he was hospitalized for three months during which time he received electric shock treatments. The head-aches finally went away, and he was placed on limited (noncombat) army serv-ice. He told me about this traumatic experience shortly after his release from an army hospital in England (about March 1945). He was in a replacement depot awaiting a new assignment.
6. Bruce Waterman, letters to author and interviews by author, 1990–94.
7. Paul Putty, interview by author, May 1991.
8. Sam Mestrezat, diary, December 1944.
9. James B. Kemp, "Personal Experiences of a Battalion Executive Officer," unpublished report, no date.
10. Charles B. MacDonald, *A Time for Trumpets*, 222.

Chapter 11

1. George Northwang, interview by author, 1997.
2. Charles P. Biggio, Jr., speech to annual convention of 99th Infantry Division Association, July 1998.

3. Colonel Butler's idea of blasting surrounded buildings with close-up cannon fire was used successfully on a much bigger scale to obtain the surrender of nearby Aachen in October 1944. Enemy troops had retreated to a massive building in the center of the city for a last stand. They surrendered, however, when Lt. Gen. Lawton Collins, commander of the U.S. First Army's VII Corps, moved several 155-mm "Long Tom" rifles to within two hundred yards of the building and began blasting away at the thick walls. The German commander said it was time to give up when the Americans started using 155-mms as "sniper weapons." (General Eisenhower reported the incident in *Crusade in Europe,* 312.)

4. Keith Fabianich, "Defense of Höfen, Germany," *Infantry School Quarterly,* July 1948, 55.

5. McClernand Butler, audiotape for his family, 1985, and interviews by author, 1990–98.

6. Actual test of wet/dry weights conducted by Joe Baibak, Painesville, Ohio, in December 1996. Test results provided by Dick Byers, 99th Division Association archivist.

7. Basic BAR Field Manual.

8. Charles B. MacDonald, *A Time for Trumpets,* 218–22.

9. McClernand Butler, audiotape for his family, 1985, and interviews by author, 1990–98.

10. Warner Anthony, interview by author, 1992.

11. McClernand Butler, audiotape for his family, 1985, and interviews by author, 1990–98.

12. Keith Fabianich, "Defense of Höfen, Germany," *Infantry School Quarterly,* July 1948, 57.

Chapter 12

1. Douglas Packard, medic for L Company, was a rare, outstanding human being. There was nothing phony about him. He was an excellent athlete (football), excellent student in all subjects, and always a hard worker. He never used the ubiquitous four-letter words. If the army honored saints, Packard should be at the top of the list. Raised in poverty in the Deep South, he impressed a well-off uncle in Baltimore, who provided him with a good education. If Packard had any weakness, it was his dedication to his crucial role as a combat infantry medic. Lieutenant Goss said Packard would go to places no one else would go to rescue our wounded. After the war, he received B.S. and M.D. degrees from the University of Maryland.

2. Dwight Eisenhower, *Crusade in Europe,* 315.

3. Omar Bradley, *A Soldier's Story,* 456, 487.

Chapter 13

1. Dwight Eisenhower, *Crusade in Europe,* 316.
2. Hugh M. Cole, *The Ardennes: Battle of the Bulge,* 459.
3. Warren Wilson, diary and notes, 1944–45.
4. Bernard Macay, notes in personal journal, August 1945.
5. Bob Wacker, "The Bloody Bulge," *The Retired Officer,* January 1995, 27–32.
6. E. P. (Bill) Everhard, interview by author, 1994.

Chapter 14

1. David Reynolds, *Rich Relations,* 395.
2. U.S. Army Center of Military History, Washington, D.C., phone query by author, 1998.
3. Noted novelist and former ASTPer Kurt Vonnegut, a private first class in the 106th, found himself in a similar situation, but his fate was much different. He joined three others trying to find the retreating American line. They did not make it. The Germans scooped them up. They sent Vonnegut to POW duty in Dresden, where he managed to survive the great air raid of February 13–14, 1945. That bloody experience inspired him to write *Slaughter House Five,* a book that made him famous.
4. Hugh M. Cole, *The Ardennes: Battle of the Bulge,* 170.
5. The Germans used a drug similar to sodium pentothal on prisoners of war believed to know particularly useful information. They found the drug much more useful than torture. Knowing this, the U.S. Army tried to keep soldiers who knew critically important information out of areas where they might be captured. Perhaps that was why riflemen, those nearest the enemy and thus the most likely candidates for capture, were kept so uninformed.
6. Richard Byers letter, copy to author, 1997.
7. Charles B. MacDonald, *A Time for Trumpets,* ending date of Battle of Bulge, 617; "greatest battle," 11.
8. Dwight Eisenhower, *Crusade in Europe,* 365.
9. Omar Bradley, *A Soldier's Story,* 494.
10. Charles B. MacDonald, *A Time for Trumpets,* 618.
11. Vincent Demma, U.S. Army Center of Military History, Washington, D.C., phone interview by author, 1998.
12. Dwight Eisenhower, *Crusade in Europe,* 364.
13. Charles B. MacDonald, *A Time for Trumpets,* 618.
14. Death figures for the 99th Division are based on official casualty lists published in William C. C. Cavanagh, *Dauntless: A History of the 99th Infantry Division,* 376–96. Evacuation figures are based on reports of the division's 324th Medical Battalion.

15. Harry Arnold, "'Easy' Memories," 106-107.

16. Warner Anthony, letter to author, January 29, 1945.

17. Duane Shipman, letters to author and interviews by author, 1996. Date and time of combat patrol and unit confirmed by "Morning Report" (S-3 Journal) of Third Battalion, 395th Infantry.

18. Duane Shipman suffered a gunshot wound in his shoulder in March 1945 as the 3rd Battalion approached the Rhine River. After the war, he became chief executive officer of Grange Insurance Group, Seattle.

19. Bruce Mather, interview by author, September 1945; and Alfred Schnitzer, interview by author, 1995.

20. Jackson W. Goss, interviews by author, 1998, and report in Silver Star citation, 1945.

21. Goss showed coolness in another tough spot during chaotic battle conditions on April 7, 1945, in Gleidorf, Germany. As reported by Thor Ronningen in *Butler's Battlin' Blue Bastards,* Goss and Colonel Butler "dodged into a corner building just as an SS trooper came in from the other side. They met almost chest-to-chest," startling all three men. Goss was quickest to react. He raised his M1 rifle and emptied it into the surprised German as he fell dead at their feet. By his fast action, Goss saved his own life and that of his battalion commander. "In a gesture of disdain," Ronningen said, Goss "rolled the dead German over on his back, crossed his hands on his chest and put a flower in his hands as though he were ready to be buried. Word of this spread rapidly, and soon there were dead bodies all over Gleidorf lying on their backs with flowers in their crossed hands."

22. Charles B. MacDonald, *The Battle of the Huertgen Forest,* 198–201.

23. Walter Scheibler, *Zwischen Zwei Fronten.*

24. *Simon & Schuster Encyclopedia of World War II,* 163.

25. *Oxford Companion to World War II,* 311.

26. John Eisenhower, *The Bitter Woods,* 224.

27. Roger J. Moore, letters to author and interviews by author, January 1996.

28. Walter E. Lauer, *Battle Babies,* 212–13.

29. Omar Bradley, *A Soldier's Story,* 446.

Chapter 15

1. In 1993, the London house I had lived in contained three living units. Before World War II, it had housed a single family.

2. Fred Redding, interview by author, London, 1993. (Redding was a retired Selfridges executive who became the store's archivist.)

3. Stephen Geis, telephone interview by author, 1996.

4. Once, when Geis went down to Whitehall to help Churchill, he took a present

for the prime minister—the best cigar the London Officers' PX had to offer. When the "call" was over, Geis gave the cigar to a grateful Churchill. Two days later, the amazed American officer received a note and present from the prime minister. Churchill thanked him for his help and enclosed an autographed copy of one of his books, *My Early Life*.

5. I learned about the German spying incident, by sheer coincidence, on November 12, 1951, when I interviewed Walter Riedel as part of my job as a newspaper editor in Pasadena, California. He revealed the spy operation when I asked him about his wartime job and about the V-2 that exploded near the Signal Center on December 6, 1944.

6. More information about this facility can be found in *The Signal Corps: The Outcome, Mid-1943 Through 1945*, 87–88.

7. Information provided to author by U.S. Army Center of Military History, Washington, D.C., 1998.

Chapter 16

1. *Oxford Companion to World War II*, 1136.
2. *World War II Almanac, 1931–1945*, 401.

Chapter 17

1. McClernand Butler, audiotape for his family, 1985, and interviews by author, 1990–98.
2. John Eisenhower, *The Bitter Woods*, 146.
3. Hugh M. Cole, *The Ardennes: Battle of the Bulge*, 63.
4. Information provided to author by U.S. Army Center of Military History, Washington, D.C., 1998.
5. Omar Bradley, *A Soldier's Story*, 445–46.

GLOSSARY

ASTP	Army Specialized Training Program (college level)
BAR	Browning Automatic Rifle
bazooka	hand-held rocket antitank weapon
burp gun	German small submachine gun
carbine	light 30-caliber semiautomatic rifle issued to infantry officers
CO	commanding officer
CP	command post
DC-3	twin-engine transport aircraft for cargo or personnel
ERC	U.S. Army's Enlisted Reserve Corps (for college students)
ETO	European Theater of Operations
German 88	highly effective rapid-fire 88-mm gun
GI	enlisted man in the U.S. Army
GI Bill	U.S. government program to help finance vocational or college education for World War II veterans
grease gun (M3)	submachine gun used by many officers
I&R Platoon	intelligence and reconnaissance unit
infantry	branch of service in the army that is trained, armed, and equipped to fight on foot
JU-52	three-motor German air transport
JU-88	Junkers 88, German twin-engine medium bomber
Kampfgruppe	German combat group of variable size
Long Tom	American 155-mm, long-barreled artillery piece
Luftwaffe	German Air Force
M1	standard issue U.S. 30-caliber semiautomatic rifle used by all rifle platoons
ME-109	Messerschmitt 109, a speedy, versatile German piston-engine fighter

machine pistol	German weapon, similar to a submachine gun
Nebelwerfer	German multiple rocket projector
OP	observation post
Panzerfaust	German hand-held disposable antitank rocket
POW or PW	prisoner of war
RAF	(British) Royal Air Force
SHAEF	Supreme Headquarters, Allied Expeditionary Force
SIGSALY	secret, secure telephone voice scrambling service for trans-Atlantic conversations between Churchill and Presidents Roosevelt and Truman and for top-level military conferences
slit trench	shallow foxhole
TD	tank destroyer
V-1 ("buzz bomb")	German jet-propelled flying bomb aimed primarily at London, Antwerp, and Liege
V-2	German long-distance rocket aimed mostly at London
WAC	(U.S.) Women's Army Corps
Wehrmacht	German Army
West Wall	German term for Siegfried Line

BIBLIOGRAPHY

Arnold, Harry S. 1985. "'Easy' Memories: The Way It Really Was" (unpublished memoir).

Biggio, Charles P., Jr. 1998. Speech to annual convention of 99th Infantry Division Association, July.

Bradley, Omar N. 1951. *A Soldier's Story.* New York: Henry Holt and Company.

Butcher, Harry C. 1946. *My Three Years with Eisenhower.* New York: Simon & Schuster.

Byers, Richard. 1983. "An Artilleryman's Recollections of the Bulge" (unpublished memoir).

Cavanagh, William C. C. 1994. *Dauntless: A History of the 99th Infantry Division.* Dallas: Taylor Publishing Company.

Center of Military History, United States Army. 1993. *Logistics in World War II: Final Report of the Army Service Forces.* Washington, D.C.: Superintendent of Documents.

Cole, Hugh M. 1994. *The Ardennes: Battle of the Bulge,* (part of series, U.S. Army in World War II) Center of Military History. Washington, D.C.: Government Printing Office.

Dear, I. C. B., ed. 1995. *Oxford Companion to World War II.* New York: Oxford University Press.

Doherty, J. C. 1994. *The Shock of War: Unknown Battles That Ruined Hitler's Plan for a Second Blitzkrieg in the West, December–January, 1944–45, Volume I.* Alexandria, Va.: Vert Milon Press.

———. 1996. *The Shock of War: Unknown Battles That Ruined Hitler's Plan for a Second Blitzkrieg in the West, December–January, 1944–45, Volume II.* Alexandria, Va.: Vert Milon Press.

Eisenhower, Dwight D. 1948. *Crusade in Europe.* Garden City, N.Y.: Doubleday.

Eisenhower, John S. D. 1969. *The Bitter Woods.* New York: G. P. Putnam's Sons.

Fabianich, Keith. 1948. "Defense of Höfen, Germany." *Infantry School Quarterly*, (July): 43–58.

Goralski, Robert. 1981. *World War II Almanac, 1931–1945*. New York: Putnam.

Fussell, Paul. 1989. *Wartime: Understanding and Behavior in the Second World War*. New York: Oxford University Press.

———. 1996. *Doing Battle: The Making of a Skeptic*. Boston: Little, Brown.

Harris, Arthur. 1947. *Bomber Offensive*. London: Greenhill Books.

Huffman, William (Bill). 1960. "Hold the North Shoulder" (unpublished memoir).

Keefer, Louis E. 1988. *Scholars in Foxholes: The Story of the Army Specialized Training Program in World War II*. Jefferson, N.C.: McFarland.

Kemp, James B. n.d. "Personal Experiences of a Battalion Executive Officer" (unpublished report of activities of 612th Tank Destroyer Battalion).

Kennett, Lee. 1987. *G.I.: The American Soldier in World War II*. New York: Charles Scribner's Sons.

Lauer, Walter E. 1951. *Battle Babies: The Story of the 99th Infantry Division in World War II*. Baton Rouge: Military Press of Louisiana.

MacDonald, Charles B. 1963. *The Siegfried Line Campaign* (part of series, U.S. Army in World War II), Office of the Chief of Military History. Washington, D.C.: Department of the Army.

———. 1985. *The Battle of the Huertgen Forest*. New York: Jove Publications.

———. 1985. *A Time for Trumpets: The Untold Story of the Battle of the Bulge*. New York: Bantam Books.

Mellin, John. 1993. "Memories, November–December 1944" (unpublished memoir), June.

Mitsch, Robert J. 1989. "Lucking Out: A Recall of World War II Survival and Observations" (unpublished memoir), November 27.

Montgomery, Bernard Law. 1958. *The Memoirs of Field Marshal Montgomery*. Cleveland: World Publishing Company.

Murphy, John. 1979. *Dorset at War, 1939–1945*. Sherbourne, Dorset, England: Dorset Publishing Company.

Niedermayer, Walter. 1990. *Into the Deep Misty Woods of the Ardennes: The Battle of the Bulge in All of Its Fury and SS-Terror*. Indiana, Pa.: A. G. Halldin Publishing Company.

Olsen, Charles A. 1946. "History of the U.S. Navy in Le Havre." Report prepared by Olsen for the city of Le Havre, June 25.

Parrish, Thomas, ed. 1978. *Simon & Schuster Encyclopedia of World War II*. New York: Simon & Schuster.

Pyle, Ernie. 1944. *Brave Men*. New York: Henry Holt and Company.

Reynolds, David. 1995. *Rich Relations: The American Occupation of Britain, 1942–1945*. New York: Random House.

Reynolds, Quentin. 1943. *Dress Rehearsal: The Story of the Raid on Dieppe.* New York: Random House.

Ronningen, Thor. 1993. *Butler's Battlin' Blue Bastards.* Lawrenceville, Va.: Brunswick Publishing Corporation.

Ruge, Friedrich. 1957. *The German Navy's Story—1939–1945.* Annapolis, Md.: U.S. Naval Institute.

Saffer, Seymour. 1993. "First Combat Patrol—First Casualties." *The Checkerboard* (99th Infantry Division Association newspaper), (April): 38.

Sassoon, Siegfried. 1991. *Memoirs of an Infantry Officer.* London: Faber and Faber.

Scheibler, Walter. 1959. *Zwischen Zwei Fronten: Kriegstagebuch des Landkreises.* Monschau, Germany: Landkreises Monschau. Translation for author by George Prager, Douglasville, Georgia.

Smithmark Publishers. 1993. *D-Day: Operation Overlord.* New York: Smithmark.

Thompson, George Raynor, and Harris, Dixie R. 1966. *The Signal Corps: the Outcome, Mid-1943 Through 1945* (part of series: United States Army in World War II), Center of Military History. Washington, D.C.: Superintendent of Documents.

Thornburg, John. 1945. "One Fly, All Die" (unpublished memoir), August.

U.S. Department of Education. 1997. *Digest of Education Statistics, 1997.* Washington, D.C.: Superintendent of Documents.

Wacker, Bob. 1995. "The Bloody Bulge." *The Retired Officer,* (January): 27–32.

Other Works Consulted by Author

Ambrose, Stephen. 1997. *Citizen Soldiers: The U.S. Army from the Normandy Beaches to the Bulge to the Surrender of Germany, June 7, 1944–May 7, 1945.* New York: Simon & Schuster.

Cawthon, Charles R. 1990. *Other Clay: A Remembrance of the World War II Infantry.* Niwot, Colo.: University Press of Colorado.

Dupuy, R. Ernest. 1986. *St. Vith, Lion in the Way: The 106th Infantry Division in World War II.* Nashville: Battery Press.

Honeycombe, Gordon. 1984. *Selfridges: Seventy-Five Years, The Story of the Store, 1909–1984.* London: Selfridges.

INDEX